*Seventh
Edition*

MUSIC
SKILLS
*for
Classroom
Teachers*

Seventh Edition

MUSIC SKILLS

for
Classroom
Teachers

Robert W. Winslow
California State University
Long Beach

Leon Dallin
California State University
Long Beach

wcb
Wm. C. Brown Publishers
Dubuque, Iowa

Book Team

Developmental Editor *Carol Mills*
Production Editor *Michelle M. Kiefer*
Designer *Mary K. Sailer*
Photo Research Editor *Faye M. Schilling*
Visuals Processor *Joyce E. Watters*
Marketing Manager *Kathy Law Laube*

wcb group

Chairman of the Board *Wm. C. Brown*
President and Chief Executive Officer *Mark C. Falb*

wcb

Wm. C. Brown Publishers, College Division

President *G. Franklin Lewis*
Vice President, Editor-in-Chief *George Wm. Bergquist*
Executive Editor *John Woods*
Vice President, Director of Production *Beverly Kolz*
National Sales Manager *Bob McLaughlin*
Director of Marketing *Thomas E. Doran*
Marketing Information Systems Manager *Craig S. Marty*
Production Editorial Manager *Julie A. Kennedy*
Manager of Design *Marilyn A. Phelps*
Photo Research Manager *Faye M. Schilling*

Consulting Editor *Frederick W. Westphal*

Contents

Preface

MUSIC SKILLS for Classroom Teachers is designed as a college textbook for courses that prepare teachers for classroom music teaching and for introductory music courses that combine the study of fundamentals with performance activities. It develops the skills—music reading, singing, and playing classroom and social instruments—needed by teachers to conduct an effective music program in the primary and intermediate grades. To avoid discouraging and confusing students without previous experience in music, subject matter is limited to that commonly used in such a program. Materials are presented systematically at the level of the adult beginner with examples drawn from music that is appealing to children and appropriate for use in the classroom. The book's many folk and familiar songs make it a valuable reference and resource book for teachers and amateur musicians.

This edition retains the basic approach and organization that proved successful in the previous editions but with substantial refinements. The chapter on playing the piano has been revised to develop performance skills to realistic levels of proficiency. The recorder chapter has been simplified and streamlined. In response to user and reviewer suggestions, the song materials have been updated, and lower ranges have been used, consistent with the function of the songs in the instrumental and theoretical chapters. The chapters on reading rhythm and pitch and on combining musical sounds have been revised to present the information more concisely and sequentially and to relate the theoretical concepts immediately to performance activities.

Suggestions for the Use of This Book

This book is organized in chapters by subject area to allow the teacher of the course complete freedom in the order of presentation. Each chapter can be studied as a unit, but it is advantageous in most situations to integrate creative and listening activities and the development of performance skills with the study of theoretical topics.

To make additional class time available for group participation in music activities, performance techniques and theoretical information are presented in a manner appropriate for individual practice and study outside of class.

Extensive cross-references facilitate the use of the song materials in multiple functions. Songs in the instrumental and theoretical chapters that are not in a comfortable vocal range can be transposed to an appropriate key for singing.

Materials recommended for the classroom include a record player and recordings, a piano, recorders, Autoharps, bells, guitars, rhythm instruments, various Orff instruments, and state and local series of school songbooks and accompanying recordings.

The piano chart in the endleaf pocket inside the back cover can be placed upright behind the piano keys as an aid when practicing at the piano. It can also be placed flat on a desk as a substitute for a piano when none is available.

Acknowledgments

We wish to recognize the contribution of the students in our elementary music education classes who tested and verified the effectiveness of these materials, first in manuscript form and then as published. We are grateful to the manufacturers and distributors of classroom and orchestral instruments for supplying the photographs used in this book. They are acknowledged individually where their photographs appear in the text.

We are indebted to the music publishers who have generously granted permission for the use of copyrighted songs. Appropriate notice is given with each example. A conscientious effort has been made to acknowledge all copyrights, but many of the songs are so much a part of our musical heritage that it is not always possible to determine the original source. For these songs we are indebted to the singers who have remembered and sung them and to the teachers who have taught them to generations of American children.

We would also like to thank the following reviewers for their contributions to this revised edition: Robert A. Cutietta, Kent State University, Ohio; Rosemary C. Watkins, Louisiana State University, Baton Rouge; Brian L. Wilson, Western Michigan University, Kalamazoo; Clifton V. Cowles, Arkansas State University; Gregory DeNardo, Bowling Green State University, Ohio; Ann C. Anderson, University of Minnesota, Duluth; Nancy Dreyer, Southwest Missouri State University; Kathryn L. Merani, Towson State University, Maryland; Glen A. Fifield, Utah State University, Logan; Martha Reynolds, Southwest Texas State University.

Robert W. Winslow

Leon Dallin

1 Singing for Fun

Singing familiar melodies and fun songs is one of the most enjoyable and effective musical activities of the elementary school program. The value of informal group singing in stimulating interest in vocal music has been demonstrated many times by teachers, camp directors, and recreation leaders.

The purpose of this introductory chapter in teacher education classes is twofold: it serves to put musically inexperienced and timid students at ease through informal activity, and it helps future teachers, through pleasurable singing, to acquire a repertoire of interesting classroom song materials. These well-known and semi-familiar tunes can be taught easily by rote* (ear imitation) to both adults and children. Above all, the instructor should cultivate a joyful spirit of singing for fun.

The use of Autoharp, ukulele, guitar, and piano accompaniments will add to the pleasure of singing. To facilitate accompaniment, chord names are indicated above the melody line directly over the note where the chord change occurs.

---

*The following are suggestions for teaching a song by rote:
1. Discuss the mood and tempo of the song.
2. Sing the entire song for the class accompanying yourself with Autoharp, guitar, or piano. (If you do not sing, play the song on the recorder, bells, piano, or record player.)
3. In the typical four-phrase rote song, the teacher can alternate singing and listening to each phrase (usually four measures). Short songs may be learned as a whole.
4. Finally the entire song is sung (or played) again, first by the teacher and then by the class.
5. Difficult passages may be repeated several times using hand cues or other visual pictures for pitch direction.
6. Orff and other classroom instruments may be added for enrichment.

DO-RE-MI

OSCAR HAMMERSTEIN II   RICHARD RODGERS

Doe... a deer, a fe-male deer, Ray... a drop of gold-en sun, _____ Me... a name I call my-self, Far... a long, long, way to run. _____ Sew... a nee-dle pull-ing thread, _____ La... a note to fol-low sew, _____ Tea... a drink with jam and bread _____ That will bring us back to Do. _____

IT'S A SMALL WORLD

WORDS AND MUSIC BY
RICHARD M. SHERMAN
ROBERT B. SHERMAN

It's a world of laugh-ter, a world of tears; it's a
There is just one moon and one gold-en sun and a

world of hopes and a world of fears. There's so
smile means friend-ship to ev-'ry one. Though the

much that we share that it's time we're a-ware. It's a
moun-tains di-vide and the o-ceans are wide, It's a

small world af-ter all. _____
small world af-ter all. _____

Fine

It's a small world af-ter all, It's a

small world af-ter all. It's a small world

af-ter all, It's a small, small world. _____

D.C. al Fine

Patriotic songs have always held a prominent place in school singing programs. They are an integral part of the American heritage. Sing them with vitality and spirit.

THIS LAND IS YOUR LAND

WOODIE GUTHRIE   WOODIE GUTHRIE

1. As I was walk - ing _____ that rib - bon of high - way _____
— I saw a - bove me _____ that end - less sky - way, _____
— I saw be - low me _____ that gold - en val - ley, _____
— this land was made for you and me. _____

Chorus

This land is your land, _____ this land is my land _____
— from Cal - i - for - nia _____ to the New York is - land, _____
— From the red - wood for - est _____ to the gulf stream wa - ters _____
— this land was made for you and me. _____

2. I've roamed and rambled and followed my footsteps
   to the sparkling sands of her diamond deserts,
   And all around me a voice was sounding,
   This land was made for you and me.

3. When the sun comes shining and I was strolling
   and the wheat fields waving and the dust clouds rolling,
   As the fog was lifting a voice was chanting,
   This land was made for you and me.

YANKEE DOODLE DANDY

GEORGE M. COHAN   GEORGE M. COHAN

I'm a Yan - kee Doo - dle Dan - dy, A
Yan - kee Doo - dle, do or die; _____ A
real live neph - ew of my Un - cle Sam,
Born on the Fourth of Ju - ly. _____ I've
got a Yan - kee Doo - dle sweet - heart,
She's my Yan - kee Doo - dle joy. _____
Yan - kee Doo - dle came to Lon - don, just to ride the
po - nies, I am a Yan - kee Doo - dle boy. _____

GEORGE WASHINGTON
TUNE: YANKEE DOODLE

CAMP SONG

1. Oh, once there was a lit - tle boy George Wash - ing - ton was he, sir. He took his brand new hatch - et out and chopped his fa - ther's tree, sir.

Chorus

Yes he did, oh, chop, chop, chop Yes he did, oh, chop, chop, chop, He took his brand new hatch - et out and chopped his fa - ther's tree, sir.

2. His father frowned and sternly cried
Who chopped my cherry treasure
George said, "T'was I, I cannot lie
I chopped it down for pleasure."

3. When Washington was very young
He took his little hatchet
And cut his father's cherry tree
Intending just to scratch it.

4. Oh who cut down this cherry tree
His father asked—"T'was I sir,
I'm very sorry but you see
I cannot tell a lie, sir."

Also sing and play *America* (p. 304), *America the Beautiful* (p. 305), and *The Star-Spangled Banner* (p. 306).

Folk Songs

The majority of the songs selected to teach music skills in this text can be classified as folk songs. These songs were handed down orally from generation to generation, expressing the emotions, feelings, aspirations, and varied geographic characteristics of the peoples of many lands.

Sing this ever-popular New Orleans Processional with a swing beat. Clapping will add to the spirit.

WHEN THE SAINTS GO MARCHING IN

U.S.

1. Oh, when the saints _____ go march - ing in, _____
_____ Oh, when the saints go march - ing in, _____
_____ Oh, Lord, I want to be in that num - ber _____
_____ When the saints go march - ing in. _____

2. Oh, when the stars refuse to shine, . . .

3. Oh, when I hear that trumpet sound, . . .

When the Saints Go Marching In can be sung as a "partner song" with the next two songs, *This Train* and *Swing Low, Sweet Chariot,* if there are enough experienced singers in the class. If not, sing only two of them in combination. Suggested procedure:

1. Learn each song well before combining them.
2. Sing two songs several times together before adding a third.
3. Be sure to assign several strong singers to each song for leadership.
4. Sing the three pick-up notes of *When the Saints Go Marching In* before beginning the other songs.

Refer to *Singing Partner Songs,* chapter 12, (p. 255) for more songs to be combined.

The key of D Major is used in this song for easy guitar strumming and vocal range.

THIS TRAIN

FOLK SONG   U.S.

This train is bound for glo-ry, this train;⎯ This train is bound for glo-ry,

this train;⎯⎯⎯ This train is bound for glo-ry,

I'm not tell-ing you a sto-ry. This train is leav-ing get on board!

SWING LOW, SWEET CHARIOT

SPIRITUAL

U.S.

Swing low, sweet char - i - ot, — Com-ing for to car - ry me home,

Swing low, sweet char - i - ot, — Com-ing for to car - ry me home

Fine

I looked o - ver Jor - dan and what did I see, —

Com-ing for to car - ry me home, A band — of an - gels

D.C. al Fine

com -ing af - ter me, — Com-ing for to car - ry me home.

The birthday serenade *Las Mañanitas* usually is sung early in the day as a beginning to the birthday celebration. The melody is a Mexican folk tune.

LAS MAÑANITAS

MEXICO

As of old, we bring a song, a greet-ing
gay at ear-ly dawn; Wak-en, friend, and join our
sing-ing, O hear the mu-sic we bring. *Fine*
I'll step out of doors at dawn-ing, I'll
climb up a mag-ic stair, And bring down the stars of
morn-ing to make a crown for your hair. *D.C. al Fine*

Estas son las mañanitas que cantaba el Rey David,
Pero no eran tanbonitas como las cantan aquí.
Despierta, mi bién, despierta, mira que ya amaneció;
Ya los pajarillos cantan, la luna ya se metió.

Despierta, mi bién, despierta, mira que ya amaneció;
Ya los pajarillos cantan, la luma ya se metió.
Estas son las mañanitas que cantaba el Rey David,
Pero no eran tanbonitas como las cantan aquí.

Also sing *La Raspe* (p. 137), an excellent example of Mexican folk rhythm.

The prominent American composer, Aaron Copland, used this popular cowboy song in his ballet suite, *Billy the Kid*.

GOOD-BY, OLD PAINT

U.S.

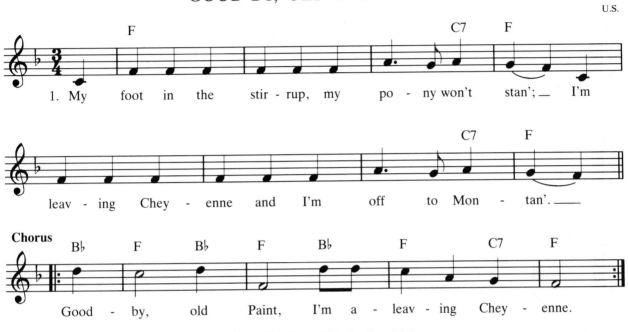

1. My foot in the stir - rup, my po - ny won't stan'; — I'm
leav - ing Chey - enne and I'm off to Mon - tan'. —

Chorus

Good - by, old Paint, I'm a - leav - ing Chey - enne.

2. I'm riding old Paint and I'm leading old Fan;
   Goodby little Annie, I'm off for Montan'.
3. Oh, keep yourself by me as long as you can;
   Goodby little Annie, I'm off for Montan'.

The beautiful old ballad *Scarborough Fair* has been popularized by Simon and Garfunkel.

SCARBOROUGH FAIR

ENGLAND

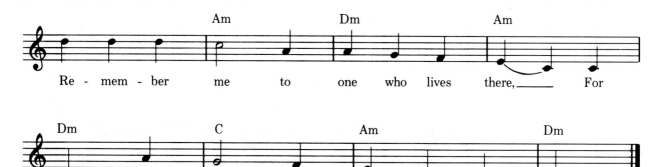

1. Are you go - ing to Scar - bor - ough Fair?

Pars - ley, sage, rose - mar - y and thyme;

Re - mem - ber me to one who lives there, _____ For

she was once a true love of mine.

Boys:
2. Bid her make me a cambric shirt,
Parsley, sage, rosemary and thyme;
Sewn without seams or fine needlework,
If she would be a true love of mine.

Girls:
3. Have him find me an acre of land,
Parsley, sage, rosemary and thyme;
Lying between sea foam and sea sand,
Or he'll not be a true love of mine.

Recreational Songs   Action, game, stunt, and camp songs provide spontaneous opportunities for informal class participation and fun for any age level from kindergarten upward. Sing and act out the following songs with gusto.

DOWN BY THE STATION

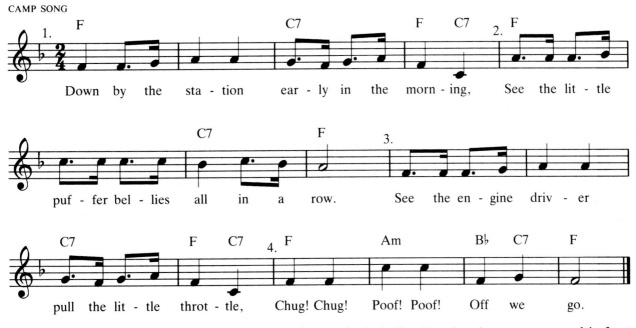

Down by the sta - tion ear - ly in the morn - ing, See the lit - tle puf - fer bel - lies all in a row. See the en - gine driv - er pull the lit - tle throt - tle, Chug! Chug! Poof! Poof! Off we go.

Imitate pulling a throttle rhythmically. Also sing the song as a round in four parts, as indicated.

As you sing the following song, act out the words.

COME ON AND JOIN INTO THE GAME

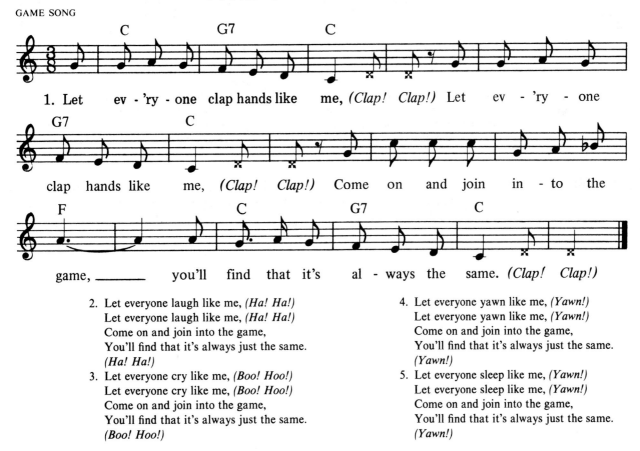

1. Let ev - 'ry - one clap hands like me, (Clap! Clap!) Let ev - 'ry - one clap hands like me, (Clap! Clap!) Come on and join in - to the game, _____ you'll find that it's al - ways the same. (Clap! Clap!)

2. Let everyone laugh like me, *(Ha! Ha!)*
   Let everyone laugh like me, *(Ha! Ha!)*
   Come on and join into the game,
   You'll find that it's always just the same.
   (Ha! Ha!)

3. Let everyone cry like me, *(Boo! Hoo!)*
   Let everyone cry like me, *(Boo! Hoo!)*
   Come on and join into the game,
   You'll find that it's always just the same.
   (Boo! Hoo!)

4. Let everyone yawn like me, *(Yawn!)*
   Let everyone yawn like me, *(Yawn!)*
   Come on and join into the game,
   You'll find that it's always just the same.
   (Yawn!)

5. Let everyone sleep like me, *(Yawn!)*
   Let everyone sleep like me, *(Yawn!)*
   Come on and join into the game,
   You'll find that it's always just the same.
   (Yawn!)

Follow the instructions indicated for the following stunt songs. Then create your own words and actions.

HOKEY POKEY

ACTION SONG

1. You put your right foot in,___ You take your right foot out,___ You put your right foot in___ And shake it all a-bout, And then you do the hok-ey pok-ey And you turn your-self a - bout, And that's what it's all a - bout. *Hey!*

2. left foot   3. right arm   4. left arm   5. head   6. whole self

For other popular action and game songs, refer to the recordings *Do the Hokey Pokey* and *The Bunny Hop,* #8073, Peter Pan Records, 88 St. Francis Street, Newark, N.J. 07105.

The stunt song *Bingo* serves as an effective icebreaker for students of all ages, especially those who are shy about singing. Sing it six times. The first time, sing it as written. The second time, omit the letter *B* in the spelling of *B-I-N-G-O* and clap instead. The third time, omit *B* and *I* and clap. Continue until the entire word has been clapped in rhythm.

BINGO

U.S.

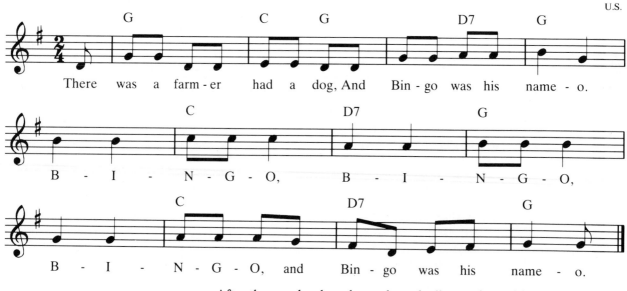

There was a farm-er had a dog, And Bin-go was his name - o.

B - I - N - G - O,   B - I - N - G - O,

B - I - N - G - O, and Bin-go was his name - o.

After the song has been learned, gradually speed up with each repetition.

IF YOU'RE HAPPY

If you're hap - py and you know it, clap your hands. *(clap clap)* If you're
hap - py and you know it, clap your hands. *(clap clap)* If you're
hap - py and you know it, and you real - ly want to show it, If you're
hap - py and you know it, clap your hands. *(clap clap.)*

If you're happy and you know it touch your head . . .
If you're happy and you know it touch your eyes . . .
If you're happy and you know it do all three . . .

Create additional words and actions.
Also sing the camp songs *Three Cornered Hat* (p. 183), *Upidee* (p. 185),
and *Upward Trail* (p. 302).

In 1893 when Mildred and Patty Hill wrote the song *Good Morning to All* for kindergarten children, they could not have dreamed that with a few changes in the rhythm and words it would become universally recognized as *Happy Birthday to You.*

GOOD MORNING TO ALL

PATTY S. HILL

MILDRED J. HILL

An excellent supplement to this chapter is Dallin, Leon, and Dallin, Lynn, *Heritage Songster,* 2d ed. Dubuque, Ia.: Wm. C. Brown Company Publishers, 1980. (332 folk and familiar songs)

2 Developing the Singing Voice

Singing is generally recognized as the basic musical activity of the elementary-school music program. Nearly all musical skills and knowledge can be developed through worthwhile singing experiences in the classroom. Therefore, it is important for the elementary teacher to be able to use the singing voice effectively. The purpose of this chapter is to help teachers develop singing skills.

Voice Registers

Voice register is a topic about which voice teachers *rarely agree* and have not developed a common vocabulary. Essentially, however, there are two voice registers in adult singing—the head and chest registers. One set of throat muscles controls the vocal mechanism for upper register singing while the resonating head cavities are used to resonate the tone. The other set controls the lower register singing, with the chest cavities the resonators. The former is frequently referred to, especially in children's singing, as *head voice* and the latter as *chest voice*. The *approximate* range of these two registers follows:

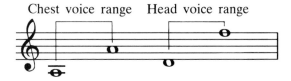

The Child's Singing Voice

The ideal singing voices of children have a light, treble, flutelike quality. The sound becomes noticeably more beautiful as they sing higher on the treble staff if they are singing freely and easily. This is evidence that the children are using head voice. Head-voice singing is a desired goal for classroom singing in all the grades.

The trend today, however, is to write children's songs in their easiest singing range—probably to encourage more participation from boys and some girls, i.e.,

or lower.

As the children gain experience, it is recommended that these songs be transposed upward to facilitate beautiful *head-voice* singing (when feasible).

One of the most important procedures for teachers to remember in developing the head voice is to pitch the songs accurately in the written keys, especially since these have been selected carefully by the nation's leading music educators. It also helps if the classroom singing is light, free, and unforced at all times.

The Classroom Teacher's Singing Voice

Many female elementary-school teachers are more comfortable singing in the alto range, using throaty chest tones. Male teachers, more often than not, like to pitch songs in the low baritone or bass range. However, children's songs are written within the easy range of the soprano voice. The most successful female teachers can sing from the middle B to the top of the treble staff with a light free tone, and the men can do likewise an octave lower. This technique is not difficult for the majority of teachers, even those with limited singing ability. The most important skills to master are the use and control of the head register and the projection of the voice high and forward into the head resonators for the upper tones.

The following suggestions and exercises are designed specifically to assist teachers in singing children's songs effectively. No attempt has been made to write a complete vocal method, nor is it our aim to develop solo singers. Teachers who find it impossible to sing songs in the written keys may choose to teach them with song bells or the recorder.

Posture and Breathing

During the singing of the forthcoming exercises and songs, the student will become aware of the need for breath support, especially if asked to sing complete phrases in one breath. Posture and breathing are interrelated in the singing act—without good posture it is impossible to breathe properly.

Exercise 1

Stand erect and poised with heels slightly apart, right foot slightly ahead of the left, weight on the ball of the right foot. Keep the head high and the chin in. Now lift the back part of the top of the head. This exercise tends to straighten the back and lift the chest. It discourages the common bad habit of raising the shoulders and projecting the chin. Think a "high chest" without tightening or crowding the neck.

Exercise 2

Standing
Stand firmly against a door or wall with heels, calves, hips, shoulder blades, and back of head touching. Then step away, trying to keep the line. Have someone check for a perpendicular line extending from earlobe to heel.

Sitting
Sit with both feet placed firmly on the floor (legs are never crossed in singing class), spine straight, chest up, chin in, *body tilted slightly forward*. Be free but poised. When a book is used, hold it upright on the desk. Never bow the head to read music.

Exercise 3

Deep breathing is the key to good singing. Poor tone quality, out-of-tune singing, and forced high tones usually result from a lack of breath control. The following suggestions will help develop proper breath support.

Breathing
Place hands firmly on hips with thumbs pressing into the back. Take four short breaths, hold the breath for four counts, exhale in four counts with four impulses. Increase this entire exercise to six and then eight counts or more. You should feel expansion at both the front and back of the waist. If not, and the shoulders and chest raise, reach arms straight up above the head. Try the exercise. Then try again, this time with hands on hips. Repeat until the lower breath impulse is felt.

Inhaling
Whenever there is time in singing, breathe through the nose. This encourages lower rib expansion and depresses the diaphragm, increasing chest capacity for breath intake. Rounding the lips and pronouncing a big "oh" when inhaling through the mouth produces about the same result. Shoulders must remain motionless.

Exhaling
To exhale correctly is more difficult than to inhale correctly. Chest and shoulders must be kept in position during exhalation and never allowed to collapse. In singing, a steady stream of breath must be exhaled with no sudden expulsion of air. An even flow of air continuously pressing against the vocal cords is necessary for the best vocalization.

Exercise 4

With hands on hips, practice panting. This should give the "feel" of the breath impulse at waist level.

Exercise 5

Take a deep breath, expand at the waist. Exhale slowly and steadily to the end of the breath with a hissing sound, "sss." Turn the head gently back and forth to release any possible tension. Keep a "high chest" to the end of the breath.

Exercise 6

With hands firmly pressed into the waist, take a deep breath and say "hmp," then "ha," sharply; then sing "ha" on G to the end of the breath. A definite impulse should be felt at the waist on all three sounds. Keep the breath against the tone.

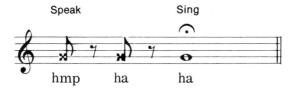

The Singing Tone

The high forward placement of head tones is best achieved through the soft, flexible humming of scale passages and easy melodies. The most used hum, "hm," is produced with the lips gently closed. The correct position for this hum is made by singing "ah" and then closing the lips but not the jaw. The singer will feel a slight vibrating sensation at the lips if the placement is correct. This practice helps the student to discover head tones.

Women should not use the hum beyond E, fourth space treble clef, because the tone becomes pinched. Men can practice light, soft humming throughout their entire vocal range. Loud or forced humming will defeat its purpose.

Exercise 7

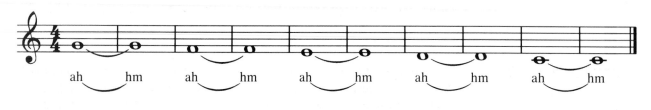

Exercise 8

Transpose up by semitones and sing softly. To *transpose* music is to change the key from that in which it is written. Each note must be written or performed a certain fixed distance higher or lower, occupying the same position in the new scale that it held in the original one.

Exercise 9

Transpose upward by semitones.

These vocalises should be sung on "ee" and "oo" vowels for additional practice in head resonance focus. The bright vowel sound "ay" can also be used.

Exercise 10

Now practice the entire descending scale with repeated tones. Try to carry a light tone to the last note of the scale. Transpose upward by semitones.

etc.

Ming, ming, ming, ming, ming.   Ming, ming, ming, ming, ming.   Ming, ming, ming, ming, ming.
Zing, zing, zing, zing, zing.   Zing, zing, zing, zing, zing.   Zing, zing, zing, zing, zing.
Moo, mee, moo, mee, moo.   Moo, mee, moo, mee, moo.   Moo, mee, moo, mee, moo.
Nee, nay, nah, no, noo.   Nee, nay, nah, noh, noo.   Nee, nay, nah, noh, noo.

Develop the sensation of head resonance further by singing familiar, easy songs. Hum lightly, sing on "mee," "moo," "loo," or "la," etc. When using "la," be sure to open the mouth and drop the jaw. Always think an "open throat." Imagine a yawn.

Range and Flexibility

Range, flexibility, and tone quality are closely related. The singer who has a wide range and a flexible voice usually can produce a lovely free tone, both high and low. These accomplishments require systematic voice building and development of the vocal organ, the larynx. The following exercises will help develop both range and flexibility. Transpose them upward by semitones to the highest comfortable pitch. Use a bright "ah" sound. Open the mouth and drop the jaw.

Exercise 11

This exercise is especially good for women's voices.

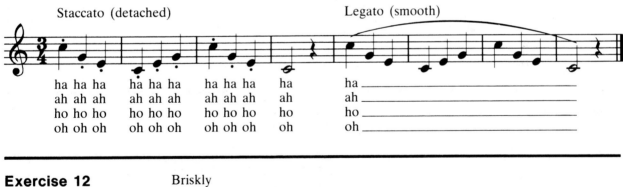

Staccato (detached)   Legato (smooth)

ha ha ha   ha ha ha   ha ha ha   ha   ha _____
ah ah ah   ah ah ah   ah ah ah   ah   ah _____
ho ho ho   ho ho ho   ho ho ho   ho   ho _____
oh oh oh   oh oh oh   oh oh oh   oh   oh _____

Exercise 12

Briskly

ah _____   ah _____   ah _____

Continue singing on the descending scale.

Exercise 13

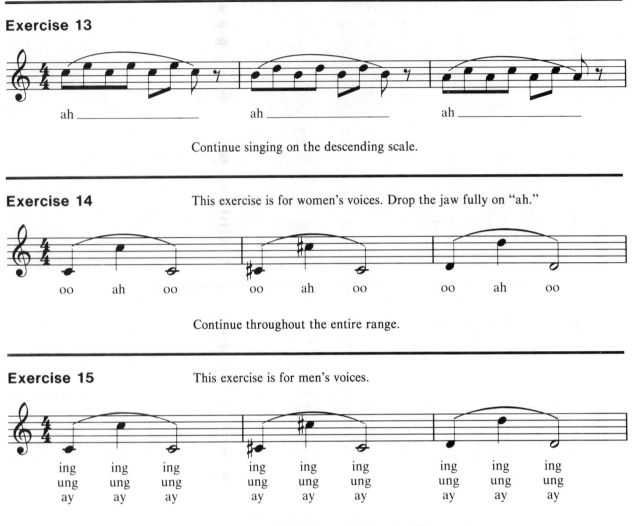

ah _____ ah _____ ah _____

Continue singing on the descending scale.

Exercise 14

This exercise is for women's voices. Drop the jaw fully on "ah."

oo   ah   oo   oo   ah   oo   oo   ah   oo

Continue throughout the entire range.

Exercise 15

This exercise is for men's voices.

ing   ing   ing   ing   ing   ing   ing   ing   ing
ung   ung   ung   ung   ung   ung   ung   ung   ung
ay   ay   ay   ay   ay   ay   ay   ay   ay

Continue throughout the range into the falsetto when necessary.

Vowels

In singing, the tone is sustained on the vowel. Beauty of tone is dependent largely upon correct vowel formations. The fundamental vowel sounds are *ee, ay, ah, oh,* and *oo.* The pure, natural vowel form, not too bright and not too dark, is the main objective.

Some voices require vowel coloring. If a voice is too bright, the "e" as in *he,* the "a" as in *hate,* and the "a" as in *and* very often are shrill and nasal. The vowel form needs to be rounded; "oo," "oh," and "ah" sounds help to round the vowel, and "ee," "eye," and "ay" provide resonance and brightness. Sing songs on these vowel forms as necessity dictates. Also practice the following exercises.

Exercise 16

For roundness, round and slightly purse the lips.

oo___ee___oo   oo___ee___oo   oo___ee___oo
oh___ee___oh   oh___ee___oh   oh___ee___oh
oh___ay___oh   oh___ay___oh   oh___ay___oh
oh___ah___oh   oh___ah___oh   oh___ah___oh

etc.

Exercise 17

For brilliance, do not allow "ah" to become "uh." This dulls the tone and flats the pitch.

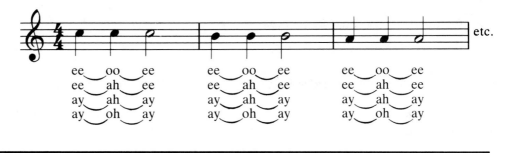

ee___oo___ee   ee___oo___ee   ee___oo___ee
ee___ah___ee   ee___ah___ee   ee___ah___ee
ay___ah___ay   ay___ah___ay   ay___ah___ay
ay___oh___ay   ay___oh___ay   ay___oh___ay

etc.

Diphthongs

A diphthong is a double vowel sound. For example, the *e* in *few* is pronounced "feeoo," and the *i* in *mine* is pronounced "maheen." The shorter vowel must be sung quickly. The longer vowel is sustained, as in "feeoo" and "maheen." Practice singing:

fee___ooo   mah_____een

Consonants

Clear, distinct articulation of consonants is necessary for good diction. Remember the following basic principles in articulating consonants.

1. Sing the consonant very quickly.
2. Try to keep an open throat (yawning sensation).
3. Think the consonant at the same pitch level as the vowel to which it is attached, with a minimum change of the vowel form used.
4. Emphasize slightly the final consonants. Try not to close the mouth on these.
5. Articulate only one of the consonants when one word ends and the next begins with the same consonant, as in *and dear.*

The consonants *t, d, s, z,* and *r* are troublesome for many inexperienced singers. Frequently the letters *t* and *d* are blurred and dropped, especially at word endings. The tendency is to sing "an" for *and,* "liddle" for *little,* and so on.

The consonants *s* and *z* must be articulated very quickly and without accent to avoid a hissing effect. The letter *r* must not be sustained at any time. Emphasize the adjacent vowel sound and pronounce the *r* quickly. The letter *r* at the end of a word may be dropped. Thus *father* is sung "fathuh," not "fathrr."

Singing Songs

Sing the following songs, applying the recommended principles. These songs can also be sung with Autoharp, guitar, and simple piano chording as accompaniment. The chord symbols are provided where each chord change occurs.

AU CLAIR DE LA LUNE
IN THE SHINING MOONLIGHT

FRANCE
L.D.

Developing the Singing Voice

FLOW GENTLY SWEET AFTON

ROBERT BURNS

JAMES SPILMAN
L.D.

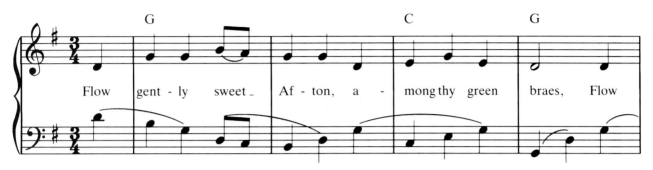

Flow gent - ly sweet _ Af - ton, a - mong thy green braes, Flow

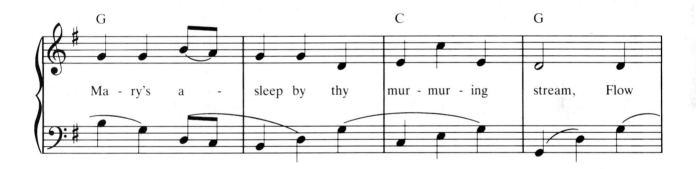

gent - ly I'll sing thee a song in thy praise; My

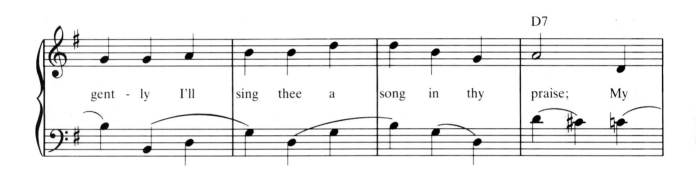

Ma - ry's a - sleep by thy mur - mur - ing stream, Flow

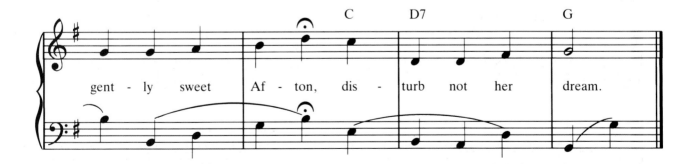

gent - ly sweet Af - ton, dis - turb not her dream.

Sing this Welsh air, concentrating on pure vowel sounds and clear consonants.

ALL THROUGH THE NIGHT

JAMES BOULTON

WELSH AIR
L.D.

Sleep my child and peace at-tend thee all through the night; _____

Guard - ian an - gels God will send thee all through the night. _____

Soft the drow-sy hours are creep-ing, hill and vale in slum - ber steep-ing,

I my lov - ing vig - il keep-ing all through the night. _____

Developing the Singing Voice

Sing this delightful English folk song slowly with a smooth flowing style. Notice the breath marks (').

THE TURTLE DOVE

ENGLAND
ARR. BY VAN A. CHRISTY

1. Fare thee well, my dear, I must be __ gone, And __ leave you __ for a __ while;
   For __ though I go I'll come back a - gain, Though I
2. So fair thou art my bon - ny __ lass, So __ deep in __ love am I;
   But I nev - er will prove false to the bon - ny lass I love, Till the
3. The crow that's black, my lit-tle tur - tle dove, Shall __ change its __ col - ors __ white;
   Be - fore I am false to the one that I love, The __

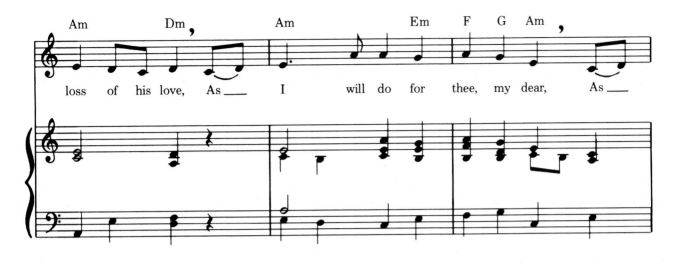

loss of his love, As ___ I will do for thee, my dear, As ___

I will do for thee. ___

From *Foundations in Singing*, 4th ed. by Van A. Christy © 1979 Wm. C. Brown Co. Publishers, Dubuque, Ia. Used by permission.

The classroom teacher should strive in every way to be as good a singer as possible for elementary school children to imitate and follow. It is not necessary to possess a strong solo voice. The aim is to develop a free musical tone and good diction. Most teachers can do it!

Suggested Assignments

1. Practice good singing posture and deep breathing in front of a full-length mirror.
2. Listen to recordings of the songbook series adopted by your state and local elementary school. Carefully study the vocal style and habits of the performing artist. Sing along with the recordings.
3. Sing songs from the various chapters of this book, applying the principles of singing stressed in this chapter.

3 Reading Rhythm

The years, the seasons, the phases of the moon, and the rising and setting of the sun are all evidence of a cosmic system, a regular and orderly sequence of events in extended time. Shorter but equally significant units of time are defined by the beating of the heart, breathing, and such physical activities as walking, running, and skipping. Quite naturally, time units organized systematically constitute an essential feature of music. The element of music that encompasses all aspects of sound organized in time is *rhythm*.

Beats and Notes

The pulse of music, which is one aspect of rhythm, can be felt by everyone, including those who have had no musical training and claim to have no musical talent. This fact is easily demonstrated. Play a recording of a John Philip Sousa march, such as *Stars and Stripes Forever*. As soon as you feel the pulse, tap your toes in time with the music. Everyone will tap at the same time, because everyone has the innate ability to sense the underlying pulse of music. The rhythmic pulses to which you are responding are *beats*. One way of notating beats is with the following symbols.

The symbols used to notate the rhythm and pitch of musical sounds are *notes*. The symbols shown are *quarter notes*. The term *note* is also used to denote a musical sound, though *tone* is a more appropriate term.

Measures and Bar Lines

With the march music still playing, stand up and march around the room. If there is insufficient space for marching, marking time in place with the feet will serve the purpose. Now you are not only keeping time with the beats in the music, but you are grouping the beats into pairs by stepping first with one foot and then with the other.

left   *right*   *left*   *right*   *left*   *right*   *left*   *right*

Listen carefully to the music and you will discover that one beat is stronger than the other. The stronger beat, which comes with the left foot in marching, marks the beginning of the group. It is stressed, or *accented*. The weaker beat that follows is unstressed, or *unaccented*. Accented and unaccented beats can be indicated by poetic scansion signs.

Groups of accented and unaccented beats form metric units called *measures*. Measures of music are divided by vertical lines called *bar lines*. Bar lines come between an unaccented beat and an accented beat. Stated another way, the beat just before a bar line is unaccented, and the beat right after a bar line is accented. Two bar lines together, called a *double bar*, indicate the end of an exercise or a composition.

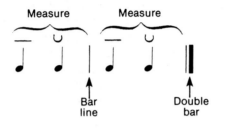

The beats in a measure are numbered consecutively, and one way of expressing musical rhythm is by counting. Continue marching to the music and count with the beats: *one, two, one, two.*

To illustrate a different kind of rhythm, play a recording of a waltz, such as the *Waltz of the Flowers*[1] from Tchaikovsky's *Nutcracker Suite*. The beat can be felt and the toes tapped in time to it, but the rhythm will not be appropriate for marching. Instead, you will want to waltz to the music.

The rhythmic group consists of one accented beat and two unaccented beats. While doing a waltz step to the music, count *one, two, three, one, two, three.*

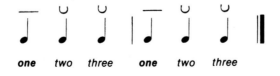

---

1. The waltz rhythm is clearer after the introduction.

Some music has a two-beat, or *duple*, rhythm; some has a three-beat, or *triple*, rhythm. Marches and waltzes illustrate the two basic patterns. Repetitions of these patterns produce the larger rhythmic and structural units of music.

Exercise 1

When recordings are played, clap with the beat. Determine whether the rhythm is basically marchlike (duple) or waltzlike (triple). Locate the accents, which will occur regularly every second or third beat, and clap more loudly on the accented beats. Count **one,** *two,* **one,** *two* when the rhythm is duple; count **one,** *two,* *three,* **one,** *two,* *three* when it is triple.

Exercise 2

Sing familiar songs, and decide which have two-beat patterns and which have three-beat patterns. They need not be marches or waltzes. These were used first only because their rhythms are most obvious. With practice you will be able to determine the underlying rhythm of any song.

2/4 Time Signature and Conductor's Beat

At the beginning of each piece of music there are two numbers, one above the other. This is the *time signature,* or *meter signature.* The lower number represents a kind of note, ordinarily the one used to express the beat. The upper number indicates the number of such beats in a measure. A 2/4 time signature, which is one used for marches, indicates that in each measure the total duration will equal two quarter-note beats.

Two Quarter notes

Conductors have a more subtle way of expressing rhythm than by marching or counting. They use *conductor's beats.* Conductor's beats are stylized patterns outlined in the air by the right hand or a baton. The basic patterns are standardized, but each conductor makes personal variations and adds embellishments. The ability to conduct is an essential skill for classroom teachers.

The first beat of a measure, referred to as the *downbeat,* is marked in conducting patterns by a downward stroke directly in front of the conductor. The lowest point is reached precisely with the accent. From this point in 2/4 time, the hand bounces to the conductor's right and up slightly. For the second beat, the *upbeat,* the motion is reversed, and the hand returns to the starting point. All conducting diagrams show the pattern for the right hand from the conductor's viewpoint, so the right hand motions of students doing the conducting exercises duplicate the pattern of the diagrams. For the left hand and from the viewer's perspective, the patterns are reversed, or mirrored.

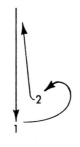

Perform the conductor's beat for 2/4 time while counting *one, two, one, two* until coordinating the hand motions with the numbers comes naturally.

A note symbol with a stem (the vertical line) like a quarter note but with an open head, is a *half note*. A half note, as the fractional name implies, has the same rhythmic value as two quarter notes.

One half note   𝅗𝅥   =   ♩ ♩   two quarter notes

Twinkle, Twinkle, Little Star is a familiar song in 2/4 time using quarter notes and half notes. The rhythm is the same for all three lines of the song, as notated, and the melody is the same for the first and third lines but different for the second line.

TWINKLE, TWINKLE, LITTLE STAR

Twin-kle,	twin-kle,	lit - tle	star,	How	I	won-der	what you	are!
Up a -	bove the	world so	high,	Like	a	dia-mond	in the	sky,
Twin-kle,	twin-kle,	lit - tle	star,	How	I	won-der	what you	are!

Sing *Twinkle, Twinkle, Little Star* while doing the conductor's beat. Next, recite the words with the rhythm of the song but without the tune. Then, count the beats and clap the rhythm, associating the rhythm with the notation.

The pitch notation is given elsewhere in the book for many of the songs in this chapter, including *Twinkle, Twinkle, Little Star*. Consult the Alphabetical Song Index for page numbers.

Two note symbols like quarter notes but with their stems joined by a beam, as shown, are *eighth notes*. Two eighth notes have the same rhythmic value as one quarter note.

One quarter note   ♩   =   ♫   two eighth notes

Hot Cross Buns is a familiar song in 2/4 time using half, quarter, and eighth notes.

HOT CROSS BUNS

Counting Eighth Notes

When learning to read rhythmic notation, it is helpful to have a system for counting and tapping eighth notes. One method is to say the number of the beat on the first eighth note and to say *"and,"* written &, on the second eighth note. The tapping of the toe, heel, or fingers coincides with the beats, and the high point of the upward motion coincides with the half beats.

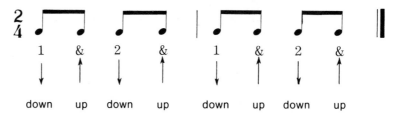

In books following the Kodály approach, the initial rhythm exercises are notated with just the stems and beams of the note symbols. Note heads are introduced later to notate the longer durations. Rhythms are chanted with syllables similar to those used in French solfège, though many variants are found in books written in English. Rhythm syllables adapted from Kodály are given for quarter and eighth notes. In the syllables the vowel *a* is pronounced "ah" and the vowel *i* is pronounced "ee."

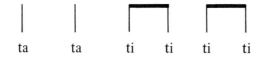

Tapping, counting, and chanting with rhythm syllables provide ways of relating the varied durations in a melody to the constant pulse of the beat. While tapping the beat, recite the rhythm of *Hot Cross Buns,* using first the beat counts and then the rhythm syllables. Numbers enclosed in parentheses are not pronounced in reciting the rhythm of the melody. When using the rhythm syllables, repeat the vowel sound on the second beat of half notes.

HOT CROSS BUNS

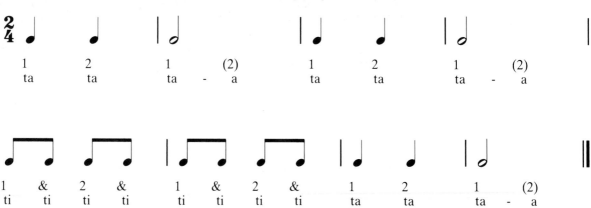

Exercise 3

Establish a steady background beat, and then perform the following rhythm patterns by counting, clapping, and/or chanting the rhythm syllables. Do each line twice without any break in the rhythm. Write the counts or the rhythm syllables under the notes as an aid to accurate performance wherever difficulties are encountered in the rhythm exercises. This and all subsequent rhythm exercises can also be performed on rhythm instruments (see chapter 7).

Repeat Signs

You were directed to do each line of the previous exercises twice, because at the end of each line there are two dots on the left side of the double bar. This is a *repeat sign*. It indicates that all or part of an exercise or composition is to be repeated. If the piece is to be repeated from the beginning, no other sign is necessary. If only part is to be repeated, that part is enclosed between a double bar with dots on the right and a double bar with dots on the left.

If the ending is different the second time, a *first ending* and a *second ending* are provided, each numbered and bracketed as shown. The first ending is performed the first time only; in the repetition the second ending is substituted.

A repeat sign is used in *Good-by, My Lover, Good-by* (p. 97) to indicate a repetition of the first half from the beginning. *Ring, Ring the Banjo* (p. 146) has facing repeat signs and first and second endings.

The abbreviation *D.C.,* for the Italian words *Da capo,* is also used to indicate repetitions. *Da capo* means to repeat from the beginning. *D.C.* can be used to direct an additional repetition of a passage already marked for one repetition by a double bar with dots. Dot-double-bar repeat signs are ignored when making *D.C.* repeats. After a repetition indicated by *D.C.* or *D.C. al Fine,* the place to end is marked *Fine. Joshua Fit the Battle of Jericho* (p. 204) and *Steal Away* (p. 261) have repetitions indicated by *D.C. al Fine.*

3/4 Time Signature and Conductor's Beat

Measures of three quarter-note beats, such as the measures in waltzes, are indicated by a 3/4 time signature.

Three
Quarter notes

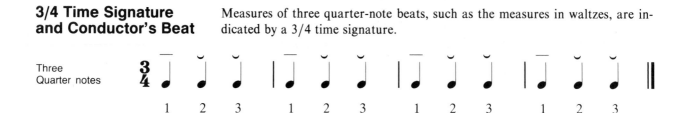

The conductor's beat for 3/4 time approximates the outline of a triangle, with a slight bounce for each beat. As always, the first beat of the measure comes with the downbeat of the pattern.

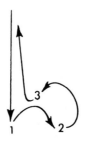

Perform the conductor's beat for 3/4 time while counting *one, two, three, one, two, three* until coordinating the hand motions with the numbers comes naturally.

A full measure in 3/4 time contains the rhythmic equivalent of three quarter notes. The note symbol with a rhythmic value equal to three quarter notes is a dotted half note, that is, a half note with a dot by the head, as shown.

One dotted half note 𝅗𝅥• = ♩ ♩ ♩ three quarter notes

Lavender's Blue is a familiar song in 3/4 time using quarter, eighth, and dotted half notes.

LAVENDER'S BLUE

Sing *Lavender's Blue* while doing the conductor's beat. Next, recite the words with the rhythm of the song but without the tune. Then, count the beats and clap the rhythm, associating the rhythm with the notation.

The counting and rhythm syllables are the same in 2/4 time and 3/4 time, except that in 3/4 time there are three beats in a measure. The vowel sound of *ta* is repeated on the second and third beats of measures filled by a dotted half note.

LAVENDER'S BLUE

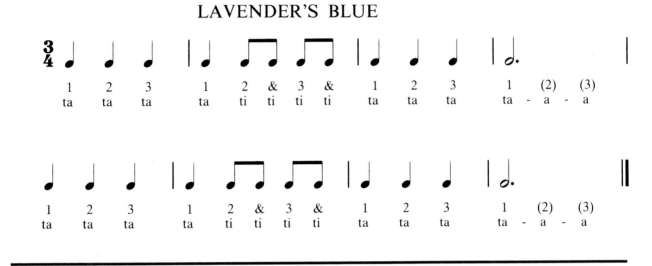

Exercise 4   Establish a steady background beat, and then perform the following rhythm patterns by counting, clapping, and/or chanting the rhythm syllables. Observe the repeat signs. Write the counts or the rhythm syllables under the notes as an aid to accurate performance whenever difficulties are encountered.

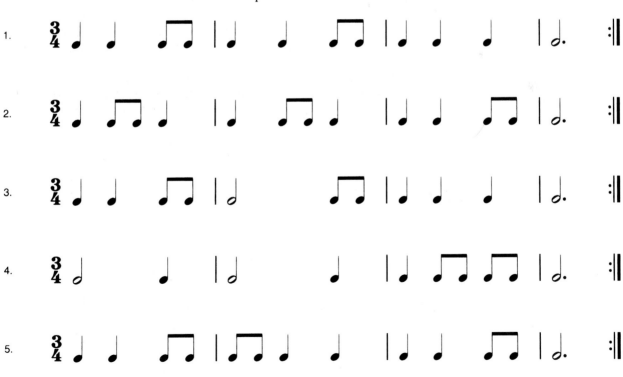

4/4 Time Signature and Conductor's Beat

Thus far, only simple duple and triple meters like those found in marches and waltzes have been considered. Although units of two or three beats are the basis of most rhythms, measures may contain more than one such unit. Two pairs of quarter-note beats constitute a measure in 4/4 time which, like 2/4 time, is also used for marches.

A measure of 4/4 time is not the same as two measures of 2/4 time. Each measure has only one *primary accent,* and it falls on the first beat of the measure. The third beat in 4/4 time is accented, but it is a lesser *secondary accent.* The second and fourth beats of 4/4 measures are unaccented. The metric pattern of 4/4 measures can be shown with scansion signs. Accented beats are marked by dashes—primary accents by a long dash and secondary accents by a short dash. This explanation of accents is valid for the folk and familiar songs in this book and for most of the standard concert literature. It does not apply to many jazz, rock, and avant-garde styles of music.

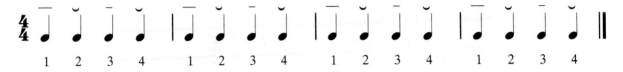

The following diagram shows the conductor's beat for 4/4 time.

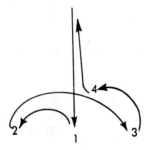

Perform the conductor's beat for 4/4 time while counting the beats until coordinating the hand motions with the numbers comes naturally.

Sing *Are You Sleeping,* or recite the words with the correct rhythm, while doing the conductor's beat. Pay special attention to the correlation between the accented syllables in the poem and the accented beats in the music.

ARE YOU SLEEPING

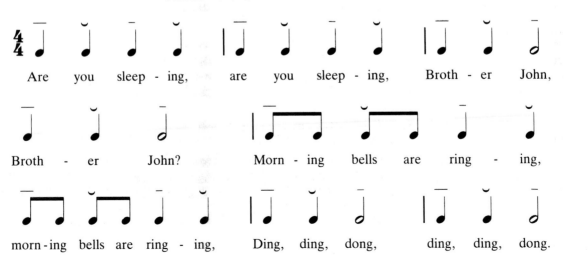

Exercise 5   The rhythmic notation of *Are You Sleeping* is given. Write the numbers of the beats under the notes occurring on a beat and an ampersand (&) under the eighth notes not on a beat. Below the numbers, write the rhythm syllables. Refer to the rhythmic notation of *Hot Cross Buns* and *Lavender's Blue* as models. Recite the rhythm with the numbers and syllables.

ARE YOU SLEEPING

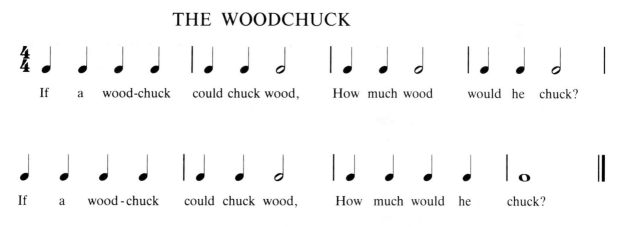

The note symbol for a full measure in 4/4 time is a *whole note*. A whole note has no stem, and its head is open like a half note but is somewhat larger and different in shape. A whole note has the same rhythmic value as four quarter notes.

One whole note      four quarter notes

In 4/4 time, whole notes most often occur at the ends of phrases and songs. *The Woodchuck* is a familiar song that ends with a whole note. See also *Au Clair de la Lune* on page 24.

THE WOODCHUCK

If   a   wood-chuck   could chuck wood,   How much wood   would he   chuck?

If   a   wood-chuck   could chuck wood,   How much would he   chuck?

While doing the conductor's beat, sing *The Woodchuck* with the words, and then recite the rhythm with the numbers. Be sure to sustain the vowel sound with the whole note in the last measure for four full beats.

Instead of a 4/4 time signature, a symbol that looks like a large C is sometimes used to indicate measures of four quarter-note beats, or *common time*. In the past, 4/4 and   **C**   time signatures were used interchangeably, but numerical time signatures are recommended in recent manuals on notation.

Ties and Dots

A curved line connecting two notes with the same pitch is a *tie*.

A tie has the effect of joining the two notes. The tone is sustained without interruption for their combined value. In vocal music tied notes have only one syllable. Ties may be used with all note values any place in the measure and across bar lines, but most often they connect fractions of beats or notes in different measures.

A *dot* after a note increases its value one half. A dotted half note equals a half note plus a quarter note. A dotted quarter note equals a quarter note plus an eighth note. A single eighth note is written like a quarter note with a *flag* (as shown) in place of the beam that connects pairs of eighth notes.

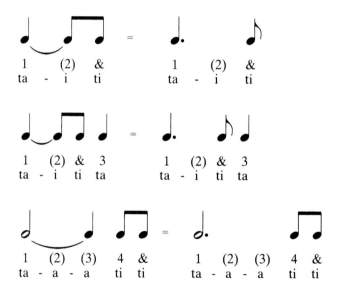

Some rhythms can be written with a tie or a dot.

In notating rhythm it is customary to use a dot rather than a tie when both are possible, though exceptions occur when the tie is to an eighth note written with a beam. Across a bar line a tie must be used, and some rhythms can only be notated with a tie.

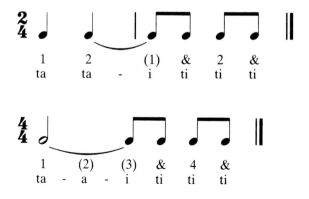

All through the Night is a familiar song that makes extensive use of dotted rhythms. The first, second, and fourth lines of the song have the same rhythm and melody, so they can be notated with a repeat sign and a *da capo* (see pp. 34–35).

ALL THROUGH THE NIGHT

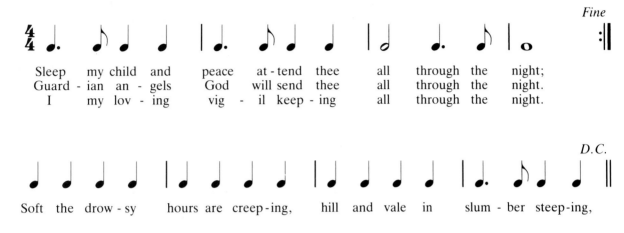

Sleep   my child and   peace   at - tend   thee   all   through   the   night;
Guard - ian   an - gels   God   will send   thee   all   through   the   night.
I   my lov - ing   vig - il   keep - ing   all   through   the   night.

Soft   the   drow - sy   hours   are   creep - ing,   hill   and   vale   in   slum - ber   steep - ing,

Sing *All through the Night* while doing the conductor's beat. Then, count the beats and clap the rhythm. Finally, recite the rhythm with the rhythm syllables.

Exercise 6   Ties and dots are used in the notation of the following rhythms. Write the numbers and rhythm syllables under the notes in the manner of the illustrative examples. Then, perform the rhythms in the ways suggested for previous rhythm exercises.

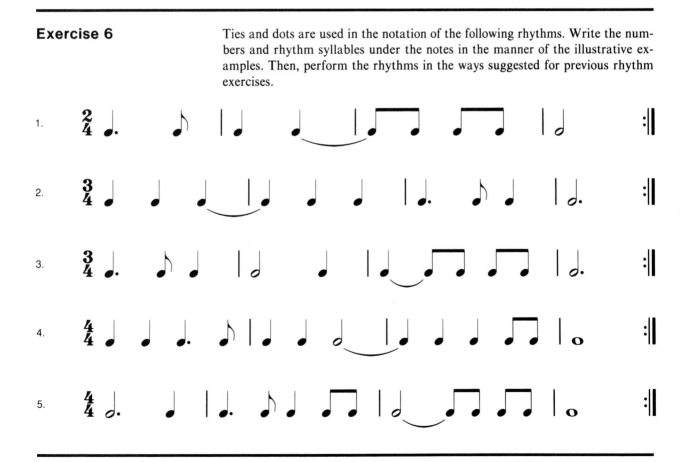

2/2 Time Signature

In all of the preceding exercises the beats have been represented by quarter notes, but beats can also be represented by half notes. When the beat is represented by a half note, the lower number of the time signature is 2. Half-note beats most often occur in measures of two beats for which the numerical time signature is 2/2. The pattern of accents and the rhythm numbers and syllables are the same as for 2/4 time.

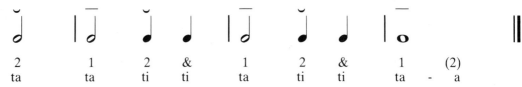

Measures of two half-note beats can be indicated by a 2/2 time signature or by a symbol like that for common time with a vertical line through it (¢) denoting *cut time,* or *alla breve* (by half notes). The symbols equivalent to 4/4 and 2/2 time signatures are common in the music of the past. Though rare in recent concert music, the symbols persist in other types of music, particularly in marches and popular music. Cut time is used for relatively fast tempos.

The conductor's beat for 2/2 and ¢ is the same as for 2/4. The appearance of the notation is changed, but not the sound, when a half note is used for the beat. When the time signature is 2/2 or ¢ , a half note receives one beat, a quarter note receives a half beat, and so on.

Anchors Aweigh is written in cut time. Do the conductor's beat (the same as for 2/4) and sing the song, paying particular attention to the relationship between the beat and the note values.

ANCHORS AWEIGH

CAPT. ALFRED H. MILES, U.S.N. (RET.)
AND CHARLES A. ZIMMERMANN

An - chors a - weigh, my boys, an - chors a - weigh. ___

Fare - well to coll-ege joys, we sail at break of day. ___

Through our last night on shore, drink to the foam, ___

Un - til we meet once more here's wish-ing you a hap-py voy-age home. ___

Exercise 7

Practice the following 2/2 (¢) rhythms in all of the ways suggested for previous rhythm exercises.

1.

2.

3.

3/8 Time Signature

In addition to quarter notes and half notes, eighth notes can also be used to represent beats. When the beat is represented by an eighth note, the lower number of the time signature is 8. The time signature for measures of three eighth notes is 3/8. Measures in 3/8 time contain the rhythmic equivalent of three eighth notes or a dotted quarter note. Consecutive eighth notes within a measure are beamed together, as shown. The pattern of accents and the conductor's beat for 3/8 time are the same as for 3/4 time, but the rhythm syllables are different. The following example shows the same rhythmic relationships notated first in 3/4 time and then in 3/8 time for comparison.

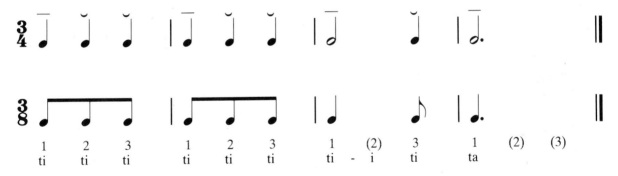

Since the same rhythmic relationships can be notated in both 3/4 and 3/8 time, it is apparent that note symbols represent only relative values, not precise durations that can be measured in seconds and fractions of seconds. The 3/8 time signature is rare in children's music. *Come on and Join into the Game* (p. 13) is an isolated example of a children's song in 3/8 time.

6/8 Time Signature and Conductor's Beat

A more usual time signature with eighth-note beats is 6/8. Measures in 6/8 time contain the rhythmic equivalent of six eighth notes. Consecutive eighth notes are beamed in groups of three, as in 3/8 time. The note symbol for a full measure in 6/8 time is a dotted half note, and the note symbol for a half measure is a dotted quarter note. The pattern of accents, the beat numbers, and the rhythm syllables for 6/8 time are shown in the following example.

The following diagram shows the conductor's beat for 6/8 time.

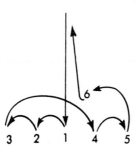

Perform the conductor's beat for 6/8 time while counting the beats and reciting the rhythm syllables of the preceding example until coordinating the hand motions with the numbers and syllables comes naturally.

Rockabye Baby is a lullaby in 6/8 time. Sing the song while doing the conductor's beat if the melody is familiar. Recite the rhythm with numbers and syllables even if the melody is not familiar.

ROCKABYE BABY

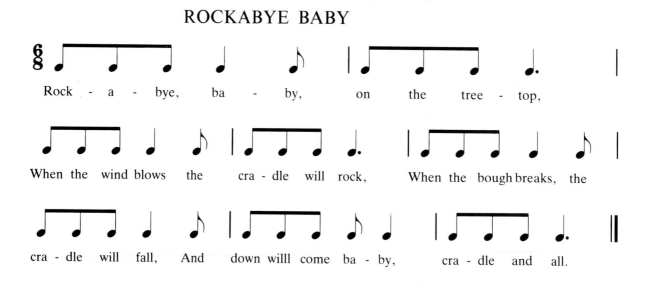

Since *Rockabye Baby* is a lullaby, it is sung slowly or, to use the musical terminology, at a slow *tempo* (rate of speed). The 6/8 time signature is also used for songs that are sung at a fast tempo. The style of *What Can the Matter Be* requires a fast tempo. Sing it in the usual way, and clap or tap the pulses. There are only two pulses in a measure. The beat is represented by a dotted quarter note, the equivalent of three eighth notes.

WHAT CAN THE MATTER BE

The conductor's beat for fast 6/8 time (in two) is the same as for 2/4 and 2/2 time. Many marches are written in 6/8 time, and these are always conducted in two. Moderate 6/8 tempos (between fast and slow) may be counted and conducted either way, in two or in six, at the discretion of the conductor or performer.

A different method of counting is required for fast 6/8 rhythms, because the dotted-quarter beats divide in thirds. The number of the beat can be used for notes occurring on the beat, with the syllables *la* (pronounced "lah") and *li* (pronounced "lee") for the divisions of the beat. In the Kodály method the same syllables are used for the beats and divisions as in 2/4—*ta* for the beats and *ti* for the divisions.

Exercise 8

Write the numbers over the notes using the eighth note as the beat and the numbers and syllables under the notes using the dotted quarter note as the beat, as in the model. Recite the rhythms with the numbers and syllables, first slowly in six and working up to a fast tempo in two. Then, tap or clap the rhythms or perform them on percussion instruments.

Slow: 1 2 3 4 5 6 | 1 (2)(3) 4 (5)(6) | 1 (2)(3) 4 5 6 | 1 (2)(3)(4)(5)(6)

Fast: 1 la li 2 la li | 1   2 | 1   2 la li | 1   (2)

Both: ti ti ti ti ti ti | ta   ta | ta   ti ti ti | ta - a

1. 6/8

2. 6/8

3. 6/8

4. 6/8

A new system of time signatures that offers certain advantages is gaining acceptance. In this system the lower number of the conventional signature is replaced by the appropriate note symbol. The system is not completely standardized, but even with minor variations the meaning is evident. The new equivalents for all of the time signatures studied thus far are shown.

$$\frac{2}{4} = \frac{2}{\text{♩}} \qquad \frac{3}{4} = \frac{3}{\text{♩}} \qquad \frac{4}{4} = \frac{4}{\text{♩}} \qquad C = \frac{4}{\text{♩}}$$

$$\frac{3}{8} = \frac{3}{\text{♪}} \qquad \frac{6}{8} = \frac{6}{\text{♪}} \text{ or } \frac{2}{\text{♩.}} \qquad \frac{2}{2} = \frac{2}{\text{𝅗𝅥}} \qquad ¢ = \frac{2}{\text{𝅗𝅥}}$$

Time signatures like 3/2, 9/8, and 12/8 are routinely included in theoretical studies, but they are rare in school music.

Rests

Durations of silence as well as durations of sound must be notated in music. For this purpose *rests* are used. There is a rest equivalent for every note value. Whole and half rests are distinguishable only in relation to a line (of the staff), as shown.

Whole rests are below the line; half rests above. The whole rest is used to notate complete measures of silence in all meters. Memorize the rest equivalents for all of the note values.

𝐨	Whole	▬		𝅘𝅥•	Dotted quarter	𝄽• or 𝄽𝄾
𝅗𝅥•	Dotted half	▬• or ▬𝄽		𝅘𝅥	Quarter	𝄽
𝅗𝅥	Half	▬		𝅘𝅥𝅮	Eighth	𝄿

Exercise 9

Write the numbers for the beats under the notes and rests. Then, while counting aloud, perform the rhythms on a rhythm instrument or by clapping or tapping.

1.

2.

3.

4.

5.

6.

Slow:
Fast:

Upbeats

When the words of a song begin with an unaccented syllable, the music begins with an *upbeat (anacrusis)*. An upbeat is one or more notes, but less than a measure, preceding the first primary accent in either vocal or instrumental music. When a piece begins with an upbeat and consequently an incomplete measure, it ends with a complementary incomplete measure, and the two incomplete measures combined are equal to one full measure, as in the following song. This song begins with a quarter-note upbeat and ends with a half note, for a correct total of three beats in 3/4 time.

OH WHERE, OH WHERE HAS
MY LITTLE DOG GONE

Oh where, oh where has my lit - tle dog gone? Oh

where, oh where can he be? _____ With his

tail cut short and his ears cut long, Oh

where, oh where can he be? _____

Rhythms can be performed by patting the left knee with the left hand and the right knee with the right hand. This is known by the German term *patschen*. Perform the rhythm of *Oh Where, Oh Where Has My Little Dog Gone*, using the right hand for the upbeat and all unaccented beats and the left hand for the accented beats. The notes for each hand are placed on the appropriate line in the following notation. (Patschen skills transfer readily to percussion instruments.)

OH WHERE, OH WHERE HAS
MY LITTLE DOG GONE

Exercise 10

For this exercise the teacher or one member of the class serves as the leader, and the other members of the class are followers. The leader, seated facing the class, establishes a meter and tempo by counting the beats with patschen. The followers imitate the leader immediately without breaking the rhythm, producing an echo effect. The leader then improvises a series of one-measure rhythm patterns, each of which is echoed by the followers. Sample 4/4 and fast 6/8 patterns are given. Members of the class can take turns serving as the leader and improvising rhythms in various meters. As facility improves, longer and more complex patterns can be used. (These exercises can also be performed on percussion instruments.)

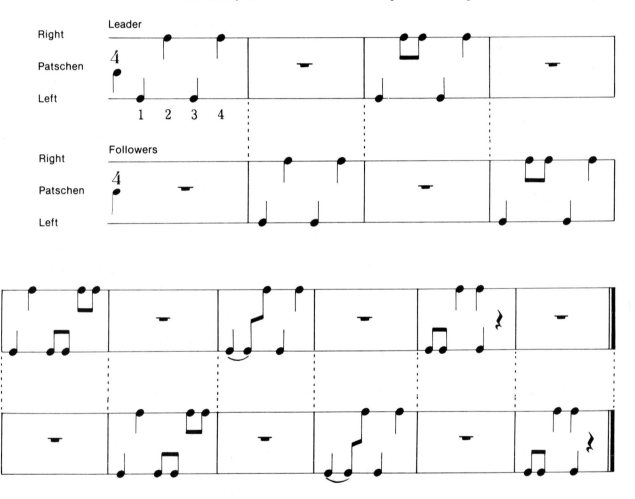

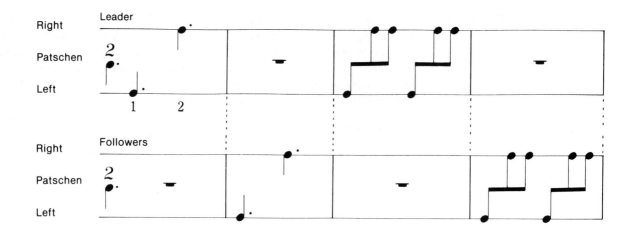

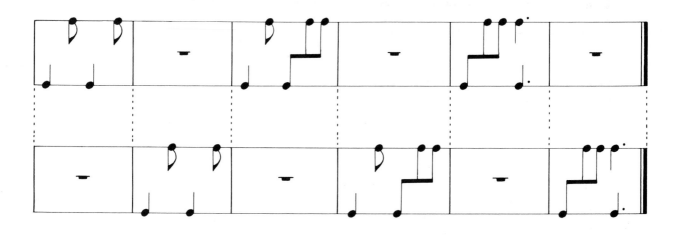

Reading Rhythm

Transcribing Rhythm

Thus far we have been concerned primarily with reading rhythmic notation, translating it into sound, and echoing rhythms. Being able to transcribe into notation rhythms that you hear or create is another useful skill. One way to start is by reciting names rhythmically while tapping a steady beat. Determine the relative duration of each syllable in the name, and then notate the rhythm in an appropriate meter with the accents in the words and music coinciding. The following are possible rhythms for the names of some celebrities. Write appropriate rhythms for your own name and for the names of your classmates.

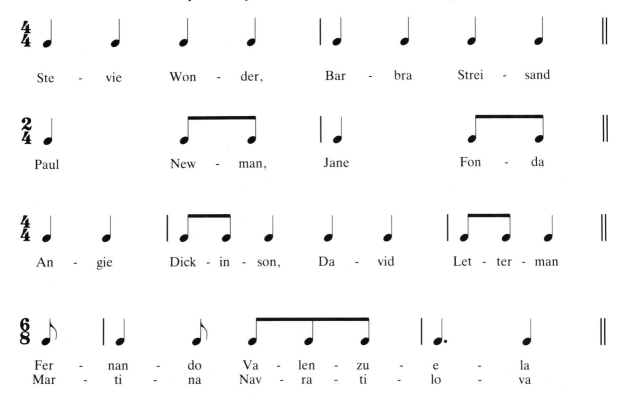

The ability to notate rhythms invented and performed by children, an invaluable asset for classroom teachers, can be developed by taking rhythmic dictation in the following manner. The teacher announces the meter and establishes the tempo by counting two measures and then claps (or performs in some other way) a four-measure rhythm pattern, which is repeated immediately. Here is a model exercise.

On the repetition the class joins the teacher in clapping the rhythm while counting the beats. Each student then writes the rhythm from memory, including the time signature and bar lines as well as the proper note values. As a sort of rhythmic shorthand, durations of a quarter note or less can be written without note heads in the manner of Kodály (see p. 34). Students then perform the rhythm, reading from the notation to check its accuracy.

Exercise 11

Here are some sample rhythms in various meters for rhythmic dictation following the procedures outlined.

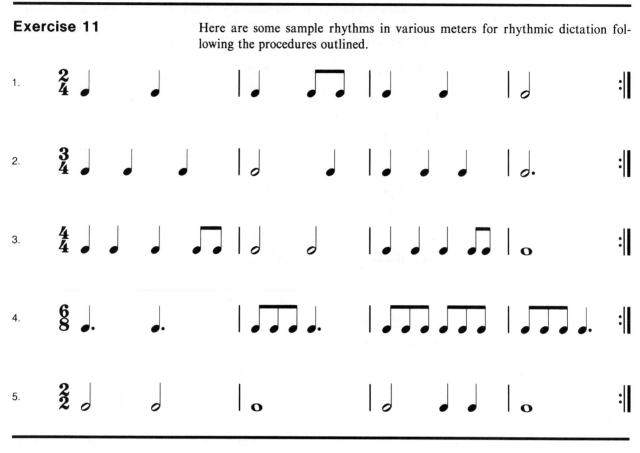

Exercise 12

Make up additional exercises and dictate them to your classmates. The difficulty and length of the exercises can be increased as proficiency in taking rhythmic dictation improves.

Subdivisions of the Beat

Beats can be divided and subdivided. Divisions of quarter-note beats are written as eighth notes (introduced early in this chapter). Equal subdivisions of quarter-note beats are written as *sixteenth notes*. The symbols for sixteenth notes are like those for eighth notes but with a second beam or flag. The symbol for a sixteenth rest is like that for an eighth rest but with a second appendage.

Sixteenth notes and rests:

One quarter note equals two eighth notes or four sixteenth notes. The Kodály rhythm syllables are shown for quarter-note beats, eighth-note divisions, and sixteenth-note equal subdivisions.

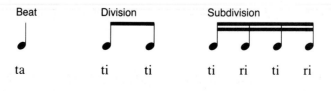

Beat	Division		Subdivision			
ta	ti	ti	ti	ri	ti	ri

Beats can also be divided unequally. The unequal subdivisions of quarter-note beats are shown. The notation on the left with ties is for illustrative purposes only. The normal notation of these rhythms is on the right.

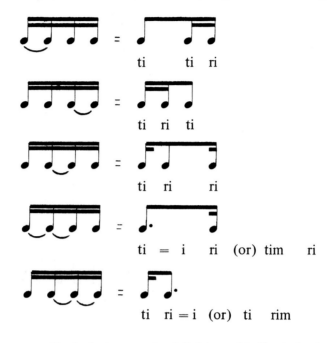

ti ti ri

ti ri ti

ti ri ri

ti = i ri (or) tim ri

ti ri = i (or) ti rim

Equivalent unequal subdivisions of half-note beats are as follows:

In the following table the relative durations of equally-divided undotted notes are shown graphically. Observe that the longer durations are represented by the simpler symbols and the shorter values by the more elaborate symbols.

1 whole note

equals

2 half notes

or

4 quarter notes

or

8 eighth notes

or

16 sixteenth notes

Dotted notes require a different table of relative durations. Observe that the dotted quarter notes in this context divide in thirds, unlike the other note values, which divide in halves. Dotted whole notes and groups of six sixteenth notes occur rarely, if at all, in familiar music but are included to parallel the preceding table.

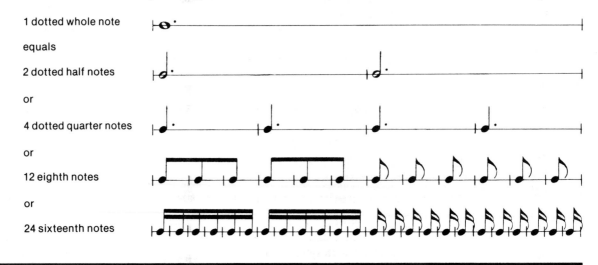

| 1 dotted whole note |
| equals |
| 2 dotted half notes |
| or |
| 4 dotted quarter notes |
| or |
| 12 eighth notes |
| or |
| 24 sixteenth notes |

Exercise 13

The following rhythm patterns exploit characteristic unequal subdivisions of beats in 2/4 and 2/2 time. Practice these patterns until you can perform them accurately and recognize them instantly.

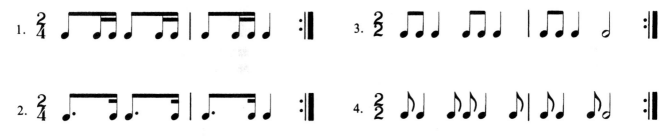

There are many possibilities for unequal subdivisions when the beat is represented by a dotted quarter note, but only the following are usual in familiar songs.

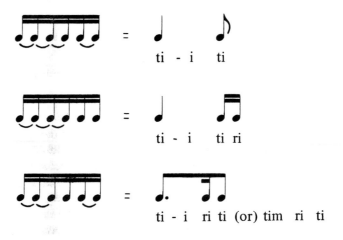

Exercise 14

Practice the following rhythm patterns, beginning slowly with the eighth value as the beat. Increase the speed in successive repetitions until the dotted-quarter value is perceived as the beat.

Exercise 15

The following rhythms from familiar songs contain equal and unequal divisions of the beat and involve most of the common rhythmic problems. Recite the rhythms with syllables and/or numbers. See if you can recognize the songs from the rhythm alone before looking at the titles listed at the end of the exercise. This material can also be used for supplementary drill in all of the response modes suggested previously.

Reading Rhythm

Here are the song titles. How many songs did you recognize from the rhythm alone?

1. *Long, Long Ago*, Bayly
2. *Auld Lang Syne*, Scotch folk song
3. *The Caissons Go Rolling Along*, Gruber
4. *The First Noel*, carol
5. *Yellow Rose of Texas*, U.S. folk song
6. *Battle Hymn of the Republic* (chorus), U.S. folk melody
7. *Joy to the World*, Mason
8. *My Old Kentucky Home*, Foster
9. *Vive l'Amour*, college song
10. *Home on the Range*, U.S. folk song

Triplets

Three notes of equal value within a beat that normally divides in halves and fourths are *triplets*. Triplets are indicated by a 3 in the middle of the beam that joins the notes of the group.

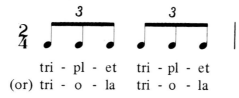

tri - pl - et   tri - pl - et
(or) tri - o - la   tri - o - la

The song *Row, Row, Row Your Boat* contains triplets.

ROW, ROW, ROW YOUR BOAT

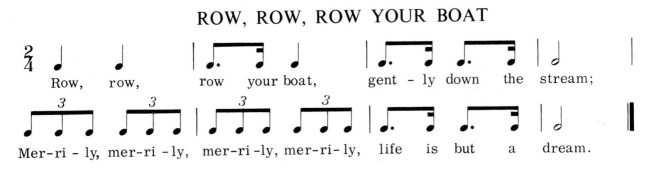

Syncopation

When the rhythmic flow momentarily fails to coincide with the beat, the effect is *syncopation*. Tying a weak beat or portion of a beat to a strong one produces syncopation. A short rest occurring where an accent is expected, a common rhythmic device in jazz, produces a similar effect.

TOM DOOLEY

Suggested Assignments

1. Place bar lines in the proper places in the following songs, and write the beat numbers and/or the rhythm syllables under the notes.

AMERICA

DECK THE HALLS

SWEET AND LOW

SHORTNIN' BREAD

2. Complete the measures with notes and/or rests.

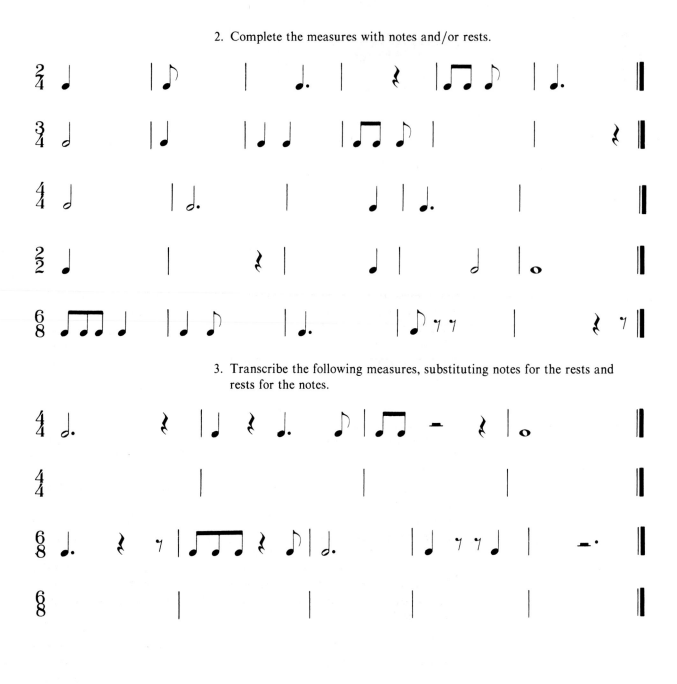

3. Transcribe the following measures, substituting notes for the rests and rests for the notes.

Reading Rhythm

4 Reading Pitch

When musical rhythms are combined with systematically organized pitches, melody results. Since melodic elements are present in virtually all music, the ability to read pitch notation is an essential musical skill. Although the note symbols already studied are used to notate both rhythm and pitch in conventional notation, rhythms and pitches can be represented by simple graphic *line notation*.

Line Notation

In line notation relative duration is represented by the length of the lines and relative pitch by the placement of the lines higher or lower on a page or blackboard. The line notation for *Under the Spreading Chestnut Tree* is given above the words.

Establish a regular beat by tapping at a moderate pace, or *tempo*. Then, while continuing the beat, recite rhythmically the words of *Under the Spreading Chestnut Tree*. Lines the length of that above the first syllable represent durations equal to one beat. Lines half as long represent durations equal to half a beat, and lines twice as long represent durations equal to two beats.

While the teacher plays or sings the melody of *Under the Spreading Chestnut Tree*, follow the line notation and act out the pitches with the right hand. Move the hand up when the pitch goes higher and down when the pitch goes lower. Whenever the same pitch recurs, represent it by the same hand position.

Finally, sing *Under the Spreading Chestnut Tree*, using the line notation to aid your memory of the teacher's performance. The relative height of the lines above the syllables accurately represents the relative pitch of the tones in the melody.

Line notation provides a simple musical shorthand useful for writing creative melodic ideas and for teaching songs to young children. Acting out the pitches with the hand serves as a preliminary exercise for more precise hand signals.

UNDER THE SPREADING CHESTNUT TREE

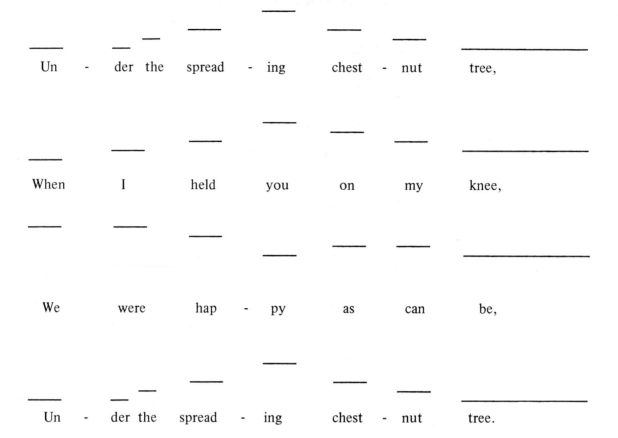

Un - der the spread - ing chest - nut tree,

When I held you on my knee,

We were hap - py as can be,

Un - der the spread - ing chest - nut tree.

The Staff and Ledger Lines

Line notation shows only the general contour of a melody. Melodic contours are represented more precisely in conventional music notation on a *staff* consisting of five equidistant lines. The five lines enclose four spaces. The lines and spaces of the staff are numbered separately from bottom to top.

Note symbols are placed on the lines, in the spaces, and above and below the staff. The stems of notes below the middle line of the staff extend up from the right side of the head. The stems of notes on and above the middle line of the staff extend down from the left side of the head. The direction of all the stems in beamed groups is dictated by the note farthest from the center of the staff. Other factors being equal, stems go down. Chords are stemmed like beamed groups.

Short, discontinuous lines called *ledger* (also spelled *leger*) *lines* are used to notate pitches beyond the range of the staff.

The Treble Clef

The location of notes on a staff shows relative pitch relationships like hand positions and line notation. With the addition of a *clef sign,* each line and space indicates a specific pitch. The clef sign most often used for vocal music, the right-hand part in piano music, and in music for guitar and most melody instruments is a *treble clef.*

The staff notation for *Under the Spreading Chestnut Tree* follows. The treble clef sign is on the staff at the beginning of each line. The time signature appears only once, following the first clef sign. The rhythmic functions of the note symbols were introduced in chapter 3.

UNDER THE SPREADING CHESTNUT TREE

FOLK SONG

ENGLAND

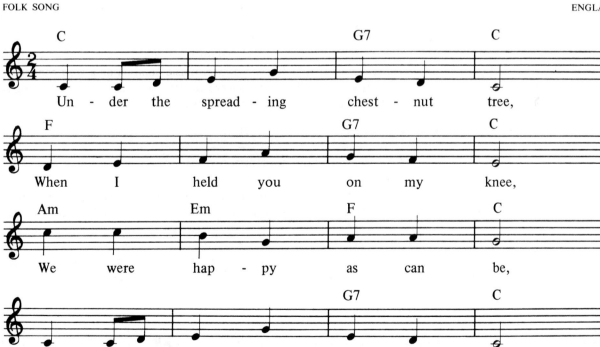

Note Names

Notes are identified by names. Every note has three: a letter, a number, and a syllable. The letter names indicate specific pitches. The number and syllable names indicate note positions in relation to a keynote and scale. The number and syllable names function in the same way, but the syllable sounds are more pleasing. The letter, number, and syllable names for the notes of *Under the Spreading Chestnut Tree* are given. Sing the melody, substituting in turn each set of note names for the words.

UNDER THE SPREADING CHESTNUT TREE

FOLK SONG

ENGLAND

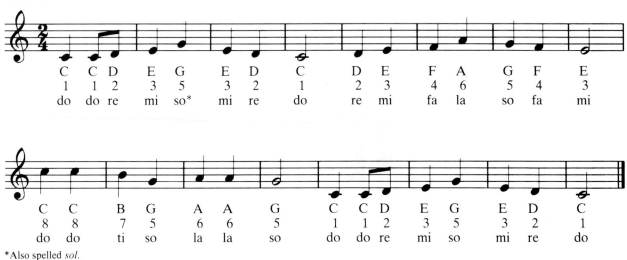

*Also spelled *sol.*

There are seven basic note names in each set, all of which are used in naming the notes of *Under the Spreading Chestnut Tree.* The note names occur in order when naming the notes written consecutively in ascending order on every line and in every space of the staff. After the seventh note, the sequence of letter and syllable names is repeated, starting again with the first. However, in this context the number designation for the next note is 8(1).

	C	D	E	F	G	A	B	C	D	E	F	G	A	B	C
	1	2	3	4	5	6	7	8(1)	2	3	4	5	6	7	8(1)
	do	re	mi	fa	so	la	ti	do	re	mi	fa	so	la	ti	do
(Kodály)	d	r	m	f	s	l	t	d'	r'	m'	f'	s'	l'	t'	d'

From any note up or down to the next note with the same names is an *octave,* meaning "eight." The numbers 1 and 8 are interchangeable. The letter names are the first seven letters of the alphabet, though the preceding example starts on C. In Kodály notation, pitches are sometimes represented by the initial letter of their syllable names, as shown. A prime sign by a letter indicates the higher octave.

A series of notes arranged consecutively in ascending or descending order forms a *scale.*

The C Major Scale

Sing the following scale both up and down with all three names. It probably has a familiar sound, because *Under the Spreading Chestnut Tree* and much of the music you know are based on a scale pattern like this. It is a *major scale*. Each scale takes its letter name from the note on which it begins and ends. This scale begins and ends on C, so it is a C major scale.

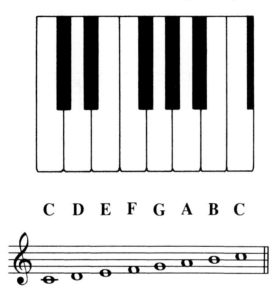

C	D	E	F	G	A	B	C	C	B	A	G	F	E	D	C
1	2	3	4	5	6	7	8 (1)	8	7	6	5	4	3	2	1
do	re	mi	fa	so	la	ti	do	do	ti	la	so	fa	mi	re	do

You may have been unaware of it when you were singing, but the pitch differences between notes of a major scale are not all the same. This is easy to see if the notes are located on a piano keyboard.

C D E F G A B C

There is a black key between C and D and between D and E, but not between E and F. There is a black key between each pair of white keys from F to B, but not between B and C. The *interval* (difference in pitch) between white keys with a black key between them and between all alternate keys, whether white or black, is a *whole step*, or *whole tone*. The interval between white keys without a black key between them and between all adjacent keys, whether white or black, is a *half step*, or *semitone*. Two half steps equal one whole step.

Major scales are made up of whole steps and half steps. In the C major scale the half steps come between E and F and between B and C. Using the other names, the half steps come between 3 and 4 *(fa and mi)* and between 7 and 8 *(ti and do)*. The pattern of whole steps and half steps is the same in all major scales.

Hand Signals

Hand signals have been used for centuries as an aid in learning music. The first system of hand signals is attributed to Guido d'Arezzo (c. 990–1050), who is also credited with being the first to use syllable names for notes. John Curwen's system of hand signals, adopted and popularized by Zoltán Kodály, associates each scale degree with a hand shape and position. The shape of the hand suggests the tendency of the tones in the scale: closed for *do*, which is most stable, open and level for *mi* and *so,* which are relatively stable, and pointing for active tones, which have a tendency to move in a particular direction. The relative pitch of each tone is represented by the position of the hand: waist level for low *do* and proportionately higher for each pitch up to high *do* above the head.

The hand signals for *Scale Song,* placed above the staff to reflect the relative pitch of the notes, are associated with corresponding number, syllable, and letter names in the words of the song. Sing the song while doing the hand signals until you instinctively associate the shape and position of the hand and the various names for the notes with the degrees of the C major scale.

SCALE SONG

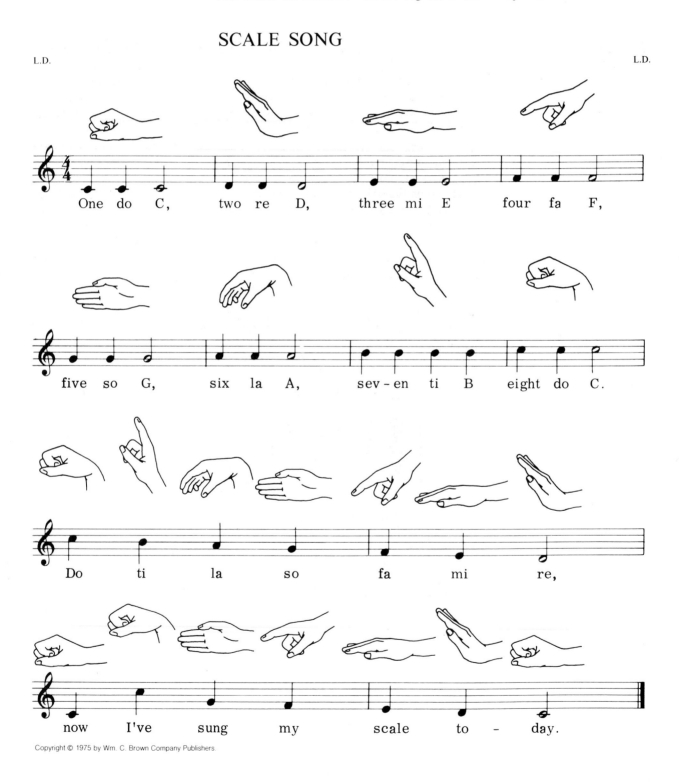

Some teachers prefer the following hand signal for *fa*.

fa

Sharps, Flats, and Naturals

Within an octave there are only seven staff positions and seven basic letter names for notes, but there are twelve different pitches. To notate the other five pitches, sharps and flats are used. A sharp (♯) to the left of a note indicates that the next higher pitch is to be sung or played. A flat (♭) to the left of a note indicates that the next lower pitch is to be sung or played. A natural (♮) cancels the effect of a sharp or a flat.

The illustration below shows where the sharp, flat, and natural notes are found in each octave of the piano keyboard. A full-sized, four-octave keyboard is enclosed in the endleaf pocket at the back of this book. The natural notes are played on the white keys; the commonly used sharp and flat notes, on the black keys. Observe that each black key serves for two notes, the sharp inflection of the note below and the flat inflection of the note above. The less usual sharp and flat notes, played on the white keys, are shown in parentheses. Two notes, like C-sharp and D-flat, that are played on the same key and have the same pitch but are written differently are *enharmonic notes*.

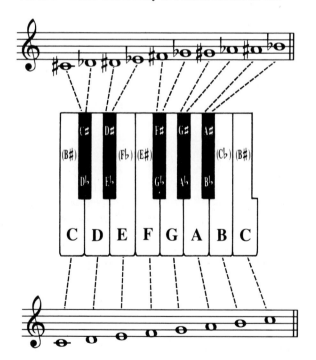

The Chromatic Scale

The sequence of notes that includes every pitch consecutively is a *chromatic scale.* The pitches of chromatic scales can be written with either sharps or flats, but it is customary to use sharps for notes that go up and flats for notes that go down. The C major syllable names are given above the letter names for both the ascending and descending chromatic scales. Observe that the only natural notes not separated by a sharp or a flat note are E-F and B-C.

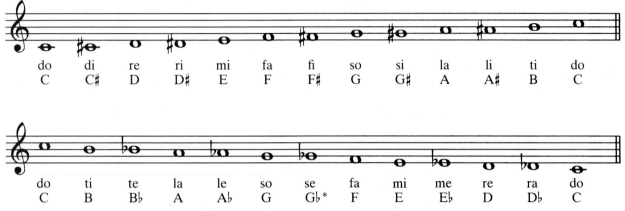

do di re ri mi fa fi so si la li ti do
C   C♯ D D♯ E F F♯ G G♯ A A♯ B C

do ti te la le so se fa mi me re ra do
C B B♭ A A♭ G G♭* F E E♭ D D♭ C

*The G-flat notation is rare. The pitch is usually written as F-sharp, even descending.

All of the musical examples should be sung and/or played. Even students with no prior keyboard experience can play scales on the piano with one finger. Songs that are introduced before music reading skills are sufficiently developed should be learned partially by rote with the assistance of the teacher.

Play the ascending and descending chromatic scales on the piano, and sing them with syllable and letter names. In this way you will become familiar with the sound, notation, and names of all the notes. The all-inclusive chromatic scale is introduced for this purpose. Only in the more complex works of the twentieth century is it used as a basis for composition. Most of our music is based on selective scales containing from five to seven of the twelve available pitches.

Pentatonic Music and Scales

Music in which only five tones are used is *pentatonic,* and the notes of such music arranged in order form *pentatonic scales.* Although numerous five-tone scale patterns are possible, the most prevalent ones contain no semitones and two gaps. *Barnyard Song* is based on a pentatonic scale of this type.

Sing *Barnyard Song* according to these directions: Omit the 3/4 measure in the first verse and sing it only once in the second verse. Starting with the third verse, sing all of the animal names and sounds from the preceding verses in reverse order before going on to "Bird goes fiddle-ee-fee."

BARNYARD SONG

FOLK SONG

U.S.

1. I had a bird, and the bird pleased me, I fed my bird by yon-der tree;
2. I had a hen, and the hen pleased me, I fed my hen by yon-der tree;

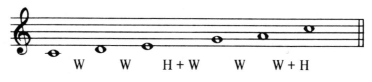

(2) Hen goes chim-my chuck, chim-my chuck, Bird goes fid-dle-ee - fee.

3. Duck: quack, quack
4. Goose: swishy, swashy
5. Sheep: baa, baa

6. Pig: griffy, gruffy
7. Cow: moo, moo
8. Horse: neigh, neigh

The pentatonic scale from which the notes of *Barnyard Song* are derived is shown below. It is like a C major scale with the fourth and seventh notes omitted: C D E __ G A __ C. The gaps are equal to a whole step (W) plus a half step (H), or vice versa.

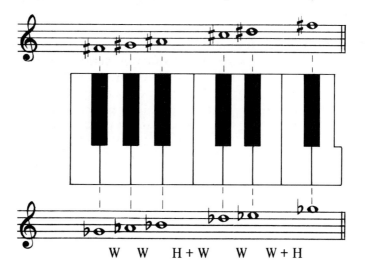

An identical pentatonic scale pattern is produced by the black keys of the piano, which can be notated with either sharps or flats.

Create spontaneous pentatonic melodies by improvising on the black keys of the piano.

Nine Hundred Miles, like *Barnyard Song,* is based on a pentatonic scale that has no semitones and two gaps. The gaps come in different places, however, creating a very different mood. The melody revolves around D, and the notes of its scale are D__ F G A__ C D.

NINE HUNDRED MILES

FOLK SONG

U.S.

1. I am walk - in' down the track, I got tears ___ in my eyes, Try - in' to read a let - ter from my home. If that train runs me right, I'll be home Sat - ur - day night, For I'm nine hun - dred miles ___ from ___ home, And I hate to hear that lone - some whis - tle blow.

2. Oh, this train that I ride on is one hundred coaches long,
   You can hear the whistle blow for miles and miles.
3. Oh, I'm gonna pawn my watch, and I'm gonna pawn my chain,
   And I'm gonna pawn my gold and diamond ring.
4. If my love bids me stay, I will never go away,
   For it's near her I always want to be.

Pentatonic scales like those illustrated contain no sharp dissonances or tendency tones. Their pitches, played in almost any melodic succession or harmonic combination, consistently produce a pleasant sound. These attributes make pentatonic scales an ideal point of departure for group improvisation and spontaneous musical activities.

The melodies of many songs contain six or fewer different notes. Except for pentatonic melodies, however, they are generally regarded as being based on one of the seven-tone scales, of which the major scale is the most common.

Major Scales, Keys, and Signatures

The C major scale has been introduced (p. 65). Songs based on the C major scale are said to be in the key of C major. *Under the Spreading Chestnut Tree* (pp. 63–64) and *Scale Song* (p. 66) are in the key of C major. Starting on C, the major scale pattern is produced by the natural notes played on the white keys of the piano. The C major scale serves as the model for the other major scales. It has half steps (marked ⌒) between 3–4 and 7–8, whole steps elsewhere. Viewed another way, it consists of two identical whole–whole–half (W W H) patterns with a whole step between them, as shown.

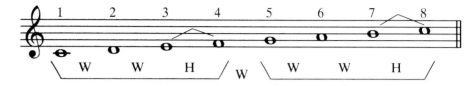

G Major

To construct a major scale starting on any note but C, one or more sharps or flats is required. For example, F-sharp is necessary to produce the correct pattern of whole and half steps in the major scale starting on G. This is a G major scale. (Use the Scale Builder in the endleaf pocket at the back of this book to determine the notes in any major scale.)

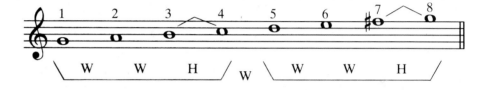

It is not customary to write the sharp by every F in the key of G major. Instead, a sharp is placed on the staff at the beginning of each line of music. This means that every F in the piece is sharp unless the sharp is canceled by a natural sign. Sharps or flats placed at the beginning of each line to indicate the key are called *key signatures*. The key signature for G major is one sharp. In the treble clef it is placed on the top line.

Are You Sleeping is in the key of G major, and it is customary to notate it with an F-sharp key signature even though the melody has only six different notes and no F or F-sharp. This song is a *round* intended for group singing. When singing rounds in class, it is advisable to learn the melody and words with everyone singing together. Then, the class is divided into the number of groups (of approximately equal size) indicated by the numbers above the music, four in this case. Group 1 begins alone. When group 1 reaches the number 2 in the music, group 2 enters at the beginning. When group 1 reaches the number 3 in the music, group 3 enters at the beginning, and so on. On reaching the end of the melody, each group goes " 'round" to the beginning and repeats the song. After the desired number of repetitions, each group completes the melody and drops out in the order of entry. Rounds are introduced at this point for advanced classes and for subsequent use. Inexperienced singers and young children can sing the simple melodies and postpone singing rounds in parts until they gain more proficiency.

ARE YOU SLEEPING

ROUND

FRANCE

Letter names are associated with specific pitches and are the same regardless of the key. Syllable and number names reflect pitch relationships within a key, and they change, in relation to the letter names, as the key changes. The note from which a key takes its name is the *keynote*. In major keys the keynote is always *do* (1). The syllable and number names of the other notes are in a fixed relationship to the keynote and to each other. Observe these facts as you sing *Are You Sleeping* with syllable, number, and letter names.

ARE YOU SLEEPING

ROUND

FRANCE

Find other songs in the key of G major and sing them, first with the words, and then with the syllable, number, and letter names.

F Major

The major scale starting on F requires a B-flat.

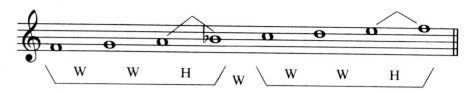

The flat in the key signature for F major, B-flat, goes on the third line in the treble clef.

Good Night is in the key of F major. The keynote, F, is *do* (1). The first note, C, is *so* (5). Sing the song first in unison (everyone singing together), using the syllable, number, and letter names, and then as a round using the words.

GOOD NIGHT

ROUND

ENGLAND

Good night to you all, and sweet be thy sleep; May an - gels a -

round you their si - lent watch keep, Good night, good night, good night, good night.

D Major

Add the necessary sharps or flats to the notes to make a major scale starting on D. Mark the whole and half steps and the four-note patterns, using the C, G, and F scales as models.

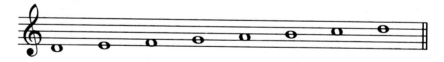

There should be sharps on F and C.

The key signature for D major appears in the following folk song, *Sweet Betsy from Pike.*

SWEET BETSY FROM PIKE

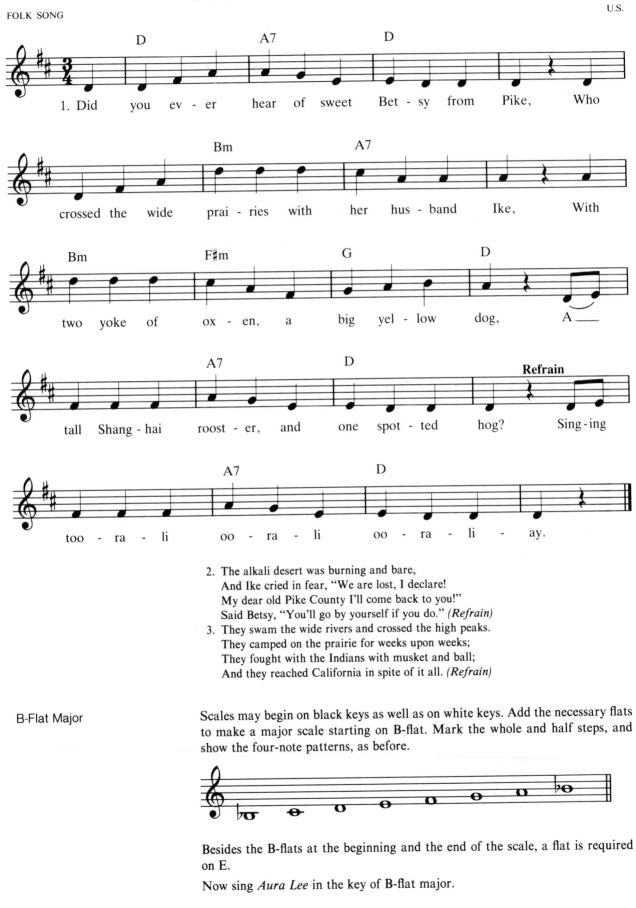

1. Did you ev-er hear of sweet Bet-sy from Pike, Who crossed the wide prai-ries with her hus-band Ike, With two yoke of ox-en, a big yel-low dog, A—— tall Shang-hai roost-er, and one spot-ted hog? Sing-ing too-ra-li oo-ra-li oo-ra-li-ay.

2. The alkali desert was burning and bare,
And Ike cried in fear, "We are lost, I declare!
My dear old Pike County I'll come back to you!"
Said Betsy, "You'll go by yourself if you do." *(Refrain)*

3. They swam the wide rivers and crossed the high peaks.
They camped on the prairie for weeks upon weeks;
They fought with the Indians with musket and ball;
And they reached California in spite of it all. *(Refrain)*

B-Flat Major

Scales may begin on black keys as well as on white keys. Add the necessary flats to make a major scale starting on B-flat. Mark the whole and half steps, and show the four-note patterns, as before.

Besides the B-flats at the beginning and the end of the scale, a flat is required on E.

Now sing *Aura Lee* in the key of B-flat major.

AURA LEE

1. As the black-bird in the spring, 'neath the wil-low tree, ____

Sat and piped I heard him sing, sing-ing Au - ra Lee.

Chorus

Au - ra Lee, Au - ra Lee, maid of gold - en hair,

Sun - shine came a - long with thee, and swal-lows in the air.

2. In her blush the rose was born,
   Music when she spoke,
   In her eyes the glow of morn
   Into splendor broke.

Finding the Keynote

A scale may begin on any note, and each one requires a particular key signature to produce the major scale pattern. Up to seven sharps or flats may appear in the key signature, but children's songs rarely have more than three or four. You must remember that the major key with no sharps or flats is C. The keynote, *do* (1), can be located for any other signature by a simple formula.

The keynote of a sharp key is always a half step above the last sharp, that is, the sharp farthest to the right in the signature. The last sharp is *ti* in the scale, and *do* is just above *ti*.

The keynote of a flat key is always the same as the next-to-last flat, that is, the flat second from the right in the signature. The last flat in the signature is *fa,* and *do* also can be located by counting down the scale from the last flat: *fa, mi, re, do.* This system must be used for F major, which has only one flat.

The following table gives the commonly used major key signatures with their names and keynotes. Key signatures with more than four sharps or flats are rare in school music.

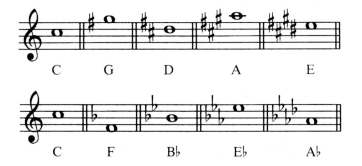

The Bass Clef

The low pitches sung by bass voices and played by the left hand on the piano cannot be written conveniently in the treble clef. For the pitches in this range another clef sign is used, the *bass clef.*

𝄢

The bass clef is also used for tenor voices when they are written on the same staff with the basses and for the large (low-pitched) instruments.

The function of the bass clef is most easily understood as a continuation downward from the treble clef. The note written on the first ledger line below the treble staff and the one written on the first ledger line above the bass staff are the same, *middle C.* Middle C is the C near the center of the piano keyboard and just below the lock or trademark.

A treble staff and a bass staff are combined to notate music for piano and mixed voices. The notes in the treble clef are played by the right hand on the piano and those in the bass clef by the left hand. For voices, the soprano and alto (women's) parts are in the treble clef, and the tenor and bass (men's) parts are in the bass clef. The same music can be used for piano and mixed voices, and this is usual in collections of familiar songs and hymns. The bar lines extend through both staffs in piano music except when there are words between the staffs.

The notation for *Prayer of Thanksgiving* is typical of multipurpose music intended for both singing and playing. Sing the song, in parts if possible, with the piano. The soprano and bass lines can be reinforced by melody instruments or played independently as a duet.

PRAYER OF THANKSGIVING

THEODORE BAKER
HYMN

NETHERLANDS

Sing the Revolutionary War ballad *Johnny Has Gone for a Soldier,* and notice how different it sounds from the songs you have been singing.

JOHNNY HAS GONE FOR A SOLDIER

FOLK SONG

IRELAND/U.S.

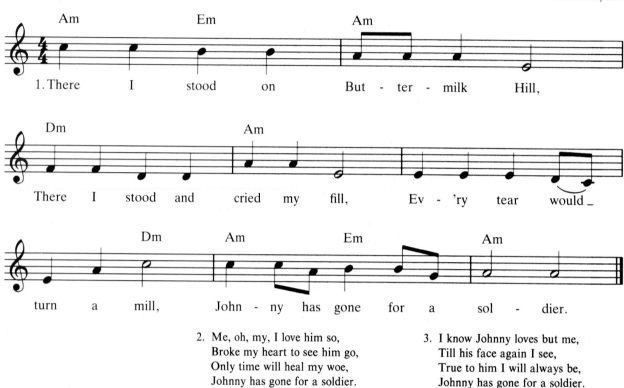

1. There I stood on But - ter - milk Hill,
There I stood and cried my fill, Ev - 'ry tear would _
turn a mill, John - ny has gone for a sol - dier.

2. Me, oh, my, I love him so,
   Broke my heart to see him go,
   Only time will heal my woe,
   Johnny has gone for a soldier.

3. I know Johnny loves but me,
   Till his face again I see,
   True to him I will always be,
   Johnny has gone for a soldier.

The sound of *Johnny Has Gone for a Soldier* is different from that of the songs in the preceding section, because it is in a minor key, A minor. The notes of the melody arranged as a scale starting on A have the pattern of whole steps and half steps shown. A scale with this pattern of whole steps and half steps is a *natural minor* scale. The A natural minor scale is written without sharps or flats and is played on the white keys of the piano. Play the scale ascending and descending.

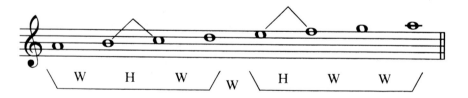

Sing *Johnny Has Gone for a Soldier* again, and listen for the distinctive minor quality produced by the descending line—C, B, A—in the first two measures and the embellished repetition of the same line in the last two measures.

The key signature for A minor is the same as for C major, no sharps or flats. The major key and the minor key with the same signature are *relative keys*. C is the *relative major* of A minor; A is the *relative minor* of C major. In school music the same syllables are used for relative keys. Any natural minor scale is like its relative major scale starting on *la* (6).

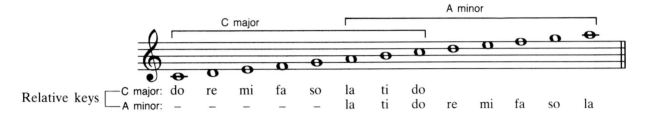

Relative keys
C major: do re mi fa so la ti do
A minor: –   –   –   –   –   la ti do re mi fa so la

The minor key and the major key with the same keynote are *parallel keys*. For example, A minor is the parallel minor of A major, and A major is the parallel major of A minor.

Many songs in minor keys contain notes borrowed from the parallel major key. The notes borrowed are the sixth and/or seventh degrees of the scale. In the key of A minor these notes are F-sharp and G-sharp, in place of F and G. With these borrowed notes the A minor scale and the A major scale are the same except for the third degree, C, which is natural in minor and sharp in major. Since parallel scales have the same keynote, it would seem logical to use the same syllables for the corresponding scale degrees and to change the vowel sound for the third degree from *mi* in major to *me* (pronounced "may") in minor, as shown. This system has the advantage of calling the keynote *do* in both major and minor and the other notes with similar functions by the same syllable names. Though not widely used, it is worth considering.

A major:
↑
Parallel keys

do   re   mi   fa   so   la   ti   do

↓
A minor:

do   re   me   fa   so   la   ti   do

The syllables for natural minor are given in both systems. In natural minor the third, sixth, and seventh degrees of the scale are a half step lower than the corresponding degrees of the parallel major scale, and the vowel sounds are changed accordingly to *me, le,* and *te* (see the chromatic scale, p. 68). Sing the A natural minor scale ascending and descending with both sets of syllables, and discuss the relative merits of the two systems.

Natural Minor

la ti do re mi fa so la   la so fa mi re do ti la
do re me fa so le te do   do te le so fa me re do

Sing *Dame Get Up,* or listen while it is played. The key is A minor, but observe that each time the note G occurs in the melody it is preceded by a sharp. G-sharp is one of the notes from the parallel major key that is frequently used in A minor.

DAME GET UP

CAROL
ENGLAND

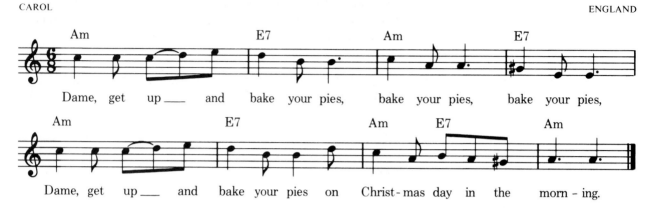

Dame, get up ___ and bake your pies, bake your pies, bake your pies,

Dame, get up ___ and bake your pies on Christ-mas day in the morn-ing.

G-sharp is used consistently in the melody and also in the chords indicated for *Dame Get Up*. When only the seventh degree of the parallel major key is used in a minor key, the form of minor is *harmonic minor*. The syllables for harmonic minor are given in both systems. Sing the A harmonic minor scale ascending and descending with both sets of syllables or with the one adopted for class use.

Harmonic Minor

| la | ti | do | re | mi | fa | si | la | | la | si | fa | mi | re | do | ti | la |
| do | re | me | fa | so | le | ti | do | | do | ti | le | so | fa | me | re | do |

Follow the notation while the teacher plays *Charlie Is My Darling* until the melody is familiar. Then, sing the song.

CHARLIE IS MY DARLING

FOLK SONG
ENGLAND

1. Char - lie is my dar - ling, my dar - ling, my dar - ling,

Char - lie is my dar - ling, the young chev - a - lier. ___

Verse

1. 'Twas on a Mon-day morn - ing right ear - ly in the year, ___ When_

Char - lie came to our ___ town, the_ young_ chev - a - lier. ___

Charlie Is My Darling begins and ends on A and is in the key of A minor, but it contains more different notes than have been found in any scale previously. Write all of the notes used in *Charlie Is My Darling* on the staff in ascending order between the A below the staff and the A on the staff.

The melody of *Charlie Is My Darling* uses all of the notes of the A natural minor scale plus F-sharp and G-sharp borrowed from the parallel major scale. The notes between A and E are the same in all forms of the A minor scale. The notes ascending between E and A in *Charlie Is My Darling* are F, F-sharp, G, and G-sharp. The scale containing all of the notes in *Charlie Is My Darling* is the *melodic minor* form of the A minor scale. Melodic minor scales are not regarded as nine-tone scales but as a seven-tone scale ascending and a different seven-tone scale descending. The descending melodic minor scale is the same as the descending natural minor scale. Sing the melodic minor scale on A ascending and descending with the syllables of your choice.

Minor keys other than A minor have one or more sharps or flats in the key signature. The key signature for E minor is one sharp, the same as for G major. *All the Pretty Little Horses* is in the key of E minor. As you sing the song, notice the prominence of the keynote at the beginning and ending of the phrases.

ALL THE PRETTY LITTLE HORSES

LULLABY U.S.

Write the key signature for E minor on the staff, and then write in scale order the notes used in *All the Pretty Little Horses*. What is the form of minor?

The distinctions between the various forms of minor exist more in theory than in practice, especially when the melodies are considered without reference to harmony. Minor melodies often have only five or six different notes, and the scale tones omitted are often the ones that distinguish the various forms of minor.

When Johnny Comes Marching Home is in the key of G minor. The key signature for G minor is two flats (B-flat and E-flat), and that key signature is used even though there is no E, flat or natural, in the melody or chords. There are F-naturals, agreeing with the key signature, and F-sharps, borrowed from the parallel major, in both the melody and chords. Listen for the effect of these features as you sing the song, preferably with an accompaniment.

WHEN JOHNNY COMES MARCHING HOME

LOUIS LAMBERT   LOUIS LAMBERT

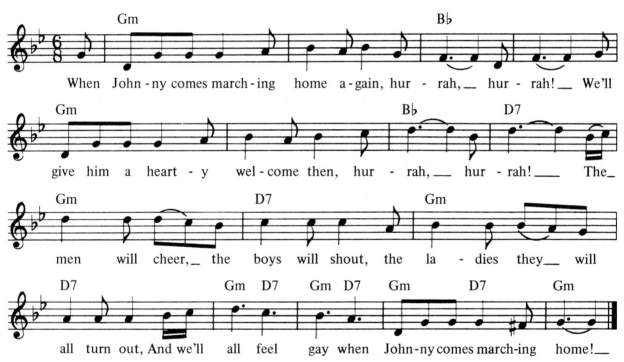

Since *When Johnny Comes Marching Home* has both F-naturals and F-sharps in the melody and harmony and these two notes occur only in the melodic form of G minor, the key of the song, to be precise, is G melodic minor.

Minor Key Signatures   Songs in minor keys can be distinguished from those in major keys by comparing the last note of the melody with the key signature. In terms of major key signatures, songs in major keys end on *do,* and songs in minor keys end on *la,* with very few exceptions.

The same arrangements of sharps and flats are used for both major and minor key signatures. When the keynote of a major key is on a line, the keynote of the relative minor key—the one with the same key signature—is on the next line below. When the keynote of a major key is in a space, the keynote of the relative minor key is in the next space below. If a sharp or a flat in the key signature applies to the keynote, the sharp or flat becomes part of the name of the key. Capital letters indicate major keys and small letters indicate minor keys when they are not otherwise modified.

The following table gives the commonly used minor key signatures with their names and keynotes. Observe that the key signatures for minor keys are the same as for major keys but that the keynotes are different. To determine the notes in all three forms of any minor scale, use the Scale Builder in the endleaf pocket.

Modes

Major and minor are sometimes referred to as *modes,* the *major mode* and the *minor mode,* but *modal music* usually implies music based on one of the other seven-tone scales with five whole steps and two half steps. Each modal scale has a distinctive pattern of whole steps and half steps and a corresponding distinctive quality. Early liturgical music was modal, as are many folk songs. *Old Joe Clark* is a representative example of the latter.

The keynote of *Old Joe Clark* is D, and it is notated with the key signature for D major, two sharps. However, every time the note C occurs, it is preceded by a natural sign canceling the sharp in the signature. C natural is also used consistently in the chords. The scale on D with F-sharp and C-natural and half steps between 3–4 and 6–7 is a modal scale (Mixolydian). The striking effect produced by this scale will be apparent immediately when you sing *Old Joe Clark*.

OLD JOE CLARK

FOLK SONG   U.S.

Adding new verses to traditional melodies is a time-honored custom. Make up additional verses fitting the sprightly mood and rhythms of *Old Joe Clark*. Then, sing the melody several times using the new words to become thoroughly acquainted with the unique quality of this particular mode. Each of the other modes has a similar characteristic quality resulting from the one note in its scale that distinguishes it from major or minor. Songs you sing and hear that differ from the major, minor, and pentatonic models are based on one of the modal scales.

Suggested Assignments

1. Write the line notation for *Are You Sleeping* and *Good Night*. If you do not remember the tunes, refer to the notation in this chapter.
2. Give the appropriate hand signal for each note as you sing ascending and descending major scales with the syllables.
3. When the teacher establishes a key and gives hand signals, respond with the corresponding syllables and pitches.

4. Give the hand signals for the pitches as you sing familiar songs. Begin with songs that are slow and in which stepwise motion predominates.
5. The following note patterns spell words. Write them.

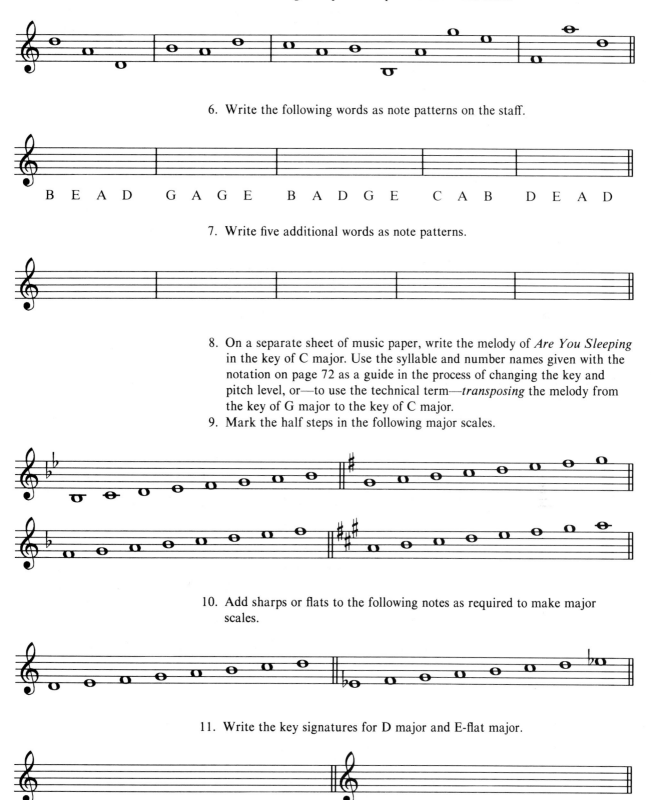

6. Write the following words as note patterns on the staff.

B E A D   G A G E   B A D G E   C A B   D E A D

7. Write five additional words as note patterns.

8. On a separate sheet of music paper, write the melody of *Are You Sleeping* in the key of C major. Use the syllable and number names given with the notation on page 72 as a guide in the process of changing the key and pitch level, or—to use the technical term—*transposing* the melody from the key of G major to the key of C major.
9. Mark the half steps in the following major scales.

10. Add sharps or flats to the following notes as required to make major scales.

11. Write the key signatures for D major and E-flat major.

12. Name the following major keys, and write the keynotes on the staff.

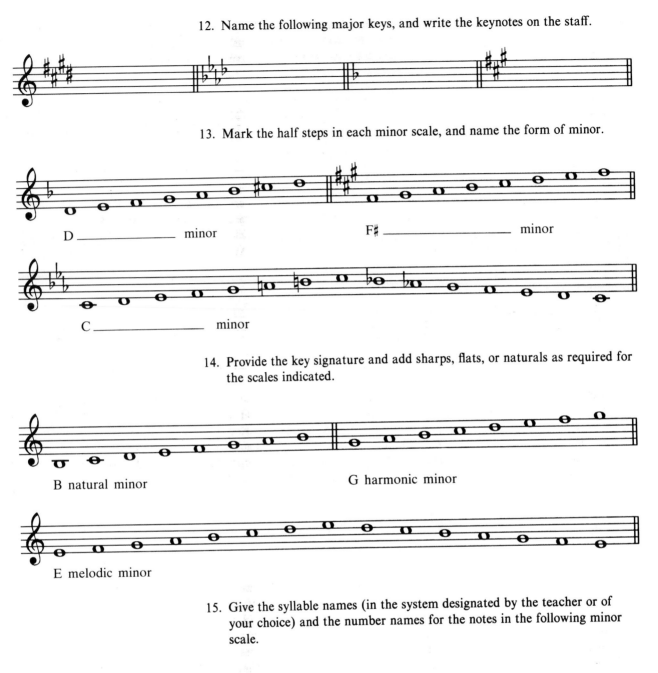

13. Mark the half steps in each minor scale, and name the form of minor.

D _____ minor   F♯ _____ minor

C _____ minor

14. Provide the key signature and add sharps, flats, or naturals as required for the scales indicated.

B natural minor   G harmonic minor

E melodic minor

15. Give the syllable names (in the system designated by the teacher or of your choice) and the number names for the notes in the following minor scale.

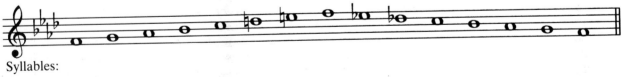

Syllables:

Numbers:

16. Find three songs in minor keys, name the songs, and identify the source. Copy the key signatures and write the first and last notes on the staff provided. Give the key and indicate whether the form of minor is natural, harmonic, or melodic.

1. Name _____ Source _____

2. Name _____ Source _____

3. Name _____ Source _____

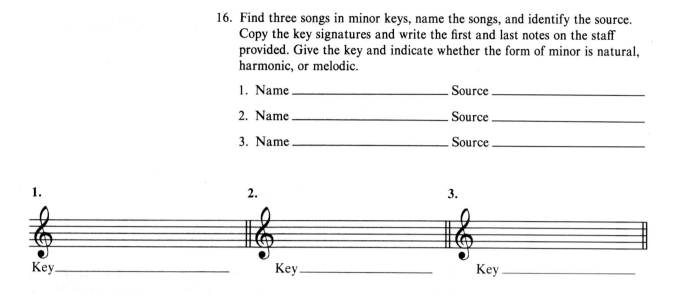

1.

Key _____

2.

Key _____

3.

Key _____

17. Find a song that you think is pentatonic or modal, and write the notes used in the melody as a scale.

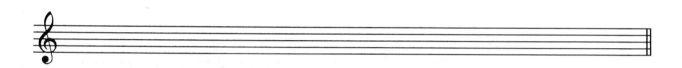

5 Combining Musical Sounds

Musical sounds are combined in a variety of ways. In succession, musical sounds become melodies. Melodies joined together, as they are in rounds and partner songs, produce *counterpoint*. Three or more notes sounding together form a *chord*, and successions of chords result in *harmony*. Musical sounds are also organized into structural units and forms. The smallest combination of musical sounds consists of just two notes.

Intervals

The difference in pitch between two notes is an *interval*. Two notes written or sounded in succession form a *melodic interval*. Two notes aligned vertically or sounded together form a *harmonic interval*. Intervals are computed by counting the scale degrees spanned by the two notes, including those occupied by the notes. Play the following harmonic intervals, and associate the sounds with the interval names. The two notes can be played on the piano with the index finger of each hand.

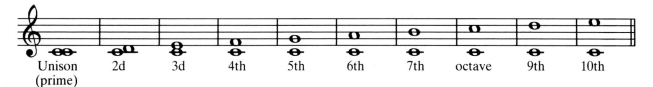

Unison (prime)   2d   3d   4th   5th   6th   7th   octave   9th   10th

Intervals exceeding an octave, known as *compound intervals,* may be called by the name of the *simple interval* formed by the same two notes within an octave (e.g., 9th = 2d, 10th = 3d).

The exact size or *quality* of intervals is indicated by the following terms and abbreviations: *major (M)*, *minor (m)*, *perfect (P)*, *diminished (d)*, and *augmented* (A). The intervals above the keynote in a major scale—for example, above C in C major—are major or perfect as indicated. Sing the following melodic intervals with the syllables, and associate the sounds with the interval names. Observe that each interval except the octave is sung both ascending and descending in performing this exercise.

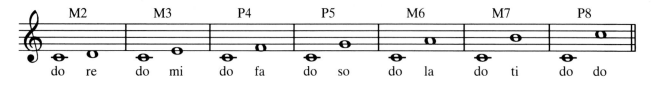

do re   do mi   do fa   do so   do la   do ti   do do

A half step smaller than *major* is *minor*. A half step smaller than *perfect* is *diminished*. A half step larger than *perfect* is *augmented*. All of the common intervals above C are shown with the precise designation of the interval, the number of semitones between the two notes (in parentheses), and the syllable names in C. Play the example, and then sing it with syllables.

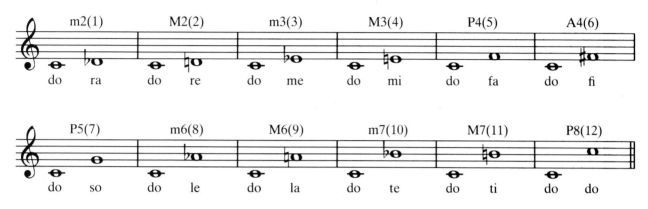

These intervals are located on the piano keyboard as follows:

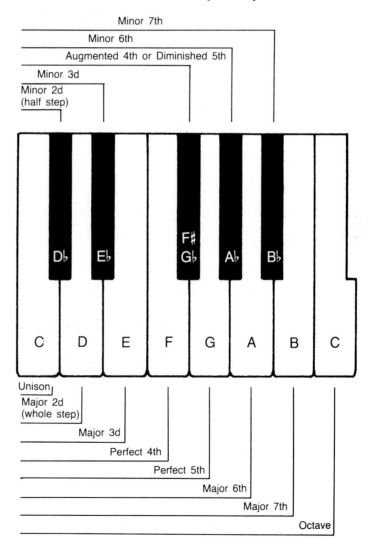

Exercise 1

The numbers (2, second, 3, third, etc.) used to identify intervals are determined by counting the number of lines and spaces spanned by the two notes. The lines and/or spaces occupied by the notes are included in the count. The quality of the intervals (M, m, P, etc.) is determined by the number of semitones spanned by the two notes (see the preceding example). Write above the staff the number identifying the interval between each pair of notes in the melody of *Rockabye Baby*. More advanced students can add the letter indicating the quality of each interval. Only major (M), minor (m), and perfect (P) intervals occur in the melody. The first five intervals have been named to serve as models.

ROCKABYE BABY

LULLABY

U.S.

Rock - a - bye ba - by, on the tree top,

When the wind blows, the cra - dle will rock, When the bough breaks, the

cra - dle will fall, And down will come ba - by, cra - dle and all.

Rockabye Baby is notated in the key of C for the interval analysis. For singing, it should be in the key of G, a fourth lower.

Triads

Any three notes written vertically or sounded together constitute a chord, but the most usual chord structures contain three alternate scale tones, which can be written on consecutive lines or in consecutive spaces of the staff. Three-tone chords of this type are *triads,* the basic elements of harmony.

Triads written with all three notes on lines or in spaces are identified by the letter name of the lowest note, the *root* of the chord. The letter name by itself indicates a *major triad* consisting, from the root up, of a major third and a minor third. The letter name followed by a small "m" indicates a *minor triad* consisting of a minor third and a major third. The letter name followed by "dim" indicates a *diminished triad* consisting of two minor thirds. A triad is associated with each degree of the scale. The type of triad depends upon the location in the scale and the mode—major, minor, etc. The triads of C major are identified by letter name and type and by scale degree written as a Roman numeral.

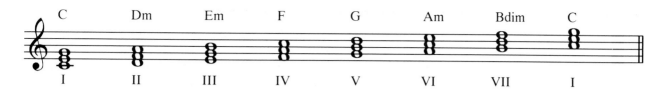

The notes of a given triad are always the same, but they can be arranged in any order. A triad is in *root position* when the root is the lowest note. A triad is *inverted* when one of the other notes is lowest. The letter name and number identifying a triad are the same no matter how its notes are arranged. Listen while the teacher plays the following C triads on the piano with the sustaining (right) pedal down to emphasize their similarity.

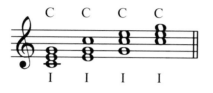

In addition to letter and number names, chords have names related to their location and function in the scale and key. The functional names, arranged in ascending order like a scale, are as follows:

I. TONIC

VII. Subtonic or leading tone

VI. Submediant

V. DOMINANT

IV. SUBDOMINANT

III. Mediant

II. Supertonic

I. TONIC

All of the triads are used, but those built on the first, fourth, and fifth degrees of the scale with their names in full capitals predominate. These are the *primary triads*. Most children's songs can be harmonized with just these three chords. They are the only ones considered further.

The primary triads (I, IV, and V) are major in major keys and minor in natural minor, but the harmonic form of minor is ordinarily used for chords. In harmonic minor the dominant (V) chord is major, as it is in major keys. The primary triads of C, F, and G major and A harmonic minor are given with their letter and number names.

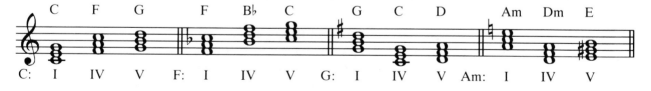

Notice that the same triad occurs in different keys. For example, the C chord is I in the key of C, IV in the key of G, and V in the key of F.

Dominant Seventh Chords

Another third is frequently added to triads. The added note is a seventh above the root (bottom note) of triads arranged in thirds. Four-note chords built in thirds are called *seventh chords,* and the one on the fifth degree of the scale is the *dominant seventh chord.* A dominant seventh chord is indicated by a 7 following the Roman numeral V or the letter name of the triad. The V7 chords in the keys of C major, F major, and G major are shown.

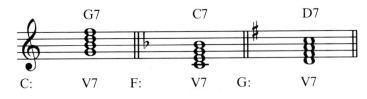

The V7 chords in the harmonic form of the parallel minor keys, C minor, F minor, and G minor would be the same, but the key signatures would be different, and the next note above the root of the chords would require a natural or a sharp.

The V7 chords can be played more easily without changing the effect appreciably by leaving out one note. The name and symbol for the chord are not affected by the omission of this note. Whenever V7 is indicated or required, this form of the chord may be used. Compare the sound of the complete and incomplete V7 chords.

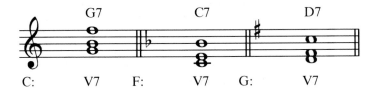

The notes in incomplete V7 chords can be rearranged and the chords inverted, as shown below.

Chord Progressions

In chord *progressions*—that is, going from one chord to another—the individual notes move smoothly and logically from chord tone to chord tone. Notes common to two chords ordinarily are repeated, and the other notes move stepwise to a note in the second chord. These principles are illustrated in all of the usual primary chord progressions in C major. If the study of chapter 6, Playing the Piano, has been integrated with the study of this chapter, you will be able to play the following progressions.

Combining Musical Sounds

Adding another minor third to a diminished triad makes a *diminished seventh chord,* the usual form of diminished chords and the one implied by *dim* following a letter name. Use the Chord Builder in the endleaf pocket to determine the notes in major and minor triads and dominant and diminished seventh chords. Practical uses of chords and progressions are explored in chapters 6 and 11.

Phrases and Sentences

In music, as in language, ideas are expressed in *phrases* and *sentences,* also called *periods.* In this book *sentence* is used because it parallels the usage in language. Sentences are complete, more or less independent, units of musical form that most often consist of two four-measure phrases. The two phrases in a typical sentence have an antecedent-consequent relationship. An incomplete idea in the first phrase is brought to a satisfactory conclusion in the second or final phrase.

Each phrase ends with a *cadence.* A cadence is a closing effect created by appropriate melodic, rhythmic, and harmonic formulas that function like the corresponding vocal inflections in speech and punctuation in written language. Just as in language there are commas and periods, in music there are *incomplete cadences* (i.c.) and *complete cadences* (c.c.). The final phrases of sentences end with complete cadences. Other phrases end with incomplete cadences.

In the following examples typical musical sentences are diagramed. A line extending under the words of a phrase turns up at the cadence, and the type of of cadence is indicated. Phrases are identified by lowercase letters. When two phrases begin alike but end differently, the second is assigned a different letter, but the letter of the first is added in parentheses to show the relationship.

Bow Belinda is a concise two-phrase sentence in which the two phrases begin alike and end differently. Sing *Bow Belinda* and observe the different effect of the incomplete and complete cadences.

BOW BELINDA

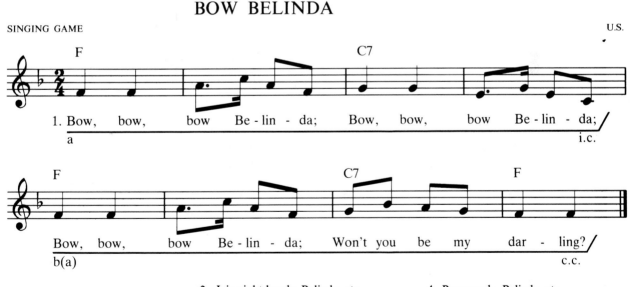

SINGING GAME   U.S.

F   C7

1. Bow, bow, bow Be-lin-da; Bow, bow, bow Be-lin-da;
a   i.c.

F   C7   F

Bow, bow, bow Be-lin-da; Won't you be my dar-ling?
b(a)   c.c.

2. Join right hands, Belinda, etc.   4. Promenade, Belinda, etc.
3. Join left hands, Belinda, etc.   5. Circle, all, Belinda, etc.

Barbara Allen illustrates a two-phrase sentence in which the two phrases are essentially different, though they share certain rhythmic features, which is usual. When the first phrase begins with an upbeat, subsequent phrases generally begin with an upbeat of the same value. As you sing the song, notice how the ascending motion from low D to high D in the first phrase is answered by the descending motion from high D to low D in the second phrase.

BARBARA ALLEN

In Scar - let Town where I was born, there
a

was a fair maid dwell - in', Made ev - 'ry youth cry___
i.c.   b

"well - a - way," her name was Bar - bara Al - len.
c.c.

Bow Belinda and *Barbara Allen* illustrate the two most prevalent types of musical sentences. Both consist of two balanced phrases and have an incomplete cadence in the middle and a complete cadence at the end. A high percentage of the sentences in familiar songs and popular music have this basic design.

God Rest You Merry, Gentlemen illustrates some of the irregularities that occur in sentence structures. It has five phrases and four incomplete cadences before the complete cadence at the end. The second phrase is an exact repetition of the first, though with different words. The third phrase introduces new material, which appears only once. The fourth phrase begins on the third beat of the measure, in contrast to the previous phrases, which begin on the fourth beat. A cadence point is reached after only three measures, but the tonic chord is avoided and the phrase is extended to the normal four-measure length. The words "comfort and joy" are repeated to accommodate the extension in the melody. The final phrase is similar to the fourth, but with essential differences. The first full measure is modified, and the extension is dropped. Without the extension, the phrase is only three measures long. The final E is harmonized with the tonic (Em) chord, and the cadence is final. Listen for these features as you sing the song.

GOD REST YOU MERRY, GENTLEMEN

CAROL

ENGLAND

One-Part Form

In music certain structural elements are stated, repeated, restated after contrasting material, and/or varied in patterns perceived as *musical form.* The patterns that occur in simple songs are often classified as *song forms,* though the same patterns also occur in instrumental music where they are more properly called *small forms* or *part forms.* The smallest musical form is a *one-part form.*

When a song consists of a single musical sentence, it contains only one complete idea and is, therefore, a one-part form. The second and any subsequent phrases may begin like the first phrase or have rhythm and pitch figures (motives) derived from it, providing a high degree of unity. *Bow Belinda, Barbara*

Allen, and *God Rest You Merry, Gentlemen,* analyzed in the preceding section, are examples of one-part form. Other examples of one-part form are, in order of complexity, *The Muffin Man* (p. 299), *If You're Happy* (p. 15), *Silent Night* (p. 131), and *When Johnny Comes Marching Home* (p. 82). Sing these songs and pay particular attention to the way the rhythmic flow and melodic contour interact at cadence points to create closing effects with varying degrees of finality.

Two-Part Form/Binary

The form resulting when two sentences are joined is *two-part form* or *binary form,* though binary sometimes implies a particular pattern of key relationships and repeats. The two sentences must be sufficiently different to provide a degree of contrast, but they typically have many elements in common.

Annie Laurie is a clear example of a two-part form. In form diagrams, sentences are identified by capital letters, phrases by lowercase letters. Phrases may divide into *subphrases,* as they do in this song, but units smaller than a phrase are usually ignored in diagraming musical forms.

ANNIE LAURIE

WILLIAM DOUGLASS

LADY JOHN SCOTT

The two sentences of *Annie Laurie* not only share rhythm patterns; they end similarly. This "rhyming" of parts is an effective unifying device. There is no convenient way to reflect it in form diagrams, but an explicit and descriptive name for binary forms with this feature is *rhymed binary.*

Song forms and their parts may be repeated individually and collectively without altering the basic concept of the form or the name for it. The musical design represented by A A A, which results when a one-part melody is used for a song with three verses, is still regarded as a one-part form.

Good-by, My Lover, Good-by is an example of two-part form in which the first part is repeated, producing an A A B design. Sing the second set of words on the repetition of the A sentence.

GOOD-BY, MY LOVER, GOOD-BY

FOLK SONG

U.S.

Songs with a chorus or refrain are frequently in two-part form. *Good-by, My Lover, Good-by* is typical. The A sentence serves for the verses and the B sentence for the refrain.

Other examples of two-part form include *Aura Lee* (p. 75) and *Buffalo Gals* (p. 188). Sing these songs and listen for the unifying and contrasting elements in the A and B parts.

Three-Part Form/Ternary

The musical form with three parts in a statement-departure-return relationship is *ternary*. The basic ternary design is represented by the letters A B A, but more often than not the first A is repeated immediately. The repetition of A can be written out or indicated by a repeat sign, as in *The Ash Grove*. With the repeat the song has a total of thirty-two measures (called *bars* in popular music) in an AA B A pattern, the standard length and form of popular songs and much jazz improvisation.

Sing *The Ash Grove* and notice how clearly the complete cadences on G, G, D, and G delineate its ternary structure and reinforce the statement-repetition-departure-return design. The two pairs of eighth notes decending scalewise in the A part and ascending scalewise in the B part provide both unifying and contrasting elements.

THE ASH GROVE

WALES

The typical ternary design represented by *The Ash Grove* is modified in many ways. Minimally, a ternary form consists of an opening phrase or sentence with or without repetition followed by a contrasting phrase or sentence and a return of the opening idea, which may be varied and abridged. Some of the possible modifications are illustrated in *Simple Gifts*. The first A is not repeated, and the contrasting part is only a phrase. The eight-measure sentence with which the melody begins is reduced to a four-measure phrase when it returns, but the essence of the initial statement is preserved. The melody of *Simple Gifts* is used as one of the themes in Aaron Copland's ballet *Appalachian Spring*. Compare the song with the version of the melody in Copland's orchestral composition.

SIMPLE GIFTS

SHAKER HYMN

Most folk and familiar songs have one, two, or three parts and a plan of organization closely related to one of the forms discussed in this chapter. As you sing and listen to songs, consciously strive to recognize their structures.

Suggested Assignments

1. Analyze the intervals between the two parts in *Tell Me Why* (p. 260) according to the instructions given for exercise 1 on page 90.
2. Using the primary chord progressions in C major on page 92 as a model, write the following progressions in F major and G major.

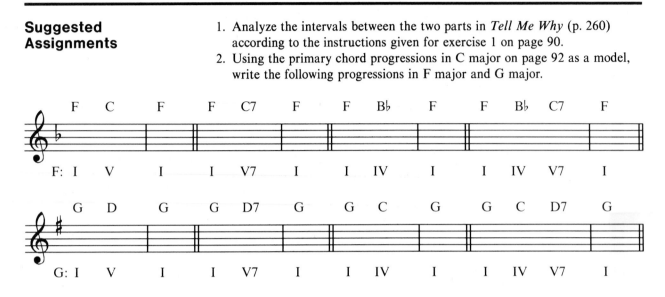

3. Write the phrase and cadence analysis below the words of *Johnny Has Gone for a Soldier*. The notation is on page 78. Use the analysis of *Barbara Allen* on page 94 as a model.

   There I stood on Buttermilk Hill, There I stood and cried my fill,

   Ev'ry tear would turn a mill, Johnny has gone for a soldier.

4. Write the phrase and cadence analysis below the words of *When Johnny Comes Marching Home*. The notation is on page 82. Use the analysis of *God Rest You Merry, Gentlemen* on page 95 as a model.

   When Johnny comes marching home again, hurrah, hurrah!

   We'll give him a hearty welcome then, hurrah, hurrah!

   The men will cheer, the boys will shout, the ladies they will all turn out,

   And we'll all feel gay when Johnny comes marching home!

5. Analyze and name the form of *Aura Lee*. The notation is on page 75. Use the analysis of *Annie Laurie* on page 96 as a model.

As the blackbird in the spring, 'neath the willow tree,

Sat and piped I heard him sing, singing Aura Lee.

Aura Lee, Aura Lee, maid of golden hair,

Sunshine came along with thee, and swallows in the air.

6. Analyze and name the form of *We Wish You a Merry Christmas*. The notation is on page 177. It is necessary to make the repeat from the beginning (D.C.) to complete the form. Use the analysis of *The Ash Grove* on page 98 and *Simple Gifts* on page 99 as models.

We wish you a merry Christmas, We wish you a merry Christmas,

We wish you a merry Christmas, and a happy New Year!

Good tidings to you, and all of your kin,

Good tidings for Christmas, and a happy New Year!

We wish you a merry Christmas, We wish you a merry Christmas,

We wish you a merry Christmas, and a happy New Year!

6 Playing the Piano

The classroom teacher who can play the piano possesses one of the most valuable of all musical skills for teaching school music. The phonograph never will be a satisfactory substitute for the teacher at the piano.

Anyone with a sense of rhythm can learn to play the piano well enough for classroom music activities. Technical facility at the keyboard is desirable but not necessary. The teacher who can play simple melodies, easy accompaniments, and basic rhythms with accuracy will succeed well.

Uses for the Piano in the Classroom

In the classroom the piano has numerous uses:

1. To help teach the melody, especially when the teacher cannot sing.
2. To give the keynote, key chord, and starting note of songs.
3. To provide accompaniments, introductions, and codas to songs.
4. To provide rhythmic music for marching, skipping, hopping, and interpretative activities.
5. To help teach part singing and harmonic feeling.
6. To introduce notation through the use of the keyboard.
7. To introduce the piano to children and encourage their study of it.

Naming and Playing the Piano Keys

The black keys are grouped alternately in twos and threes on the piano keyboard. The white keys, named with the first seven letters of the alphabet (A B C D E F G), can be located quickly in relation to these groups of black keys as follows:

1. The white key C is located directly to the left of the group of two black keys. Find and play all the C keys on the piano. Notice especially the fourth C, counting from left to right on the keyboard—the twenty-fourth white key. This is called *middle C,* falling about the middle of the keyboard, slightly to the left of the piano maker's label. Middle C is midway between the treble and bass staffs.
2. The white key D is located between the group of two black keys. Find and play all the D keys.
3. The white key E is located directly to the right of the group of two black keys. Find and play all the E keys.

Chart of the complete piano keyboard

4. The white key F is located directly to the left of the group of three black keys. Find and play all the F keys.
5. The white key B is located directly to the right of the group of three black keys. Find and play all the B keys.
6. Locate and play all the G and A keys in the same manner in relation to their position among the black keys. Then, practice finding all the notes at random with increasing speed.
7. The black keys get their names from the white keys on either side of them using the term sharp (♯) or flat (♭) added to the name of the white key. For example, the black key between C and D can be either C-sharp moving upward to the nearest key to the right or D-flat moving downward to the nearest key to the left.

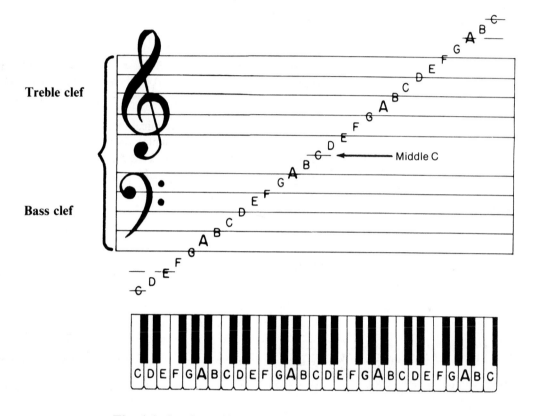

The right hand usually plays the notes on the treble staff, and the left hand plays the notes on the bass staff.

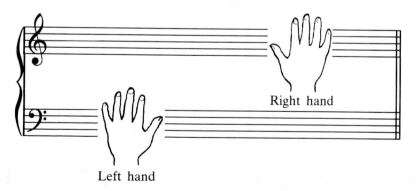

Playing with the
Right Hand

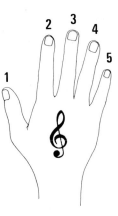

Right-hand finger numbers

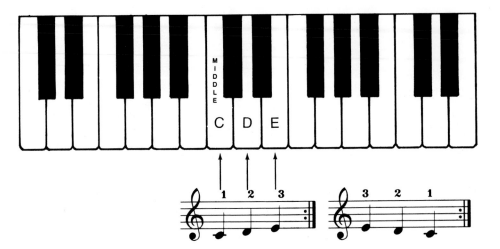

WALTZ TIME

Playing with the
Left Hand

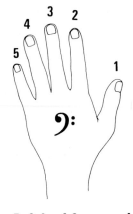

Left-hand finger numbers

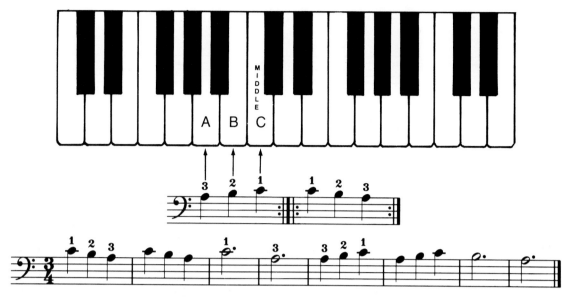

Playing with Both Hands

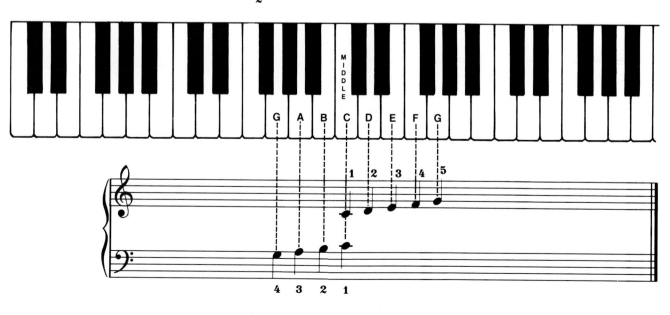

MARCH TIME

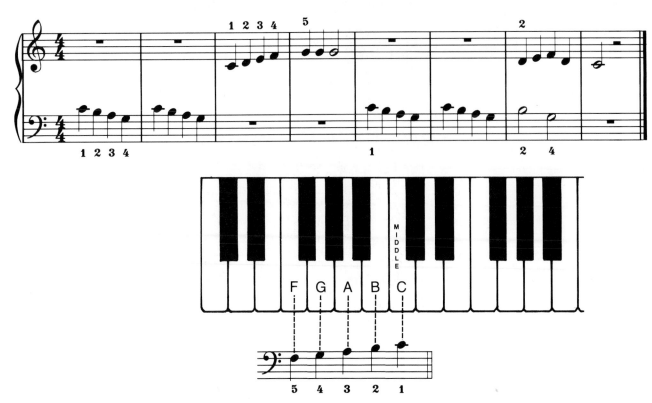

CAMPTOWN RACES

STEPHEN C. FOSTER

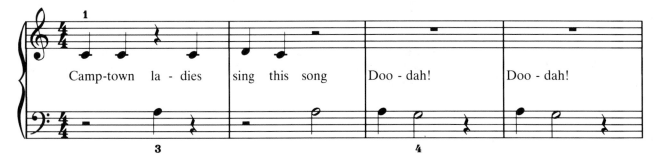

Camp-town la - dies sing this song Doo - dah! Doo - dah!

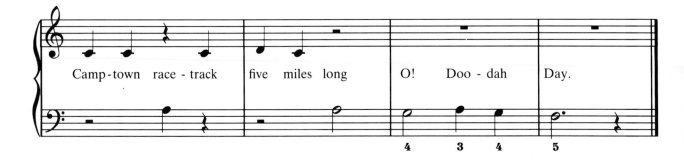

Camp-town race - track five miles long O! Doo - dah Day.

Five-Finger Positions

The Right-Hand C Position

1. Place the right thumb on middle C and play up the scale. Curve and raise the fingers. Strike the keys; do not press them.

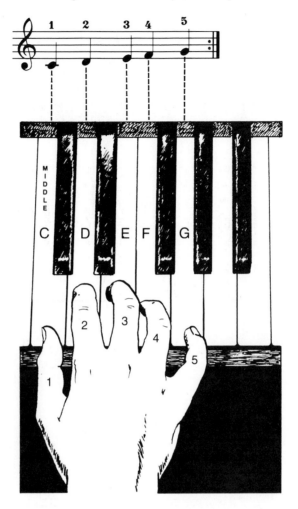

2. Play these five notes up and down with the hand in the same position. Try not to look at your hands; learn to visualize the keyboard. Also play with eyes closed.

The Left-Hand C Position

Take the Piano Chart from the endleaf pocket, and place it above and align it with the piano keys for reference while practicing. Place the fifth finger of the left hand on C below middle C, and play up the scale to G.

Practice the following exercises with each hand separately when necessary.

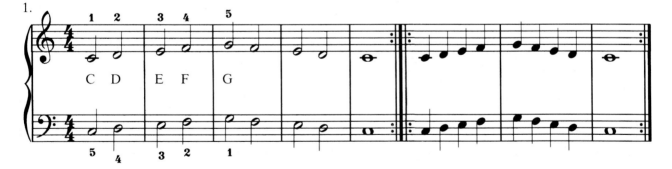

Playing the Piano

2.

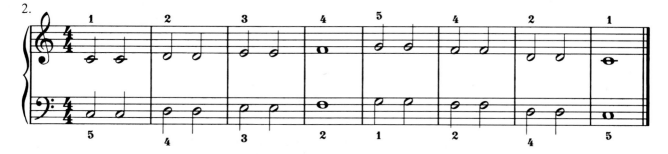

3.

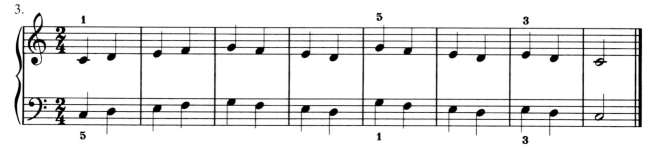

THE WOODCHUCK

U.S.

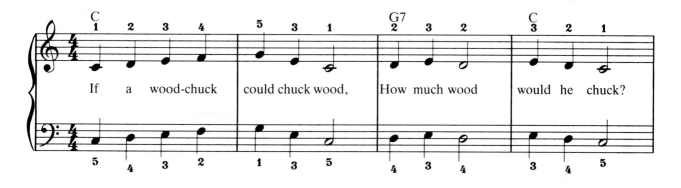

If a wood-chuck could chuck wood, How much wood would he chuck?

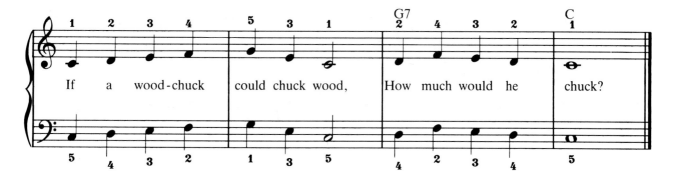

If a wood-chuck could chuck wood, How much would he chuck?

CHORALE THEME

J. S. BACH

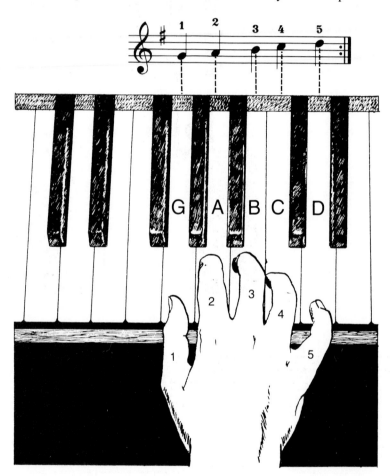

The Left-Hand G Position   Place the fifth finger of the left hand on G just below middle C and play up the scale to D.

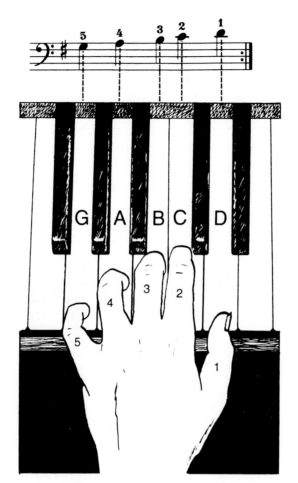

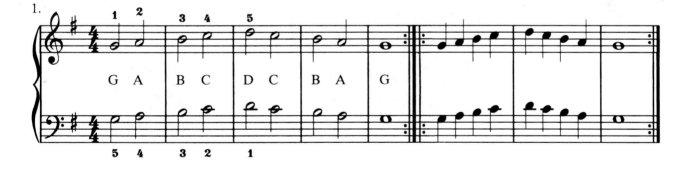

1.

G   A   B   C   D   C   B   A   G

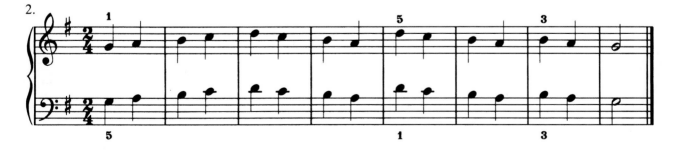

2.

HOT CROSS BUNS

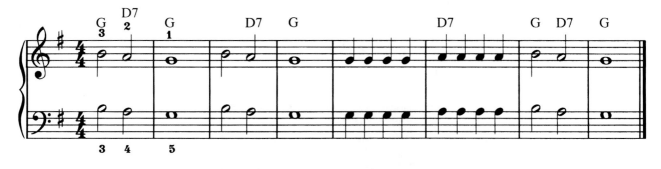

Preparatory exercise for *Lightly Row*. Play it several times.

LIGHTLY ROW

GERMANY

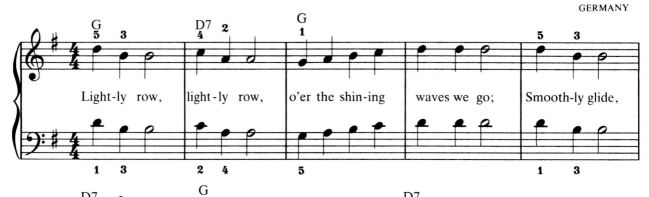

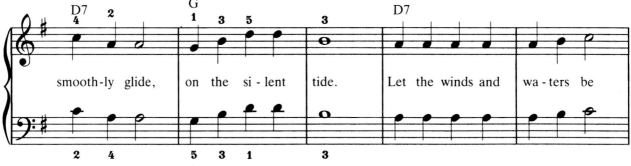

Five-Finger Position
in F Major

Place the right thumb on F above middle C. Play from F up to C, extending the fourth finger slightly forward to strike B-flat.

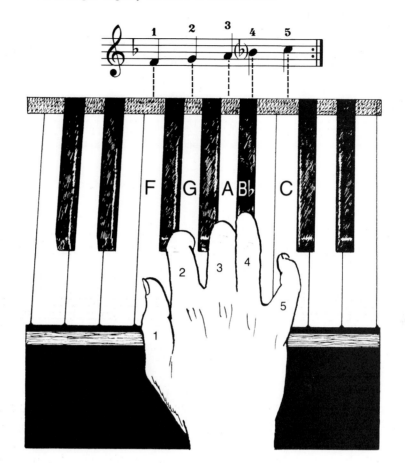

The Left-Hand F Position

Place the fifth finger of the left hand on F below middle C and play up to middle C.

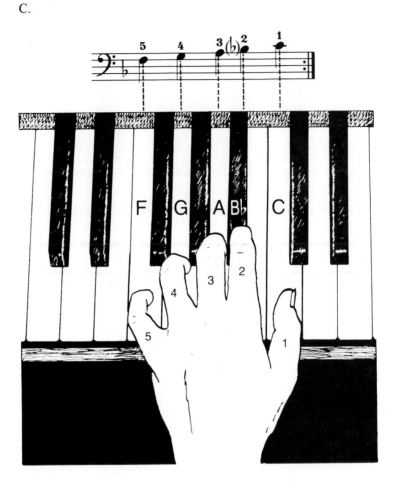

Remember to play the following exercises with each hand separately when insecure.

Playing the Piano

SINGING ON THE PLAYGROUND

GERMANY

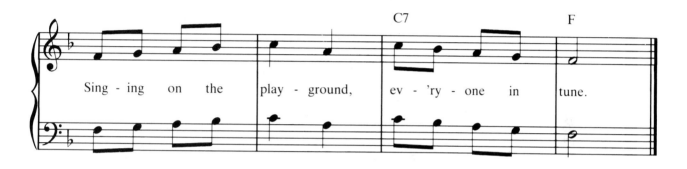

Sing - ing   on   the   play - ground,   sing - ing,   play - ing,

Sing - ing   on   the   play - ground,   ev - 'ry - one   in   tune.

OLD GRAY GOOSE

U.S.

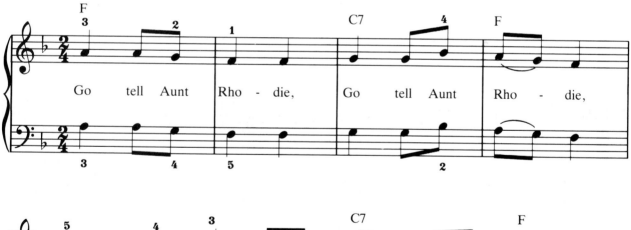

Go   tell   Aunt   Rho - die,   Go   tell   Aunt   Rho - die,

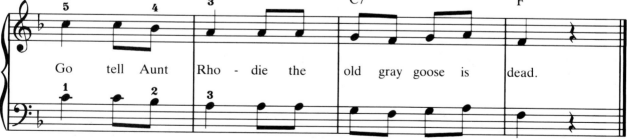

Go   tell   Aunt   Rho - die   the   old   gray   goose   is   dead.

Accompanying and Harmonizing Melodies

Bass accompaniment exercise

THEME FROM THE SURPRISE SYMPHONY

JOSEPH HAYDN (ADAPTED)

GERMAN FOLK TUNE

(ADAPTED)

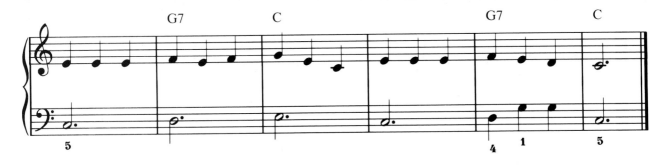

Playing Basic Chords
in C Major

Play the notes of the chord separately, and then sound them simultaneously.

C Chord—1

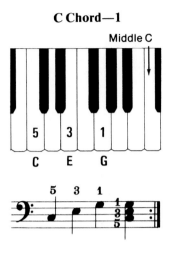

PLAYGROUND TUNE

Also play *Starlight* (p. 175) using the C chord.

G7 Chord—V7

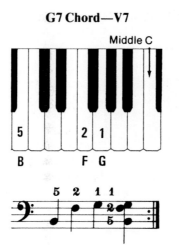

Practice the chords below several times before playing the songs that follow. Play the chords with eyes closed. Practice with each hand separately. The notation ♩‑‑‑♩ indicates notes and fingering in common; keep finger in position.

MERRILY WE ROLL ALONG

TRADITIONAL

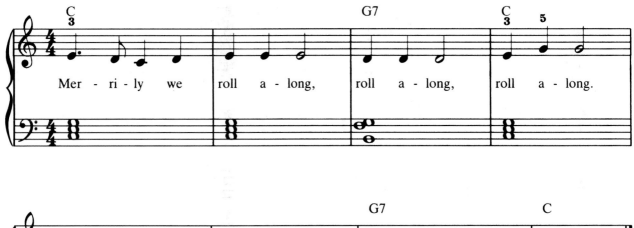

Mer - ri - ly we roll a - long, roll a - long, roll a - long.

Mer - ri - ly we roll a - long o'er the deep blue sea.

SOME FOLKS DO

STEPHEN FOSTER

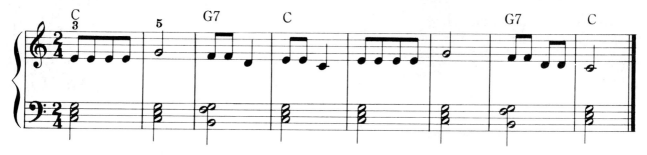

**Playing Basic Chords
in G Major**

Play the notes of the chord separately, and then sound them simultaneously.

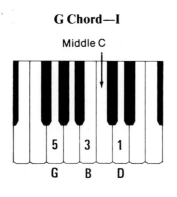

Chords:

THE CUCKOO

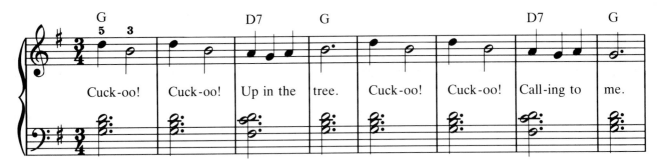

Cuck-oo! | Cuck-oo! | Up in the | tree. | Cuck-oo! | Cuck-oo! | Call-ing to | me.

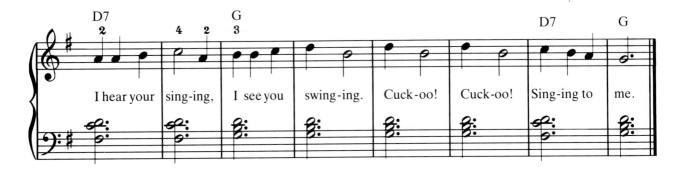

I hear your | sing-ing, | I see you | swing-ing. | Cuck-oo! | Cuck-oo! | Sing-ing to | me.

Playing Basic Chords in F Major

Play the notes of the chord separately, and then sound them simultaneously.

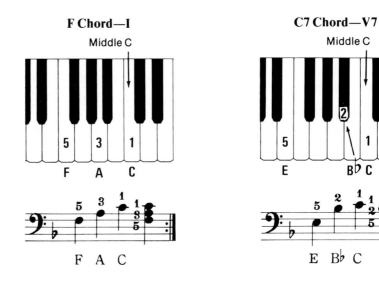

F Chord—I

Middle C

F A C

C7 Chord—V7

Middle C

E B♭ C

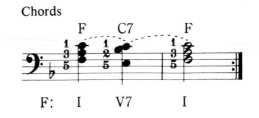

Chords

F: I V7 I

AUF WIEDERSEHEN

GERMANY

Auf wie - der - sehen   Auf wie - der - sehen

Now that our school's at an end   we'll say good - bye to our friends.

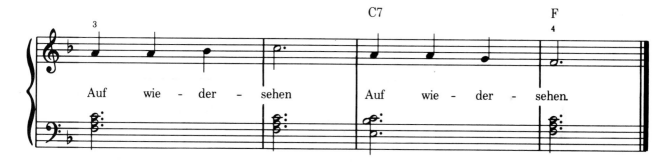

Auf wie - der - sehen   Auf wie - der - sehen.

Chording Melodies in Minor Keys

The hand positions, common notes, and fingerings in the chord progressions are the same for both major and minor.

Playing Basic Chords in A Minor

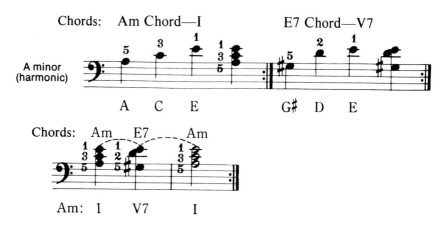

FOLK TUNE

Also play *Minka* (p. 205), using the Am and E7 chords.

Playing Basic Chords
in E Minor

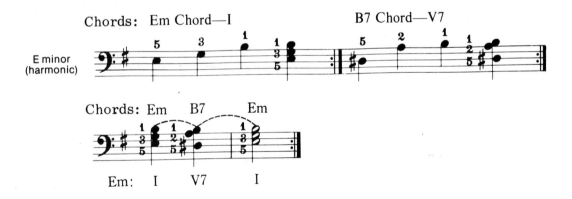

Playing the Piano

SLEEP MY BABY

Eve - ning time is com - ing soon, Birds have hushed their ___

sing - ing, Shad - ows gent - ly fill the ___ room, Send your cares a -

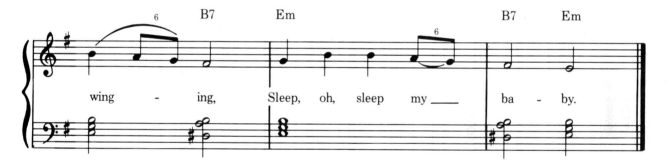

wing - ing, Sleep, oh, sleep my ___ ba - by.

Playing Basic Chords
in D Minor

Chords: Dm ———— I   A7 ———— V7

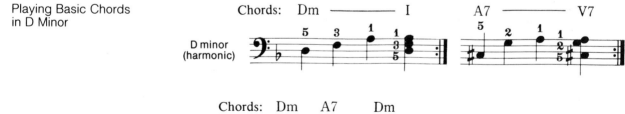

D minor
(harmonic)

Chords: Dm   A7   Dm

Dm: I   V7   I

DANCE

HUNGARY

Important note: Practice all of the piano chords in Appendix C in both treble and bass clefs (pp. 317–18).

Using the IV Chord with I
and V7 in C Major

F Chord—IV

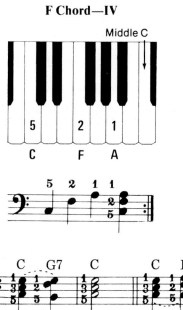

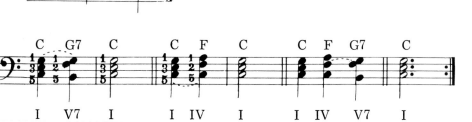

Extending the Five-Finger Position

The range of notes can be extended by expanding the hand position. Fingerings involving a change of hand position are circled.

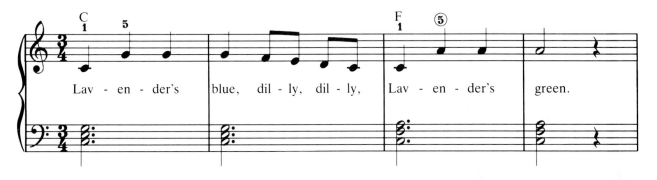

LAVENDER'S BLUE

ENGLAND

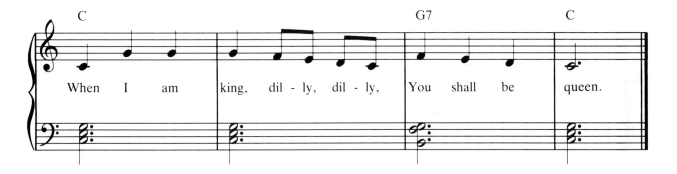

Lav - en - der's blue, dil - ly, dil - ly, Lav - en - der's green.

When I am king, dil - ly, dil - ly, You shall be queen.

Twinkle, Twinkle, Little Star may be played or sung as a canon with the second part starting one measure after the first part.

TWINKLE, TWINKLE, LITTLE STAR

FRANCE

Playing the Piano

Playing Accompaniment Patterns

Chords can be played in various patterns to make more interesting accompaniments. The following are particularly useful in playing accompaniments for familiar songs.

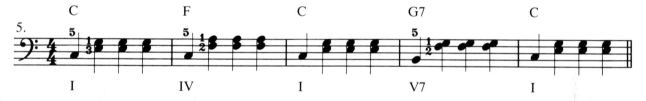

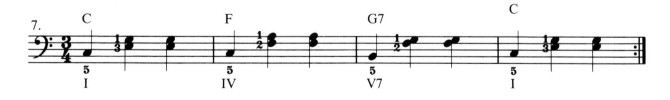

JINGLE BELLS

J. S. PIERPONT

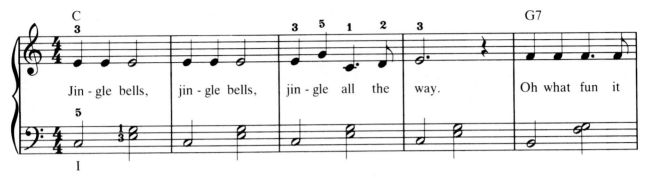

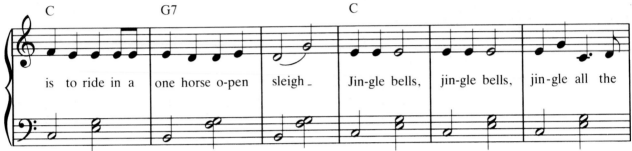

Repeat using patterns 1 and 4 (p. 127).

Important note: Play this song with each hand separately first. Observe right hand fingering.

DU, DU, LIEGST MIR IM HERZEN

FOLK SONG

GERMANY

liegst mir im Sinn; Du, du, machst mir viel Schmerz - en;

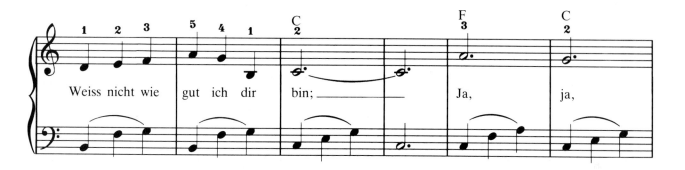

Weiss nicht wie gut ich dir bin; Ja, ja,

ja, ja, weiss nicht wie gut ich dir bin.

Accompanying Singing and
Playing with Bass Accents
and Chords (Ump-Pah Style)

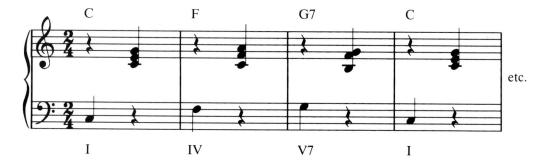

etc.

I   IV   V7   I

Improvise chord, bass accent, and broken-chord accompaniments for the following melodies.

NORWEGIAN DANCE

C-I   G7-V7   C-I   G7-V7   C-I

G7-V7   C-I

G7-V7   C-I   G7-V7   C-I

A-HUNTING WE WILL GO

ENGLAND

C-I   G7-V7

Oh a - hunt - ing we will go, a - hunt - ing we will go. We'll

C-I   F-IV   C-I   G7-V7   C-I

catch a lit - tle fox and put him in a box and nev - er let him go.

A broken-chord accompaniment is very effective with *Silent Night*.

SILENT NIGHT

JOSEPH MOHR

FRANZ GRUBER

Suggested Assignments

1. Play melodies, using the right hand only, from state and locally adopted songbook series or community songbooks.
2. Play chords indicated by letter markings for songs in school music books. Then, combine melody and chord accompaniments. Create different kinds of accompaniments for these songs, using various patterns studied in this chapter.
3. Create accompaniments for the songs in chapter 1 and the other melodies in this book.
4. Create accompaniments for songs where no chords are indicated.
5. Play chords and accompaniment figures in keys other than those used in this chapter—D, A, E, B-flat, E-flat, and A-flat major. Apply these to songs in the standard school songbook series.
6. Play accompaniments indicated in the teachers' manuals of standard school songbook series.
7. Play the songs from chapter 2 with accompaniments.
8. *Important:* play the piano chords from Appendix C (pp. 317–18) in both treble and bass clefs.

7 Playing Classroom Percussion Instruments

Playing Rhythm Instruments

Experience with percussion instruments is invaluable, not only for developing rhythmic sensitivity and coordination, but also for building other musical insights, such as a feeling for musical structure. Also it provides another interesting musical activity for teachers and children with singing problems and limited musical background.

Many rhythm instruments used in the classroom are shown here. Others include bongo and conga drums, wrist- and hand-played bells, gongs, claves, guiros, coconut shells, temple blocks, wood blocks, and pom-poms. These, as well as instruments made by children themselves, bring added joy to the music period.

Rhythm Sticks

One stick is struck against the other, producing a clicking sound. If one stick is notched, a gourd effect can be produced by rubbing the other over it.

Tone Blocks

Small, medium, and large tone blocks are available; they produce hollow tones of high, medium, and low pitch. The tone is sounded by striking the hollow barrel with the mallet midway between the two slots.

Sand Blocks

Sand blocks are rubbed together to produce a deep swishing sound.

Jingle Sticks (Clogs)

The jingle stick is struck against the palm of the hand for single beats. A roll is made by rotating the wrist. Five jingle sticks can be substituted for one tambourine.

Castanets

The castanet with a handle is struck against the palm of the hand for a single click. Roll effects are produced by rotating and snapping the wrist. Finger castanets are worn on the thumb of each hand and are played by the fingers with a crisp, short, tapping action.

Maracas

The Latin-American rhythm instruments called maracas are played by shaking easily, using the wrist as a pivot.

Tambourines

The tambourine is held with fingers in a slot of the wood frame. For light beats, strike the bottom edge of the tambourine with the open hand or tap with a striker or the fingers. For accented beats, strike with the knuckles. For a roll effect, rotate the wrist freely and shake.

Triangle

To produce a clear tone on a triangle, strike the side opposite the open corner with the straight end of the metal striker. A wooden striker produces a softer ring. For a roll effect, rotate the beater in the corner against both sides, using free wrist action. The triangle should always be suspended with a cord loop for full vibration.

Drums

All sizes and types of drums can be played with the hand or a mallet. To prevent muffling, drumheads must be completely free from contact with any object while being played. For this reason slings are provided with some drums.

Cymbals

Crash effects with cymbals are produced by an up-and-down sweep of the arms. For single beats and gong effects, hold one cymbal with a sling and strike it with a mallet. Finger cymbals are fitted on the thumb and forefinger of each hand and played by clashing them together. The player can also hold one cymbal and strike it with a mallet.

Classifying the Rhythm Instruments

Rhythm instruments can be classified and used according to their distinctive quality of sound, as follows:

Clicking Instruments	**Swishing Instruments**	**Ringing or Tingling Instruments**
rhythm sticks	sand blocks	
wood blocks	maracas and other shakers	finger cymbals
tone blocks	pom-poms	wrist bells
temple blocks		sleigh bells
claves	**Booming Instruments**	triangles
coconut shells	drums	tambourines
castanets	tom-toms	jingle sticks
guiros		
	Clanging Instruments	**Orff Percussion Instruments**
	hand cymbals	See pages 153–60.
	gongs	

Arranging the Instrumentation

Which instruments produce the most appropriate sound effects for different types of music? Small instruments usually play the fastest rhythmic patterns, and large instruments provide basic beats and accents. The ringing or jingling instruments provide sound effects for gay, light, higher-pitched music, while the drums produce background for deep, rhythmic music.

National characteristics of music can be enhanced by the selection of instruments used to play rhythmic patterns associated with various countries and peoples. For example, tambourines, shakers, and castanets suggest Mexican or Spanish music; tom-toms and drums, Indian music; bongo drums, claves, guiros, and maracas, Latin-American music.

For clarity of sound, only a few instruments are played at one time, especially when used to accompany classroom singing. A feeling for musical form and structure can be taught by having a different group of instruments play each phrase or section of the music.

Reading Rhythm Instrument Scores

Printed rhythm instrument scores are seldom used in the modern classroom. The following sample scores are provided to demonstrate typical uses for different instruments.

A simple score for *Yankee Doodle* (see p. 176 for melody) could be arranged as follows:

YANKEE DOODLE

Pattern

Tambourines
Triangles
Finger cymbals

Underlying Beat

Rhythm sticks
Tone blocks

Accent

Drum
Hand cymbal

135

To illustrate phrase contrast and national characteristics, *Down in Mexico* can be played by rhythm instruments in the following manner:

DOWN IN MEXICO

Playing Classroom Percussion Instruments

Play and sing *La Raspe,* creating rhythmic patterns on castanets, tambourines, maracas, claves, and other instruments.

LA RASPE

TR. MAURICE TALBOT

MEXICO

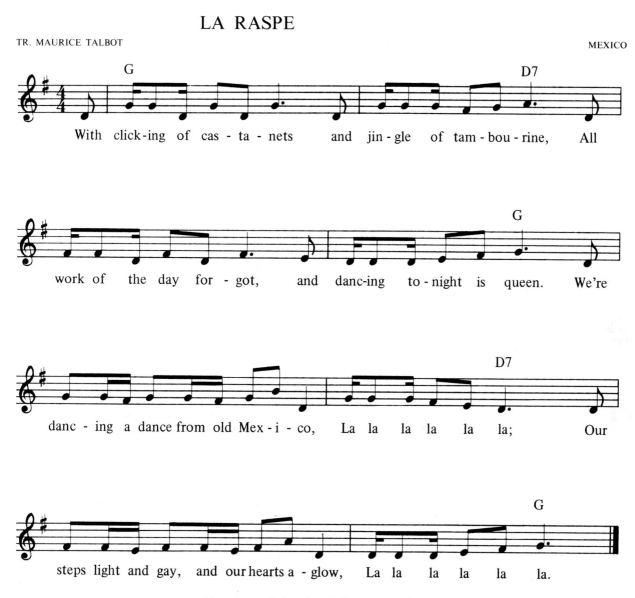

With click-ing of cas - ta - nets and jin - gle of tam - bou - rine, All

work of the day for - got, and danc-ing to - night is queen. We're

danc - ing a dance from old Mex - i - co, La la la la la la; Our

steps light and gay, and our hearts a - glow, La la la la la la.

Also play and sing *Las Pollitas* (p. 293), creating appropriate instrumentations.

CALYPSO JOE

R. W. W.

CARIBBEAN FOLK TUNE

Refrain

I know a boy down on Nas - sau ____ isle,

Joe is his name, he's got a win - ning ____ smile. "How a - bout a shine, Mis - ter,

just a ____ dime?" Sings lit - tle Joe in ca - lyp - so ____ time.

Verse

If you should come to his town some - day, ____ he'll

cap - ture your heart with his plead - ing way, ____ Sing - ing and clap - ping his

tune so bright, ____ He'll nev - er let you ____ out of sight. ____

Playing Classroom Percussion Instruments

The following typical calypso rhythmic patterns can be used to accompany *Calypso Joe* and most other calypso tunes. These patterns can be used as two- and four-bar introductions and codas (endings).

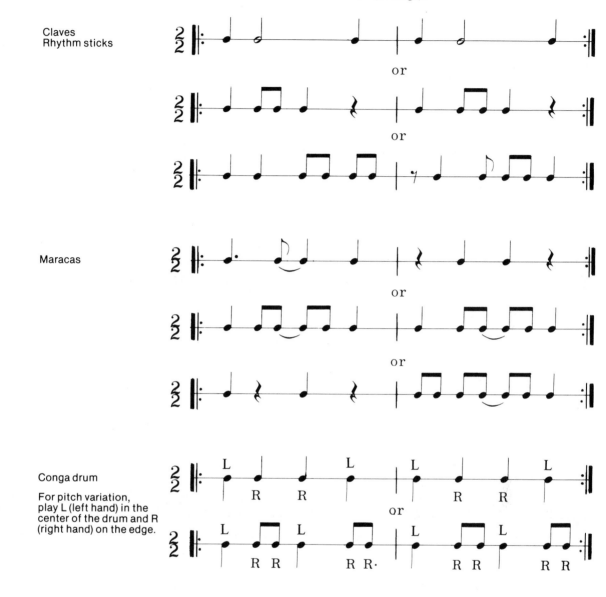

Claves
Rhythm sticks

Maracas

Conga drum

For pitch variation, play L (left hand) in the center of the drum and R (right hand) on the edge.

Suggested Assignments

1. Sing folk songs of various countries from state and local music texts, and play rhythm instruments that you think are appropriate for the music.
2. Create and write your own rhythm instrument scores for several compositions, using different time signatures.
3. Form a classroom orchestra with rhythm instruments, melody instruments, and Autoharp. Take a turn with others in conducting the orchestra.

Playing Bells

Uses for Bells in the Classroom

Bells have proved to be an effective aid in teaching children to enjoy and understand music. For teachers and children with limited musical background, bells are especially helpful in learning simple melodies. Bells can be used as follows:

1. To teach rote songs to children. Teachers who do not sing or who have low-pitched voices can play the tune. Also, difficult tonal patterns and phrases can be learned quickly by having them played several times on the bells.
2. To pitch and start songs. In pitching the song, bells can be used to sound the keynote, check the pitch at phrase and song endings, etc. Some teachers prefer the bells since the key chord, 1–3–5 *(do-mi-so)*, can be played more easily. Interesting introductions can be made with bells. The first or last phrase of the song or a simple tonal pattern can be used to start the song.
3. To provide simple accompaniments, descants, and codas for children's songs.
4. To create special sound effects in the music, such as imitating chimes, clocks, church bells, and sleigh bells.
5. To provide creative opportunities by having children take turns constructing their own tunes.
6. To provide ear training through tone matching activities to help out-of-tune singers locate and sing pitches that have been played on the bells.
7. To make up a classroom orchestra with wind melody and percussion instruments, Autoharps, and piano.

Courtesy of Walberg & Auge, 86 Mechanic St., Worcester, Massachusetts.

Song Bells (Melody Bells)

Song bells are available in sets of various sizes, ranging from eight bars to the popular and very useful two-and-a-half octave set pictured.

Step Bells

Step bells are available in two sizes—an eight-note C to C diatonic set, and a seventeen-note C to E chromatic set. These special bar bells are mounted on a staircase frame. They are used in the classroom to show visually the relationship between pitch, half and whole steps, and scale elevation. Step bells are an invaluable audiovisual aid for students who do not understand pitch direction.

Playing Classroom Percussion Instruments

Courtesy of Rhythm Band, Inc., Fort Worth, Texas.

Courtesy of Scientific Music Industries, Inc., 1255 S. Wabash Ave., Chicago, Illinois 60805.

Seven-Note Pentatonic Resonator Bell Set

| Pink
1
F | Lt. Blue
2
G | Gray
3
A | Green
4
B♭ | Yellow
5
C | Rose
6
D | Dk. Blue
7
E | Red
8
F |

| 1
F
do | 2
G
re | 3
A
mi | 4
B♭
fa | 5
C
so | 6
D
la | 7
E
ti | 8
F
do |

Tone Educator Bells

Tone Educator Bells are available in two sizes, a twenty-bell set (one-and-a-half octaves, C through G) and a twenty-five bell set (two octaves, G through G). These bells can be removed from the case and played individually or in various combinations. They can be used in any key since they are built chromatically. (Resonator Bells are similar to Tone Educator Bells; the two can be used interchangeably.)

Swiss Melodé Bells

The Melodé Bells are a set of eight Swiss-type copper bells tuned to the key of F. These bells, which are individually colored in eight different hues, are accurately pitched and maintain their pitch under all conditions. Each bell is keyed to the scale by color, number, and letter as shown. The color of the bells is of great interest to young children, and some will relate color to pitch. Soon, however, the color seems to be disregarded and the pitch, number, or letter name is used, thereby introducing concepts related to music notation.

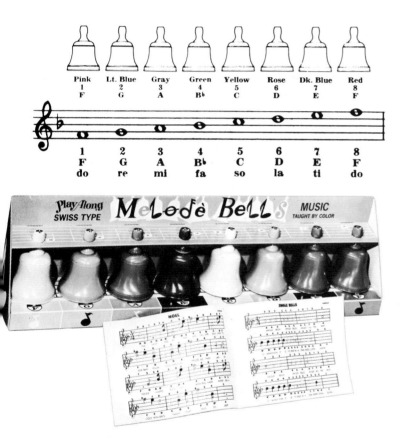

Courtesy of Scientific Music Industries, Inc., 1255 S. Wabash Ave., Chicago, Illinois 60805.

Uses for Tone Educator Bells in the Classroom

A unique feature of Tone Educator Bells is that the player can choose from the set only the bells that are needed for any given song. For example, the beginner in music can start with as few as three bell blocks to play such tunes as *Hot Cross Buns* and *Merry Bells,* and then go to five-tone songs like *Jingle Bells* and *Lightly Row,* six-tone songs like *Twinkle, Twinkle, Little Star,* and so on, adding bells for wider range songs. (See the following pages for these songs.) This is a practical way to introduce sharps and flats one at a time.

A musical game can be played by having individual class members hold one of the bell blocks needed for a certain tune. Each plays the note for the bell block held when signaled by the teacher or student director. Both familiar and original tunes can be played in this way, with all children in the room taking turns in the activity.

It is important to note that Tone Educator Bells can be used effectively as an introduction to studying and playing harmony. These bells provide beautiful chordal accompaniments for classroom singing. Individual students are given single notes of a chord from the set of Resonator Bells, and all the notes of a given chord are sounded simultaneously to produce the required harmony. Refer to *Ring, Ring the Banjo* (p. 146).

How to Play the Bells

The mallet should be held firmly. Use a bouncing blow, flexing the wrist quickly just as the bar is struck. The use of two mallets struck alternately facilitates playing fast passages. When two mallets are used, a roll can be made by a fast movement of the wrists and hands for sustained notes.

Line Notation

Teachers and children who do not read music can learn to play simple tunes on the bells through the use of *line notation*. (See chapter 4, pp. 61–62.) The number or letter over a word indicates the bar to be struck to produce the melody note. These can be written on the bars with chalk or crayon. The approximate duration of the notes is indicated by the relative lengths of the lines. At first use songs that move stepwise, such as *Hot Cross Buns*. (See p. 179 for the staff notation of this song.)

HOT CROSS BUNS

NURSERY SONG

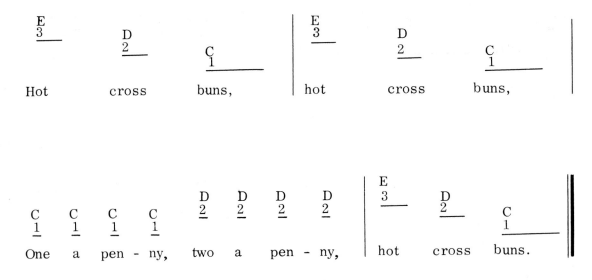

Playing Classroom Percussion Instruments

MERRY BELLS

WALES

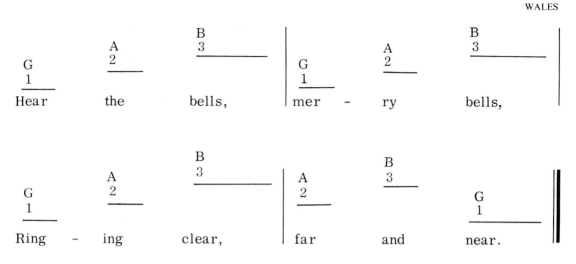

G 1 Hear
A 2 the
B 3 bells,
G 1 mer -
A 2 ry
B 3 bells,

G 1 Ring -
A 2 ing
B 3 clear,
A 2 far
B 3 and
G 1 near.

Using Staff Notation

Note: Play the following exercises and songs using staff notation. Practicing the exercises and songs for piano right hand position starting on p. 104, chapter 6, will be helpful at this point.

C D E F G F E D C   C E G E C

C D E F G A B C B A G F E D C   C E G C G E C   C G C G C C

VALENTINE SONG

U.S.
ADAPTED R. W. W.

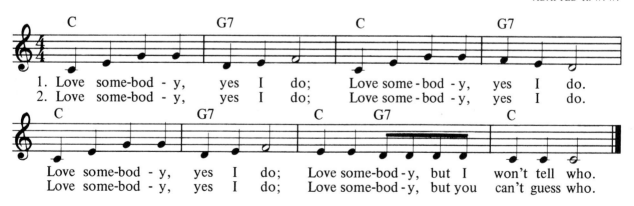

C   G7   C   G7
1. Love some-bod - y, yes I do; Love some-bod - y, yes I do.
2. Love some-bod - y, yes I do; Love some-bod - y, yes I do.

C   G7   C   G7   C
Love some-bod - y, yes I do; Love some-bod - y, but I won't tell who.
Love some-bod - y, yes I do; Love some-bod - y, but you can't guess who.

Playing Classroom Percussion Instruments   143

BIG BEN CLOCK

ENGLAND
ADAPTED R. W. W.

STEEPLE BELLS

FRANCE

Stee - ple bells are gen - tly ring - ing, Hear them ring - ing,

"Peace on earth" is what they're say - ing. Hear them ring - ing.

EVENING BELLS

NURSERY SONG

Those eve - ning bells, those eve - ning bells, how many a tale their

mus - ic tells, of youth and home and that sweet time when

last I heard their sooth - ing chime.

Also play and sing *Joy to the World* (p. 182).

WHITE CORAL BELLS

ROUND

ENGLAND

1. White cor - al bells up - on a slen - der stalk,
2. O, don't you wish that you could hear them ring?

Lil - ies of the val - ley deck my gar - den walk.
That will hap - pen on - ly when the fair - ies sing.

JINGLE BELLS

J. PIERPONT

Jin - gle bells, jin - gle bells, jin - gle all the way.

Oh what fun it is to ride in a one - horse o - pen sleigh. —

Jin - gle bells, jin - gle bells, jin - gle all the way.

Oh what fun it is to ride in a one - horse o - pen sleigh!

Also play and sing the bell songs *Lovely Evening* (p. 246) and *The Bell Doth Toll* (p. 291).

The following songs can be performed by one or more players.

JACOB'S LADDER

SPIRITUAL

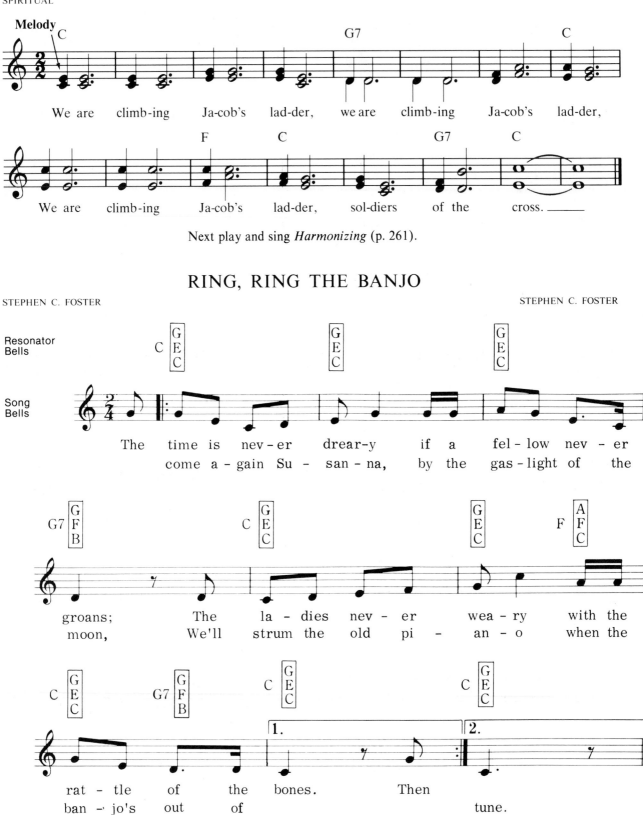

Next play and sing *Harmonizing* (p. 261).

RING, RING THE BANJO

STEPHEN C. FOSTER   STEPHEN C. FOSTER

THERE'S MUSIC IN THE AIR

GEO. F. ROOT

Also play and sing two-part songs from chapter 12.

Courtesy of Schulmerich Carillons, Inc., Sellersville, PA.

Handbells

One of the most colorful and interesting musical activities to be introduced in recent years for schools and community is the playing of handbells. Every school should have at least one set which can be shared by classroom teachers from grade 5 upward. Previous training in the use of other bells mentioned in this chapter, especially Tone Educator or Resonator Bells, is recommended. Melodies, chords, and accompanied melodies can also be played on the handbells with more spectacular results and audience appeal.

The pitch names and octaves are clearly marked on the Schulmerich Handbells pictured herein. The lowest pitched bell in a three-octave set is C4 (middle C), and the highest bell is C7. Handbell sets are available in the ranges indicated below:

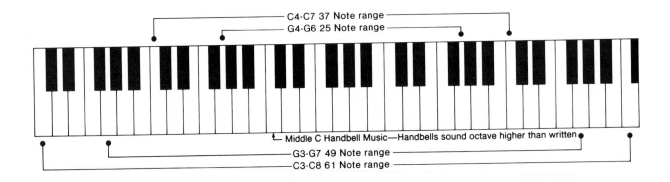

E5 F5 F#5 G5 G#5 A5 A#5 B5 C6 C#6 D6 D#6 E6 F6 F#6 G6 G#6 A6 A#6 B6 C7

C4 C#4 D4 D#4 E4 F4 F#4 G4 G#4 A4 A#4 B4 C5 C#5 D5 D#5

Limited space in this chapter prohibits the writing of a method for playing the handbells. Therefore, the reader is referred to two excellent texts by Dr. James Fisher, *Learning Packages for Handbells,* Volumes I and II published by Schulmerich Carillons, Inc., Carillon Hill, Sellersville, Pennsylvania 18960. These provide complete instructions and music.

Suggested Assignments

1. Play songs from state and local school songbook series. Include several part songs. Practice finding and sounding the keynote and the key chord (1-3-5-8-5-3-1) for these songs.
2. Create and play your own melodies.
3. Practice the chromatic scale on the bells up and down between the lowest and highest notes, and gradually increase the speed.

The Orff Approach

The Orff approach to teaching music is based on a program developed by Carl Orff at the Guentherschule, a school of music, dance, and gymnastics in Munich, Germany. His ideas have won acclaim and acceptance by music educators throughout the world. Orff's uniquely creative approach introduces music to children through their own speech and rhythmic movement, and through singing and playing percussion and melody instruments.

A brief introduction to some of the Orff approaches to music education and the skills involved is presented here. Teachers and students who wish to pursue this very important topic further should refer to the classic text *Elementaria,* by Carl Orff's longtime associate, Gunild Keetman.

Speech and Rhythmic Experiences

Chanting

Chanting results from the instinctive connection between speech and rhythm. Through the rhythm of the words, children naturally and delightfully relate to their carefree world of play and imagery, whether they are chanting traditional nursery rhymes or creating their own rhymes about their activities, their friends, or their pets.

Clapping, the simplest form of bodily movement, occurs spontaneously as children begin to feel the rhythm of the words.

Chant and clap the rhythms of the following:

Tom - my, Mar - y, come and play with me.

Ring a - round a ros - y, a pock - et full of po - sies, ash - es, ash - es, we all fall down.

Cyn - thi - a, Tim - o - thy, skip with me.

"Baa, baa, black sheep, have you an - y wool?" "Yes sir, yes sir, three bags full, One for my mas - ter and one for my dame, And one for the lit - tle boy that lives in the lane."

Orff teachers have found that, through repeated use in combinations of various rhythms, these patterns imprint themselves quickly and soon are readily recognized and reproduced in music reading and writing.

Echo Clapping

In *echo clapping,* the teacher claps a rhythmic pattern of one, two, or more measures, which is to be imitated by the children. This exercise is designed to develop listening skills, quick reaction, rhythmic memory, and feeling for form. Clap the following:

Improvise various other rhythmic patterns in duple and triple meter with gradually increased difficulty to include dotted rhythms, syncopation, triplets, and the like.

Other Bodily Movements (Patschen, Stamping, Finger Snapping)

In addition to chanting and clapping, a prominent feature of the Orff approach to rhythmic training is the use of various bodily movements such as patschen (patting knees with hands), stamping feet, and snapping fingers. Wheeler and Raebeck include many excellent exercises for rhythmic experiences in their valuable book, *Orff and Kodály Adapted for the Elementary School.*[1] A few of these exercises are shown here; practice the patterns indicated. For patschen, simultaneously pat the left knee with the left hand and the right knee with the right hand. (See pp. 48–50 for additional experiences with patschen.)

1. Wheeler, Lawrence, and Raebeck, Lois. *Orff and Kodály Adapted for the Elementary School.* 3d ed. Dubuque, Ia.: Wm. C. Brown Company Publishers, 1984. Rhythm exercises used by permission.

For Primary Grades

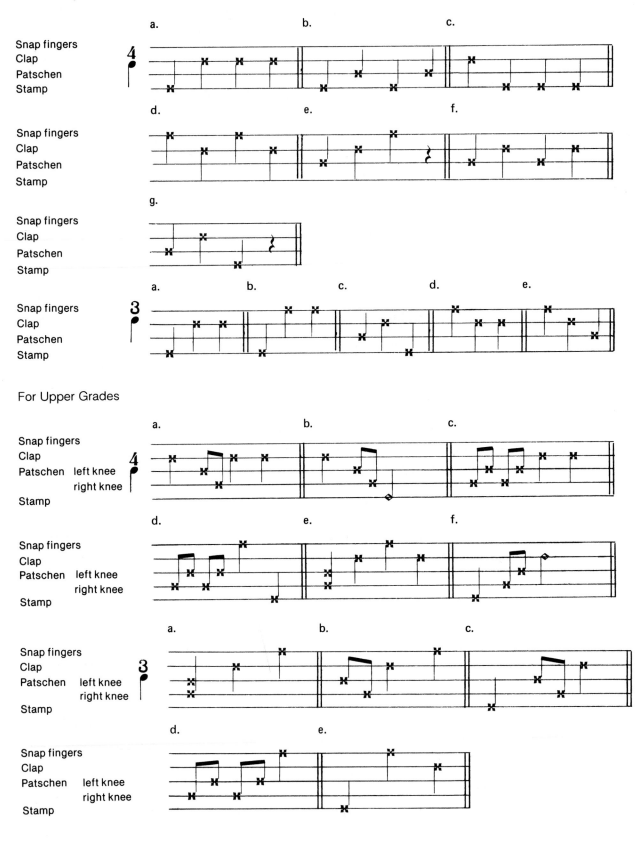

For Upper Grades

Playing Classroom Percussion Instruments

The playing of these unique and fascinating instruments provides creative and joyful experiences in bridging the gap between rhythm and melody in the Orff curriculum. The instruments described below are basic to that program.

Melodic Tonebar Instruments

A distinct advantage of melodic tonebar instruments is their *removable* bars. When playing simple melodies and accompaniments that call for only a few notes, the bars not needed can be removed, thus, children can find the right note quickly. These instruments are made of wood or metal to produce varied tone qualities and effects. All of them are diatonic (same as the white keys of the piano). Extra F♯ and B♭ bars can be added for variety and change of key.

Wood-Barred Instruments
Tonebars for xylophones are made of rosewood or fiberglass and set on a resonator box or an aluminum tube resonator. The tone quality is mellow-dry. There are soprano, alto, and bass xylophones; their ranges are as follows (*8* indicates that the pitch is an octave higher than written):

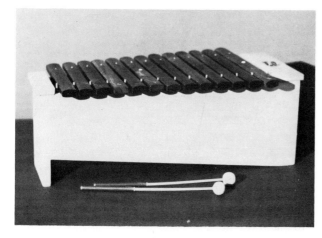

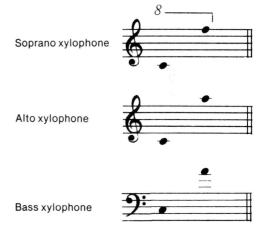

Soprano xylophone

Alto xylophone

Bass xylophone

Metal-Barred Instruments
Metallophones. Tonebars for metallophones are also removable. They are made of metal alloy and set over box resonators. The tone quality is rich, mellow, and bell-like. Resonator Bells or Tone Educator Bells may be substituted for metallophones. There are soprano, alto, and bass metallophones; their ranges are as follows:

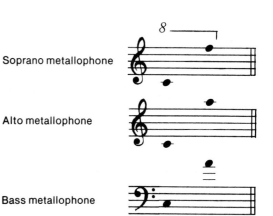

Soprano metallophone

Alto metallophone

Bass metallophone

Glockenspiels. Tonebars for glockenspiels are made of tempered steel and are set on wooden resonator boxes. The tone quality is a bright, ringing, bell-like sound. Large sets of melody or song bells may be substituted if necessary. There are soprano and alto glockenspiels; their ranges are as follows (*15* indicates that the pitch is two octaves higher than written):

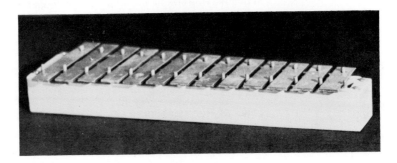

Soprano glockenspiel

Alto glockenspiel

Tuned Percussion Instruments

The drums shown below are used in pairs to give an octave range. They are usually tuned to *do* and *so* (scale steps 1 and 5), sometimes to *do* and *re* (steps 1 and 2), *so* and *la* (steps 5 and 6), or *do* and *la* (steps 1 and 6). The heads are made of skin or resonant plastic, and hand screws are used for tuning. They are played with wool- or felt-headed mallets. Wheeler and Raebeck recommend the twenty- and fourteen-inch timpani to meet the needs of the average classroom.

These two drums are especially useful in accompanying songs pitched in the C, D, F, and G *pentatonic* scales, as shown below:[2]

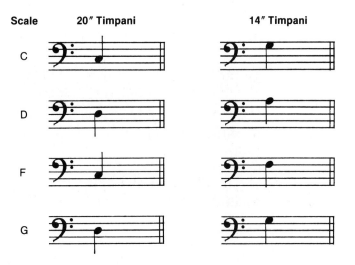

Pentatonic scales are based on a five-note scale—steps 1–2–3–5–6 of the major scale. All melodies used with Orff instruments are *pentatonic,* thereby avoiding clashing dissonant harmonies. C and G are the most commonly used in the Orff approach.

Also refer to pages 68–70, in chapter 4.

Untuned Percussion Instruments

See the beginning of this chapter for photographs and/or descriptions of the following percussion instruments.

triangles (several sizes)	rhythm sticks
tone blocks	rattles
sand blocks	maracas
finger cymbals	tambourines

Other Orff Instruments for the Classroom

String Instruments
viola da gamba
cello
guitar
ukulele (baritone)
Autoharp
dulcimer

Wind Instrument
recorder (soprano)

2. Wheeler, Lawrence, and Raebeck, Lois. *Orff and Kodály Adapted for the Elementary School.* 3d ed. Dubuque, Ia.: Wm. C. Brown Company Publishers, 1984.

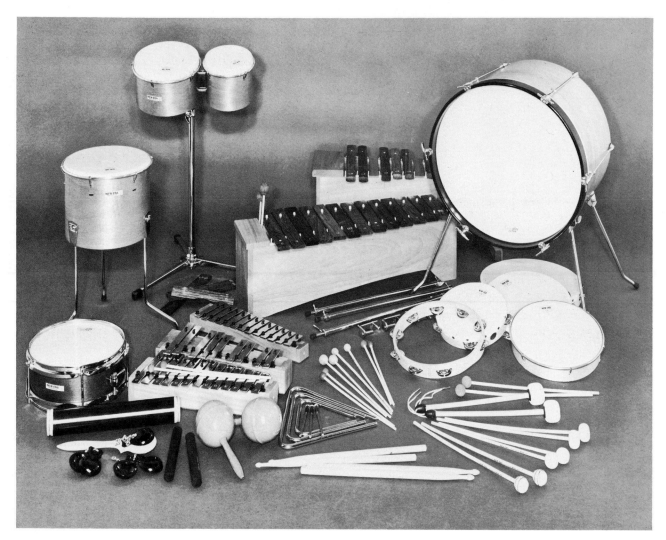

Courtesy of Selmer, Elkhart, Indiana.

Orff Instruments

Rhythmic and
Melodic Ostinati

Another important purpose of the Orff school is to provide the student with co-
pious experiences in creating rhythmic and melodic ostinati (musical patterns
repeated to form accompaniments as well as melodies for movement, singing, and
playing instruments). These develop a feeling for meter, form, and basic note
values as well as melodic concepts and the natural, free use of the singing voice.
The children chant first in two-note patterns, then in three-, four-, and five-note
patterns, calling to their friends and imitating bird calls, street cries, and familiar
jingles and nursery rhymes. A typical starting point is the child's play chant on
a descending minor third interval (e.g., G-E, 5–3).

JOHNNY

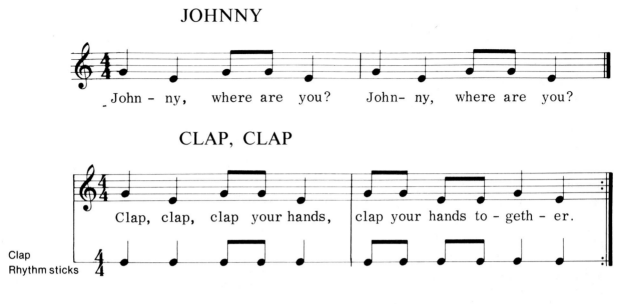

John - ny, where are you? John- ny, where are you?

CLAP, CLAP

Clap, clap, clap your hands, clap your hands to - geth - er.

Clap
Rhythm sticks

Three-Note Pattern

Rhythm sticks, triangle, and tambourine can be substituted for clapping rhythms, and drums can be substituted for stamping rhythms.

RAIN, RAIN

Rain, rain, go a - way, come a - gain some oth - er day.

Clap

Snap fingers

Stamp

Rain, rain, go a - way, lit - tle Cin - dy wants to play.

Clap

Snap fingers

Stamp

POLLY PUT THE KETTLE ON

Five-Note Pattern
(Pentatonic)

Any one or more of these ostinati may be used as a two- or four-measure introduction before the voice part enters. A concluding part (coda) may be added by having one or more of the ostinati continue for two or four measures after the melody has ended. One ostinato at a time may drop out with a gradual decrease in volume (diminuendo).

SOURWOOD MOUNTAIN

APPALACHIAN SONG

ARR. R. W. W.

Also try these melodic ostinati:

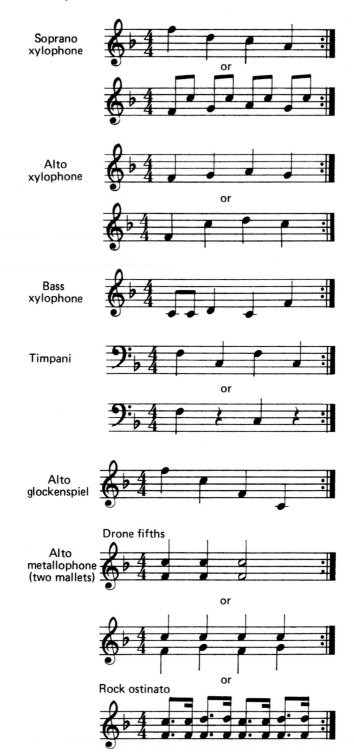

A basic hard rock beat, like that of the rock ostinato above, against any pentatonic folk tune or improvised melody provides a spirited classroom experience.

Now try these rhythmic ostinati. (Numerous others with bodily movement are given in this chapter, beginning on page 151.)

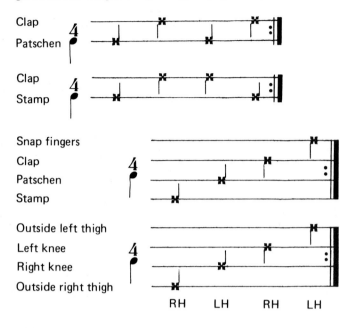

Now try these rhythmic ostinati. (Numerous others with bodily movement are given in this chapter, beginning on page 151.)

Suggested Assignment

Create your own ostinati and instrumentations for the following pentatonic melodies.

Old Paint (p. 215)
Li'l Liza Jane (p. 250)
Steal Away (p. 261)
Old Texas (p. 254)
Auld Lang Syne (p. 263)
Cindy (p. 190)

Sources for Orff Instruments

De Gouden Brug (The Golden Bridge), distributed by Rhythm Band, Inc., P.O. Box 126, Fort Worth, Texas 76101.

Kid Stuff, distributed by Kid Stuff Division of Master Musical Instruments, P.O. Box 3681, Center Line, Michigan 48015.

Kitching Educational Division of Ludwig Industries, 1728 N. Damen Ave., Chicago, Illinois 60647.

Lefima Instruments, distributed by Custom Music Company, 1414 S. Main St., Royal Oak, Michigan 48067.

M.E.G. (Music Education Group), Classroom Musical Instruments, Box 1501, Union, New Jersey 07083.

New Era Instruments, distributed by Rhythm Band, Inc., P.O. Box 126, Fort Worth, Texas 76101.

Premier Instruments, distributed by Selmer, Box 310, Elkhart, Indiana 46514.

Sonor Instruments, distributed by M. Hohner, Inc., Andrews Rd., Hicksville, New York 11802.

Studio 49, distributed by Magnamusic-Baton, Inc., 10370 Page Industrial Blvd., St. Louis, Missouri 63132.

8 Playing the Recorder

The recorder has been popular as a social instrument with young and old alike for many centuries. It is recognized as a musical instrument, not a musical toy. A pleasing flutelike tone and a range of two octaves of well-tuned notes can be produced. A wealth of great music has been written for the recorder through the ages.

The recorder can serve as an aid in learning to read music and to provide invaluable preband and preorchestra experience for children. Classroom teachers can have fun learning to play, developing their own musical skills at the same time. Men and women with low voices can use this melody instrument in teaching children's songs.

C recorders can be used effectively together with bells, Autoharps, guitars, and Orff instruments. Try various combinations of instruments in performing the songs in this and other sections of the book.

Description of the Instrument

Most recorders have eight holes. Some of them have a key to cover the eighth hole. Others have two small holes in place of the eighth hole, as pictured.

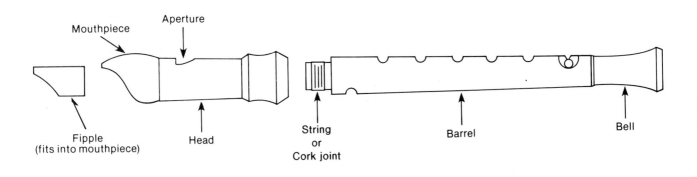

Mouthpiece   Aperture

Fipple (fits into mouthpiece)   Head   String or Cork joint   Barrel   Bell

Kinds of Recorders

Four-part harmony (soprano, alto, tenor, and bass) can be played using C-Soprano, C-Tenor, F-Alto, and F-Bass recorders. In schools the C-Soprano is generally used, with the occasional addition of the F-Alto for low harmony parts. Instruction in this chapter is limited to the C-Soprano recorder.

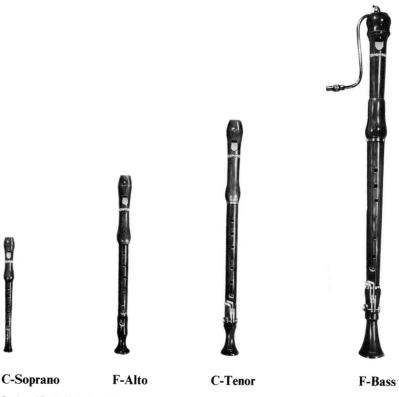

| C-Soprano | F-Alto | C-Tenor | F-Bass |

Courtesy of Trophy Music. Co., 1278 W. 9th St., Cleveland, Ohio 44113.

Care of the Recorder

An all-plastic, two-piece recorder, which is both economical and practical for school use, is available. The serious student of the recorder, however, should use one made of wood.

The wood recorder requires greater care than the plastic recorder.

1. A new wood recorder should be oiled before it is played. Take the instrument apart and oil each part with a swab lightly moistened with woodwind oil. Do not oil the fipple or the aperture. Allow the oil to dry for about twelve hours before playing the recorder. Oil the instrument three or four times a year. Do not oil it just after playing; wait until it is dry.
2. A new wood recorder should not be played more than fifteen or twenty minutes at a time. The wood must become adjusted to moisture and warmth.
3. Hold the instrument in the hands until it is warm. A recorder should be warm before it is played to protect the wood from cracking.
4. When playing, blow gently. Overblowing causes bad tone quality and will eventually damage the upper register of the instrument.

5. After playing, dry each section of the instrument with a swab. Do not touch the delicate fipple or the aperture when drying the head piece.
6. When the recorder is not in use, keep it in its case. Never store it near heat or sunlight; avoid sudden changes of temperature.

Baroque and German Fingering Systems

Baroque fingering was the authentic fingering of recorders from the Baroque period until the early 1900s. The main difference between Baroque and German fingering systems lies in the fingering for F and F♯. Baroque fingering has the advantage of an easier F♯ in both low and high octaves, which facilitates passages involving this note (see the chart on p. 167). About 1920, the German fingering came into use, simplifying the forked (Baroque) fingering of low F and high F (see the chart on p. 167).

Music teachers who use the recorder as a preorchestral instrument for children prefer the German fingering because of its direct relationship to orchestral woodwind fingerings.

The Recorder and Other Melody Wind Instruments

Song Flute, Tonette, and Flutophone are closely related in fingering to the C-Soprano recorder and can be used together in the classroom (up to a point), as indicated by the Comparative Fingering Chart, which follows. Those who own one of these melody instruments or prefer it to the recorder (they cost a little less) may use the same exercises and songs in this chapter through *Upidee* (p. 185). Beyond this point the sharps and flats become difficult and are less in tune; they can be played only up to D, fourth line treble clef (see the fingering chart, p. 168).

Comparative Fingering Chart

Recorder

Song Flute, Tonette, Flutophone

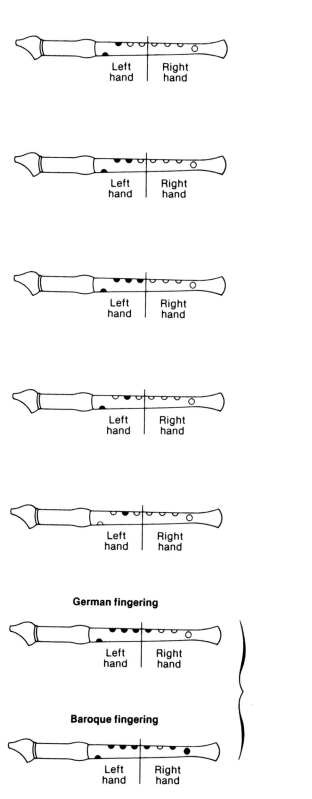

B

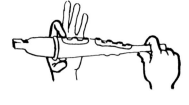

A

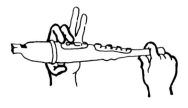

G

C

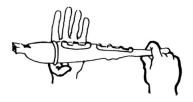

German fingering

D

Baroque fingering

F

Playing the Recorder

165

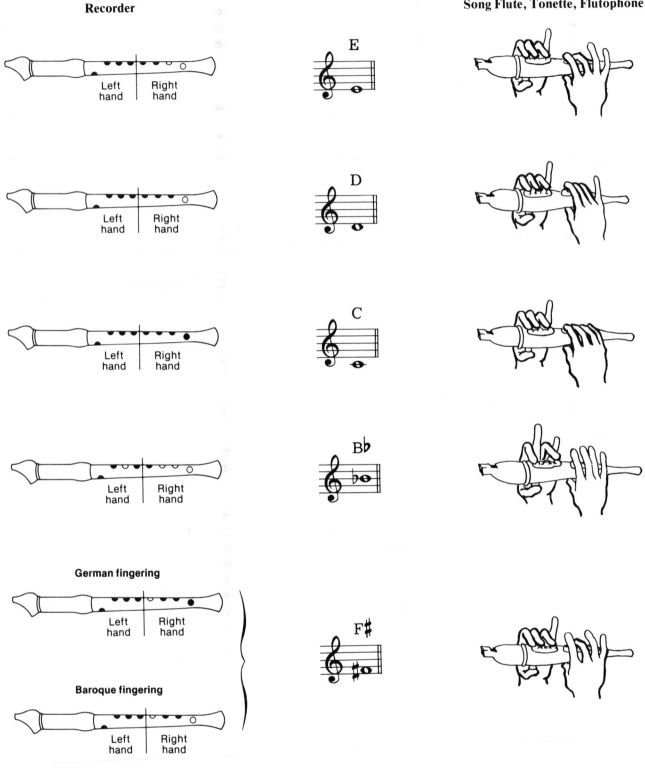

German fingering

Baroque fingering

Fingering Chart for Soprano Recorder

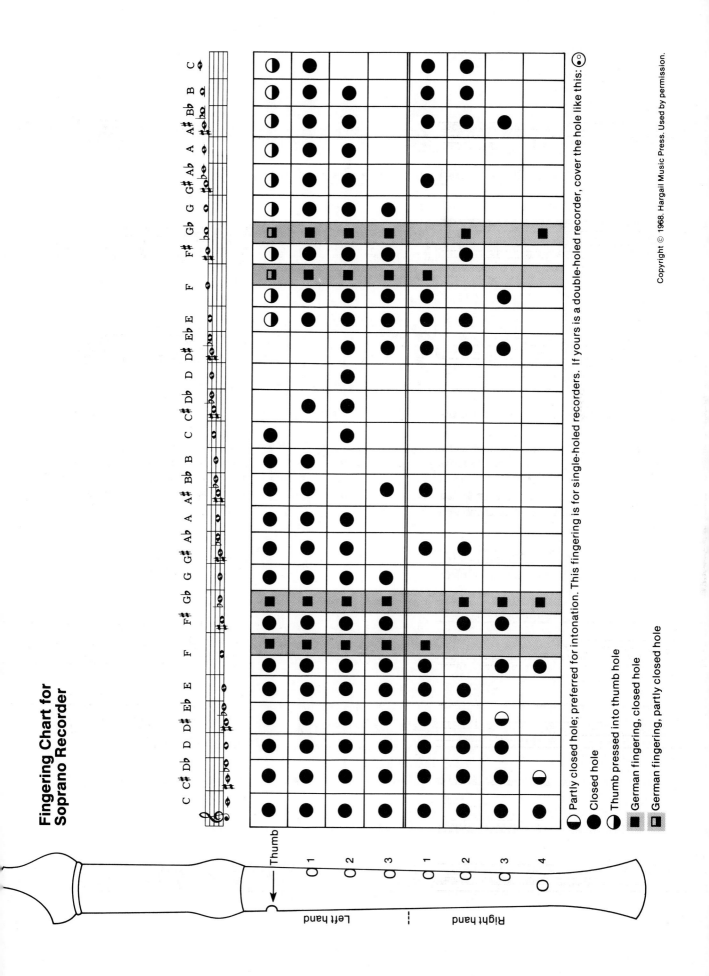

Copyright © 1968. Hargail Music Press. Used by permission.

◑ Partly closed hole; preferred for intonation. This fingering is for single-holed recorders. If yours is a double-holed recorder, cover the hole like this: ●○

◑ Partly closed hole; preferred for intonation. This fingering is for single-holed recorders.
● Closed hole
◐ Thumb pressed into thumb hole
■ German fingering, closed hole
▣ German fingering, partly closed hole

Thumb

1
2
3

1
2
3
4

Left hand

Right hand

Fingering Chart for Song Flute, Tonette, and Flutophone

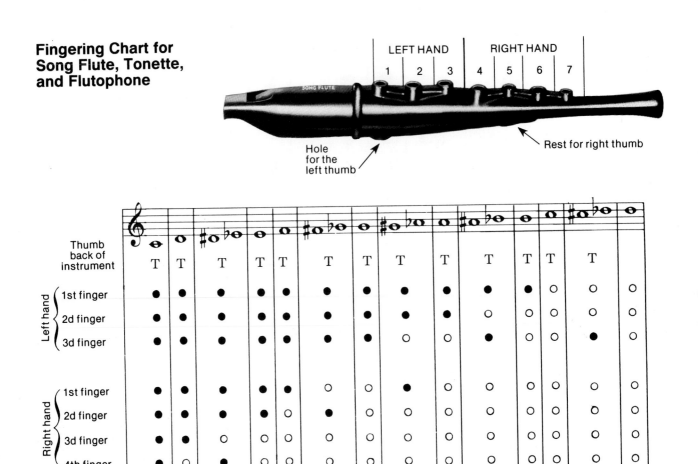

T - Thumb hole covered
● - Hole covered
O - Hole open

Playing the Recorder

The range of the C-Soprano recorder is as follows:

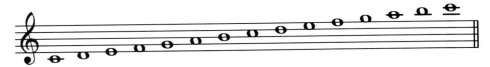

Holding and Fingering Positions

The first three fingers of the left hand are used to cover holes 1, 2, and 3. The hole on the underside is covered with the left thumb. The four fingers of the right hand are used to cover holes 4, 5, 6, and 7. The right thumb rests on the back of the instrument.

Producing the Tone

The mouthpiece is held with the lips. The tone is started by pronouncing the syllable "tu" and sustained with a steady stream of air. Only a small amount of air is needed; *do not overblow*.

The instructional material, exercises, and songs for the recorder through page 185 (with notes no higher than D, fourth line treble clef) are equally effective on the Song Flute, Tonette, and Flutophone. See the fingering chart above for different fingerings.

Using the Left Hand
Playing B, A, and G

First try this fingering without playing. Find the holes by feeling. Bring the fingers down firmly; lift them quickly.

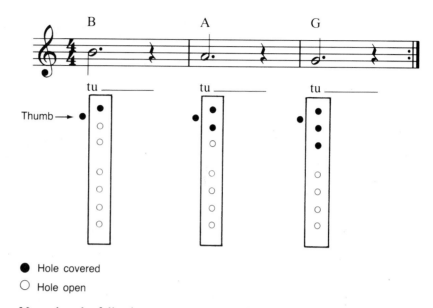

● Hole covered
○ Hole open

Now play the following preparatory exercise and songs.

HOT CROSS BUNS

NURSERY SONG

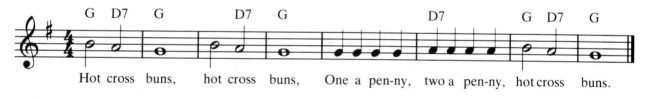

Hot cross buns, hot cross buns, One a pen-ny, two a pen-ny, hot cross buns.

FRENCH TUNE

FRANCE

FAIS DO DO

FRANCE

Fais do - do, and let us go dream - ing.

Fais do - do, come dream - ing with me.

GOOD NEWS!

SPIRITUAL

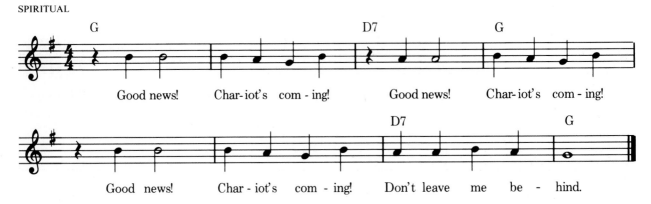

Good news! Char-iot's com - ing! Good news! Char-iot's com - ing!

Good news! Char - iot's com - ing! Don't leave me be - hind.

Playing C   Thumb and second finger of left hand. Play with clean attacks and releases.

Now play the following songs.

POLKA

Learn both parts.

DUET

TO PAREE

FRANCE

To Pa - ree, to Pa - ree, Po - ny gray will car - ry me. Off we

go round the track, Po - ny gray will bring me back.

SHAVE AND A HAIRCUT

Shave and a hair - cut, two bits!

* Alto part

*For advanced players.

CHOPSTICKS

TRADITIONAL

*Alto part

(Accent)

Playing D

Second finger only. When playing D, the mouth and right-hand thumb and third finger support the recorder. Always lift the fingers only a short distance from the holes in order to be ready for notes requiring them.

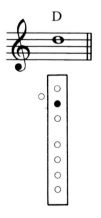

Review of All Fingerings for
the Left Hand

Gradually increase speed.

Playing Tunes with the Left
Hand Only

When you play the following with others, always hold the starting note until
everyone has it.

LIGHTLY ROW

GERMANY

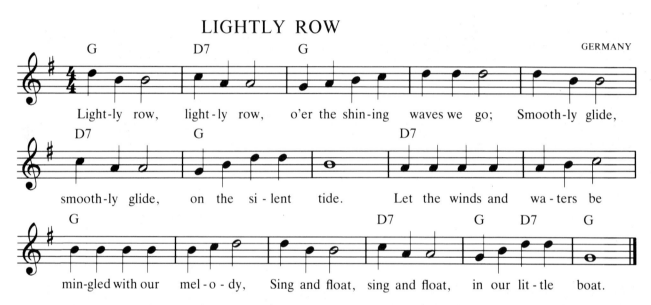

Light-ly row, light-ly row, o'er the shin-ing waves we go; Smooth-ly glide,

smooth-ly glide, on the si - lent tide. Let the winds and wa - ters be

min-gled with our mel - o - dy, Sing and float, sing and float, in our lit - tle boat.

THE BEE

GERMANY

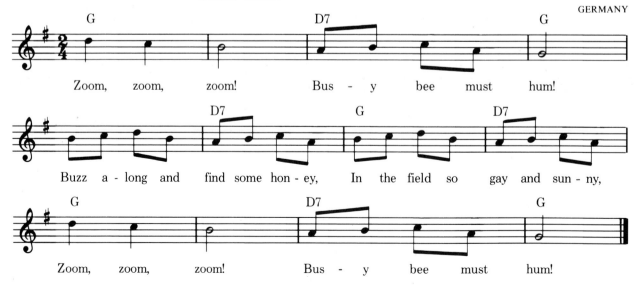

Zoom, zoom, zoom! Bus - y bee must hum!

Buzz a - long and find some hon - ey, In the field so gay and sun - ny,

Zoom, zoom, zoom! Bus - y bee must hum!

POLICE CALL

Before playing *The Recorder Band,* practice *Police Call* several times to prepare for the difficult interval on line three indicated with an asterisk (*).

THE RECORDER BAND

R. W. W.

GERMANY

I am a mu - si - cian, I come from *(name your town).* I

play in a re - cord - er band the best one in the land.

I can play this tune with on - ly my left hand.

CHORALE FROM JESU, JOY OF MAN'S DESIRING

J. S. BACH

Je - su, Joy of man's de - sir - ing,

Ho - ly wis - dom Love _____ most _____ bright.

Using the Right Hand
Playing F

1. Cover the holes for the left hand *firmly* as if to play G.
2. Play F using the first, third, and fourth fingers of the right hand.

Review of all fingerings thus far.

MERRILY WE ROLL ALONG

TRADITIONAL

Mer - ri - ly   we   roll   a - long,   roll   a - long,   roll   a - long.

Mer - ri - ly   we   roll   a - long   o'er   the   dark   blue   sea.

FIDDLE-DEE-DEE

ENGLAND

Fid - dle - dee - dee,   Fid - dle - dee - dee,   The   fly   has mar-ried the   bum - ble bee.

Playing E

STARLIGHT

TRADITIONAL

Star - light, star - bright, First star I see to - night.

Wish I may, Wish I might, Have the wish I wish to - night.

Playing D

Blow gently on all low notes.

Check fingering for low D carefully. *Cover all holes firmly.*

SNAKE DANCE

Dm   A7   Dm   A7   Dm

TRUMPET VOLUNTARY

PURCELL

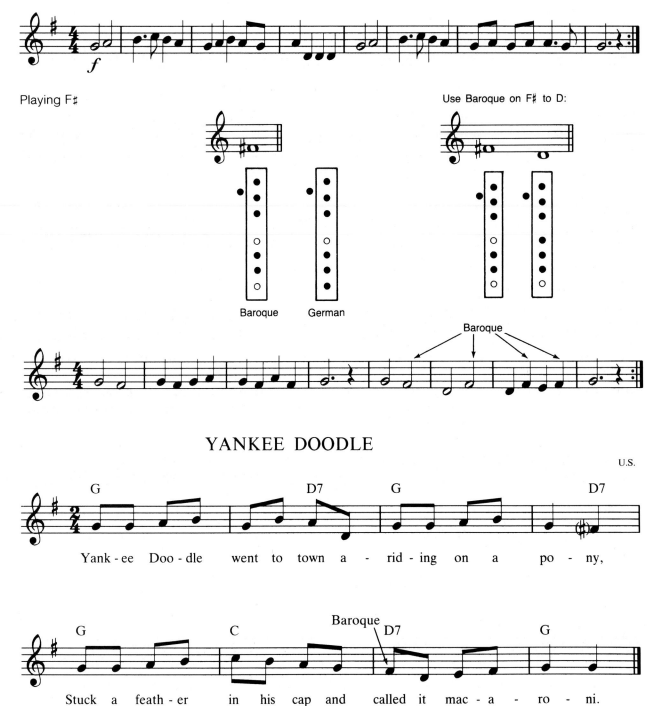

Playing F♯

Baroque   German

Use Baroque on F♯ to D:

Baroque

YANKEE DOODLE

U.S.

G   D7   G   D7

Yank - ee Doo - dle   went to town a - rid - ing on a   po - ny,

G   C   Baroque D7   G

Stuck a feath - er   in his cap and   called it mac - a - ro - ni.

WE WISH YOU A MERRY CHRISTMAS

CAROL ENGLAND

We wish you a mer-ry Christ-mas, We wish you a mer-ry
Christ-mas, We wish you a mer-ry Christ-mas, and a
hap-py New Year! Good ti-dings to you, and all of your
kin, Good ti-dings for Christ-mas, and a hap-py New Year.

Playing Slurs

A *slur* is a curved line connecting two or more notes of different pitches. To play a slur, tongue the first note and finger the remaining notes while blowing a steady stream of air into the instrument.

YOU CAN'T LOVE TWO

U.S.

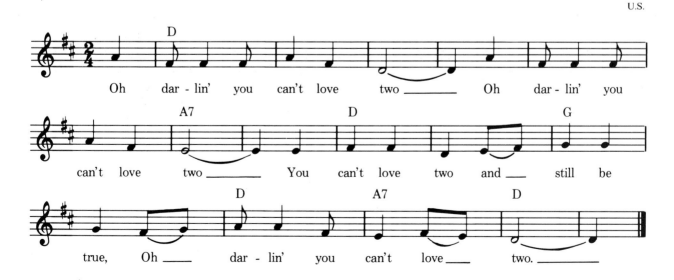

Oh dar-lin' you can't love two _____ Oh dar-lin' you
can't love two _____ You can't love two and _____ still be
true, Oh _____ dar-lin' you can't love _____ two. _____

FANTASIE IMPROMPTU

FREDERIC CHOPIN

O COME ALL YE FAITHFUL

TR. F. OAKLEY

J. F. WADE

| G | | D7 | | G | D7 | G | C | G | D7 | Em |
O come all ye faith-ful, Joy-ful and tri - um -phant, O

| A7 | D | A7 | D | G | D | G | D | A7 | D |
come ye, O come — ye to Beth - le - hem.

| G | D7 | G | D7 | G | D7 | G | Em | Am | D7 | G |
Come and be - hold Him, Born the King of an - gels; O

| D7 | G | D7 | G | D7 | G | D7 | G | D | G |
come let us a - dore Him, O come let us a - dore Him. O

| C | G | D | A7 | D7 | G | C | G | D7 | G |
come let us a - dore Him, ___ Christ ___ the Lord.

Playing Low C   Cover the holes firmly with flat-finger position (especially the third finger).

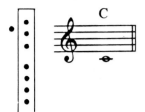

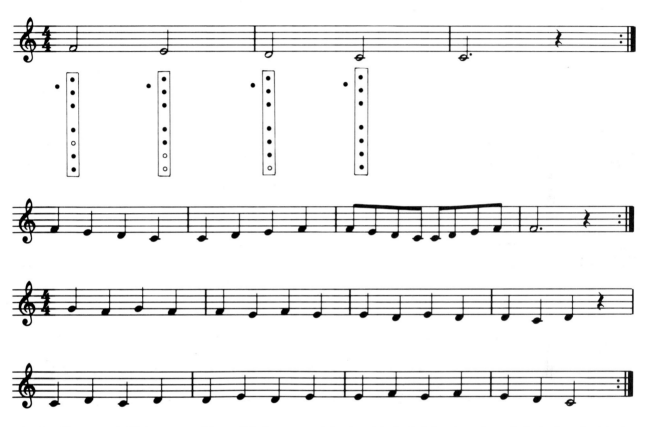

Playing Tunes with Right
Fingers

Keep all holes covered firmly with the left hand as the melody is played with the right hand.

HOT CROSS BUNS

ENGLAND

Hot   cross   buns,   hot   cross   buns.

One   a   pen - ny,   two   a   pen - ny,   hot   cross   buns.

CHORALE THEME

J. S. BACH

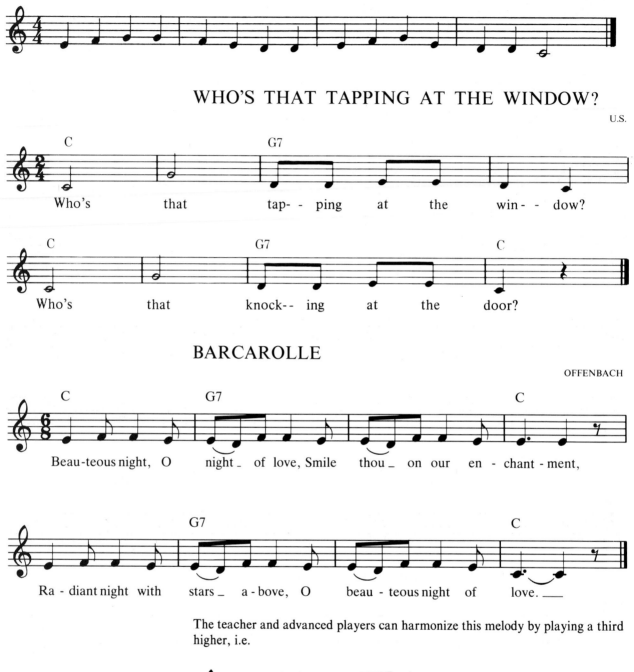

WHO'S THAT TAPPING AT THE WINDOW?

U.S.

Who's that tap- - ping at the win - - dow?

Who's that knock- - ing at the door?

BARCAROLLE

OFFENBACH

Beau-teous night, O night _ of love, Smile thou _ on our en - chant - ment,

Ra - diant night with stars _ a - bove, O beau - teous night of love. __

The teacher and advanced players can harmonize this melody by playing a third higher, i.e.

etc.

MEXICAN FOLK SONG

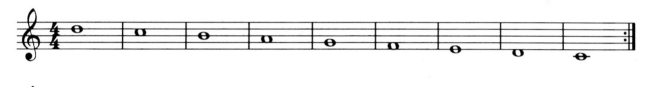

C MAJOR SCALE AND ARPEGGIO

Tongue all notes first. Then slur as written.

JOY TO THE WORLD

ISAAC WATTS

LOWELL MASON*

Joy to the world! the Lord is come; Let earth re - ceive her King; Let
ev - 'ry __ heart __ pre - pare __ Him __ room __ And heav'n and na - ture __
sing, and _ heav'n and na - ture _ sing, And _ heav'n and heav'n _ and na - ture sing.

*This melody is frequently but questionably attributed to Handel.

Phrasing

In some compositions, the slur encompasses an entire phrase. (Read the section on phrases and sentences, beginning on page 93.) As in playing slurs that have only a few notes, maintain a continuous flow of air through the instrument until you reach the end of the slur. Try not to breathe until you reach the *breath mark* (') at the end of the first long slur.

SONG WITHOUT WORDS
PRAELUDIUM NO. 2 FOR ORGAN

MENDELSSOHN

Also play *The Turtle Dove* (p. 27) for additional experience in phrasing.

F PENTATONIC

MORNING

GRIEG

JAPANESE HYMN

Playing B♭

Alternate fingering

THREE CORNERED HAT

CAMP SONG

F

C7

My hat, it has three cor - ners, _____ Three _ cor - ners
(German) Mein Hut, er hat drei Eck - en, _____ Drei _ Eck - en

F

has my hat, _____ A hat with - out three
hat mein Hut, _____ Und hat er nicht drei

C7

F

cor - ners, _____ Could _ nev - er be my hat. _____
Eck - en, _____ Dann _ ist er nicht mein Hut. _____

The accompaniments for *Little Lost Dog* (p. 186) can be played with *Three Cornered Hat* exactly as written.

EVENING SONG

CARL MARIA VON WEBER

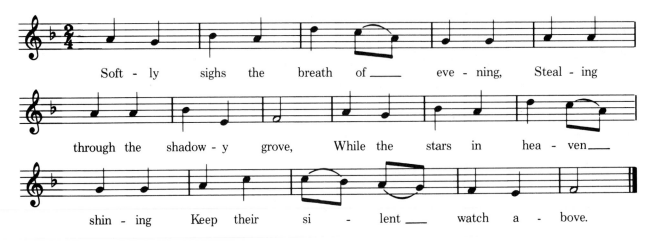

Soft - ly sighs the breath of ____ eve - ning, Steal - ing

through the shadow - y grove, While the stars in hea - ven ____

shin - ing Keep their si - lent ____ watch a - bove.

MELODY

SCHUMANN

SYMPHONIC THEME

TCHAIKOVSKY

Also play the melody as a canon by having half of the class start one measure later.

Refer to the popular canon, *Old Texas,* (p. 254), for additional experience.

UPIDEE

The shades of night were fall-ing fast, tra-la-la, tra-la-la, as

through an Al-pine vil-lage passed, tra-la-la-la-la, a

youth who bore, mid snow and ice, a ban-ner with the strange de-vice:

Chorus
Melody

Up - i - dee - i, dee - i - da, up - i - dee, up - i - da,

Up - i - dee - i, dee - i - da, up - i - dee - i - da!

Also play *Lovely Evening* (p. 246) in unison and as a round, and play *Steal Away* (p. 261) in two-part harmony.

LITTLE LOST DOG

Also play *Three Cornered Hat* (p. 183) with the same accompaniment parts.

Playing C♯ (D♭)

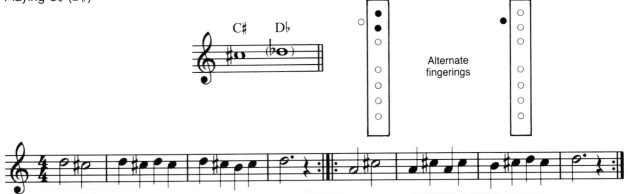

Alternate fingerings

D MAJOR SCALE AND ARPEGGIO

LAVENDER'S BLUE

ENGLAND

Lav - en - der's blue, dil - ly, dil - ly, lav - en - der's green;

When I am King dil - ly, dil - ly, you shall be Queen.

Who told you so? dil - ly, dil - ly, Who told you so?

'Twas my own heart dil - ly, dil - ly, that told me so.

Sing and play this song with Autoharp and guitar accompaniment.
For another version of this folk song, see page 125.

BUFFALO GALS

COOL WHITE

As I was walk-ing down the street, — down the street, —

down the street, — A pret-ty gal I chanced to meet, — O,

she was fair to see. _____ O Buf-fa-lo gals won't you

come out to-night, won't you come out to-night, won't you

come out to-night; O Buf-fa-lo gals won't you

come out to-night and dance by the light of the moon?

Also play *Sweet Betsy from Pike* (p. 74).

Open thumb hole.

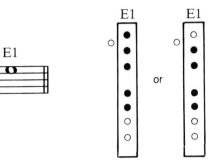

High E has two fingerings indicated E1 and E2. E1 is presented first since it is used with the first octave notes already learned.

GERMAN TUNE

THE BLACKSMITH
ARIA FROM MOZART'S OPERA
THE MARRIAGE OF FIGARO.

W. A. MOZART

Oh, the black-smith's a fine stur-dy fel-low, Hard his hands but his heart's true and

mel-low; See him stand there his huge bel-lows blow-ing, With his

strong, brawn-y arms free and bare; See the fire in the fur-nace a-

glow-ing, Bright its spar-kle, its flash, and its glare.

MELODY

ARBAN

The following *Etude* (study) is based on the G pentatonic scale.

ETUDE

Improvise and create your own melodies in duple and triple meter on the G pentatonic scale.

CINDY

APPALACHIAN SONG

U.S.

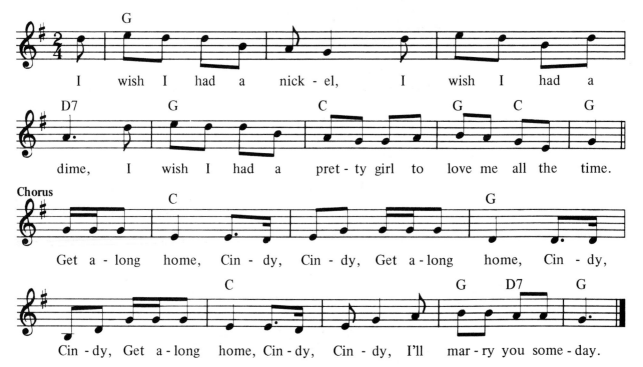

I wish I had a nick - el, I wish I had a dime, I wish I had a pret - ty girl to love me all the time.

Chorus

Get a - long home, Cin - dy, Cin - dy, Get a - long home, Cin - dy, Cin - dy, Get a - long home, Cin - dy, Cin - dy, I'll mar - ry you some - day.

Accompaniment Ostinati

Read *rhythmic and melodic ostinati* (p. 156).

Any two or more of the following ostinati may be combined and played as accompaniment for *Cindy*.

Melodic Ostinati
Resonator Bells may be used with these four ostinati:

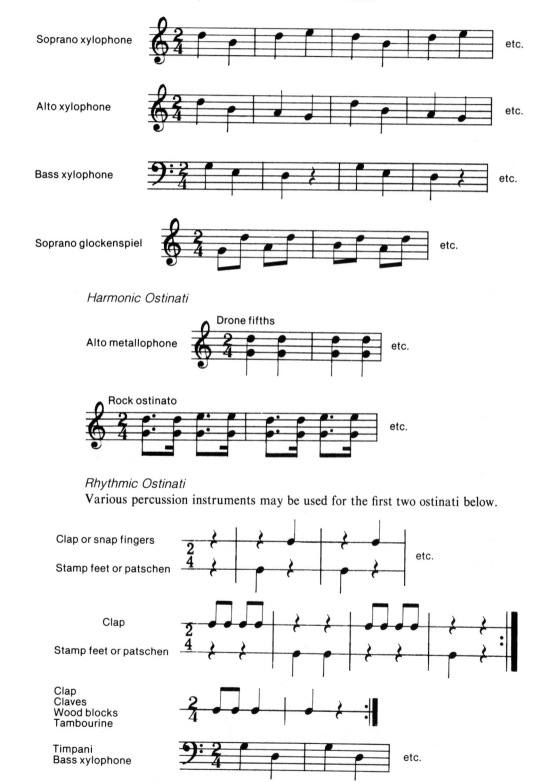

Soprano xylophone

Alto xylophone

Bass xylophone

Soprano glockenspiel

Harmonic Ostinati

Alto metallophone — Drone fifths

Rock ostinato

Rhythmic Ostinati
Various percussion instruments may be used for the first two ostinati below.

Clap or snap fingers

Stamp feet or patschen

Clap

Stamp feet or patschen

Clap
Claves
Wood blocks
Tambourine

Timpani
Bass xylophone

THE PAPAYA TREE

FOLK SONG

R. W. W.
PHILIPPINES

O big pa-pa-ya tree, so straight, so strong and high; a
mes - sage take for me far up in - to the sky. Please
tell the glow - ing sun we thank him for his light, O
tall pa-pa-ya tree don't grow be - yond my sight.

Playing E2

Half-open thumb hole marked ◖ .

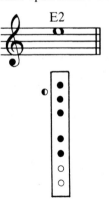

From E2 upward in the high register of the recorder, the thumb covers only half of the thumb hole.

Practice first low E and then E2 as follows:

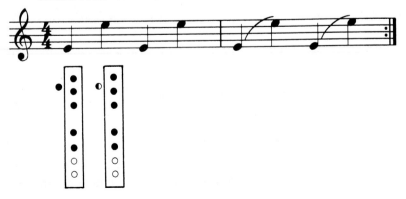

Playing the Recorder

Playing High F

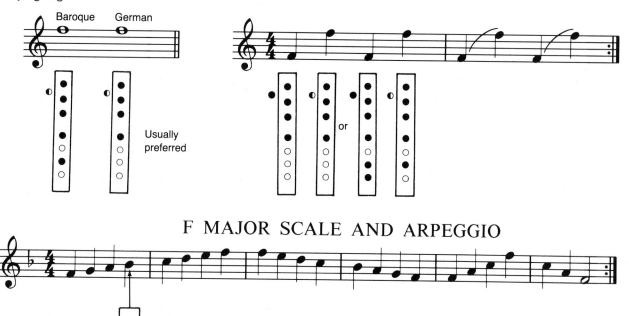

F MAJOR SCALE AND ARPEGGIO

THE DESPERADO

He was a des-per-a-do from the wild and wool-y West, He
came in-to Chi-ca-go just to give the West a rest. He
wore a big som-bre-ro and a gun be-neath his vest, and
ev-'ry-where he went he gave his war whoop!

Also play *There's Music in the Air* (p. 147) and *Sourwood Mountain* (p. 159).
Add ostinati—accompany with Orff instruments or bells.

Playing the Recorder

INTERLUDE
FROM "JESU, JOY OF MAN'S DESIRING"

J. S. BACH

GAVOTTE

GLUCK

Playing the Recorder

MARCHING SONG

R. W. W.
SILESIAN FOLK TUNE

GERMANY

9   Accompanying with Autoharp

The Autoharp, ChromAharp (similar to the Autoharp), and guitar are commonly used today either as substitutes for or supplements to the piano for accompanying school music singing. The Autoharp is one of the most colorful and versatile social musical instruments available. It is used extensively in schools, camps, churches, and in many homes. Almost anyone can learn to play it in a few easy lessons. The classroom teacher who does not have access to a piano can play ready-made harmonies and song accompaniments simply by pressing the appropriate buttons and strumming the strings in rhythm on an Autoharp.

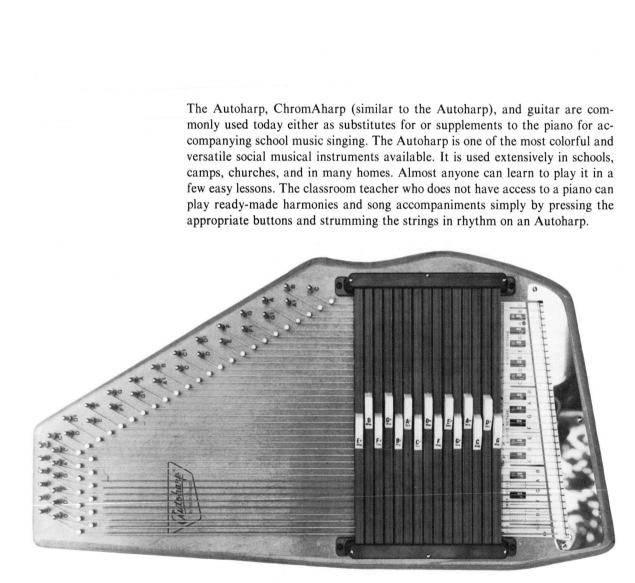

Courtesy of Oscar Schmidt-International, Inc., Garden State Road, Union, New Jersey.

Description of the Autoharp

The two most commonly used Autoharps are the 12-bar and the 15-bar models, both having thirty-six piano-type strings and a piano-related music scale to the right of the chord bars. Under the chord bars are felts designed to stop vibration of all strings except those required for the chord being played. The names of the chord bars are indicated on the instrument. Each string is attached to a tuning pin.

Care of the Instrument

Keep the Autoharp in its box at all times when it is not in use. Store it in a dry place with an even temperature. Handle carefully when moving it; bumping or jarring will impair its tuning.

Registers and Range

The Autoharp has a range of nearly four octaves, which can be divided into three registers—low, medium, and high. The special sound of each register may be used for variation of rhythmic and tonal effects, as demonstrated in the next few pages.

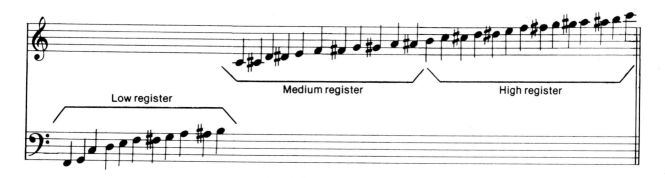

Tuning the Autoharp

The Autoharp is tuned by placing the tuning key on the pin attached to the string to be tuned. The key is turned to the right to tighten the string and raise the pitch, to the left to loosen the string and lower the pitch. Pick the string while slowly turning the key until the desired pitch is reached. The vibration of adjacent strings can be stopped by placing a felt pick between them. The instrument is tuned to a piano, chromatic pitch pipe, or any fixed-pitch instrument. Both the 12- and 15-bar models show piano keys under each of the strings, which facilitates tuning to the piano.

Fortunately, it is not necessary to retune the entire Autoharp very often; usually only a few strings are out of tune at the same time. To locate these, press a chord bar and run your thumb or a pick slowly across the entire instrument. A player with a good ear will be able to locate the strings that are out of tune. After tuning these strings, proceed to the next chord. The usual order for chord tuning is (1) C major, (2) F major, (3) G major, and (4) the remaining chords.

When the entire Autoharp is out of tune, tune each string to a well-tuned piano. Start with the lowest string, the second F below middle C, and proceed upward. If using a chromatic pitch pipe, start tuning at the C in the middle octave of the Autoharp (the bottom note on the C chromatic pitch pipe). Tune upward by half steps for one octave. Then tune all other octaves with this, the middle octave of the Autoharp.

A variation of these tuning procedures, recommended for both speed and accuracy, is as follows:

1. Find the string for middle C. Sound middle C on the piano, and tune all the other C strings on the Autoharp.
2. Tune all the E strings and G strings in the same way, always starting with the middle octave. This completes the C major chord (C-E-G). Check results by pressing the C chord bar and strumming. Adjust individual notes as needed.

3. Tune the notes of the G7 chord—all the B, D, and F strings (the G strings were tuned in the C major chord).
4. Tune the notes of the F major chord. This requires only the tuning of A strings since the F and C strings were tuned in the C and G7 chords.
5. Play each chord slowly to check pitch accuracy.
6. Tune all the remaining notes individually.
7. As a final check, play all of the chords to locate strings that may possibly still be out of tune.

Playing the Autoharp

There are several ways to hold the Autoharp, but usually the instrument is placed on the player's lap or on a desk or table so that the names of the chord bars can be read easily. Many experienced performers prefer to hold it upright, chord bars facing outward, with the wider end of the instrument resting on the lap.

Photographs courtesy of Joanne Harris, Mission Viejo, California.

Using the Chord Bars

There are no fixed rules for fingering the chord bars. In fact, some skillful players create their own fingering by sometimes jumping from one chord bar to another with one finger. However, the following suggestions will help inexperienced players.

1. Usually the index, middle, and ring fingers of the left hand press the chord bars. The chord bars for the 12-bar Autoharp are grouped together for convenient fingering of the three basic chords for each of five keys—C, F, and G major, and A and D minor (see the illustration of the 12-bar Autoharp on the next page). If the index finger is placed on the bar for the key chord (e.g., in the key of C this chord bar is C) and the middle finger is placed on the adjacent chord bar with the number 7, fingering will automatically be correct.

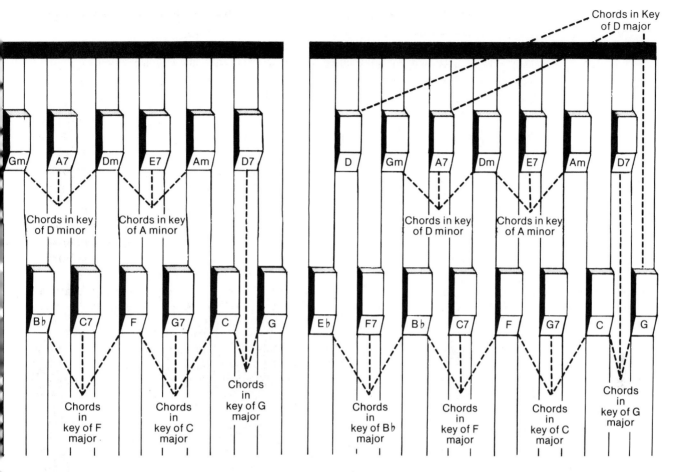

12-Bar Autoharp

15-Bar Autoharp

2. The 15-bar Autoharp provides the player with two more keys, B♭ and D major, with the addition of the E♭, D, and F7 chord bars. The three-chord hand position used on the 12-bar instrument (index finger on the key chord) is the same for all keys except D major (see the illustration of the 15-bar Autoharp above). For this key, place the middle finger on D, the index finger on A7, and the thumb on the G bar.
3. Press the chord bars firmly to avoid a blurred sound.
4. Memorize the location of the chord bars and learn to find the desired chords without looking down, as in the touch system used in typing. This facilitates making quick chord changes while keeping the eyes on the music.

Strumming

1. Strum the Autoharp with the thumb of the right hand. Felt or plastic picks may be used also, depending upon the tonal effect called for in the music itself.
2. Strum on the important beats of the measure and almost always on the first beat. Varied rhythmic patterns will be developed with experience and training.

3. On accented beats strum all strings from bottom to top with a rapid sweeping motion to get the full chord at once. The more strings used, the more resonant the tone. Short strokes in the middle or upper registers can be used for unaccented beats and light tonal effects; for example:

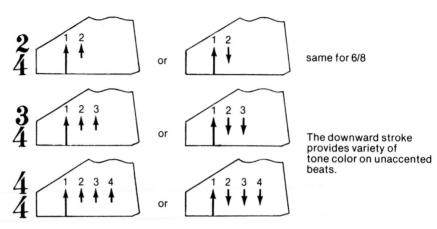

same for 6/8

The downward stroke provides variety of tone color on unaccented beats.

4. Strive for a beautiful musical tone quality by strumming smoothly and without excessive pressure on the strings. Raise the right elbow slightly, and keep the wrist flexible and relaxed.

Playing Introductions to Songs

Song introductions on the Autoharp that establish both the tempo and key may be played as follows:

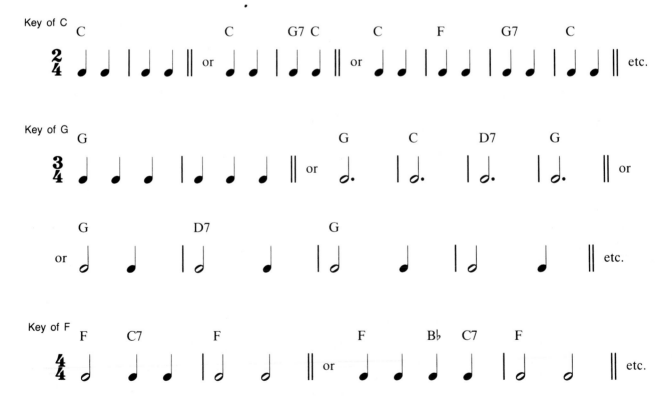

Accompanying Songs

Most of the newer songbooks for children include songs in which letter names for the chords are indicated over the melody line. The chord must be changed on the note over which a new letter appears. The following are some suggestions for effective accompaniments.

1. Try always to coordinate precisely the pressing of the chord bar with the stroke of the thumb or pick for a smooth sound.
2. Play softly enough for good balance when accompanying young children's singing; their voices are typically light.
3. Observe the rhythmic accents, and keep the beat steady.
4. Strive to capture the mood of the music; e.g., a light flowing style for a lullaby and a firm, crisp, accented style for a march.
5. Strum in the lowest octave of the Autoharp on accented beats, using the upper strings for unaccented beats when an "oom-pah" accompaniment fits the music; e.g., 3/4 "oom-pah-pah" or 4/4 "oom-pah-pah-pah."

One-Chord Accompaniments

Hold the C-chord bar down for the entire song, strumming at the marks (/).

MY GOOSE

ROUND

Why should-n't my goose sell as well as thy goose,

When I paid for my goose twice as much as you?

CLOCKS AND WATCHES

ROUND   GERMANY

Big clocks tick so slow-ly, tick, tock, tick, tock, Lit-tle clocks tick

fast-er, tick tock, tick tock, tick tock, tick tock, Watch-es on your

wrists tick fast-er, tic-ka, toc-ka, tic-ka, toc-ka, tic-ka, toc-ka, tick.

This song can be strummed one full stroke per measure or one long and two short strokes. Play the tune also in the key of F major, using F and C7 chords.

MY BOAT

HAWAIIAN FOLK SONG

U.S.
COLLECTED AND ADAPTED BY
ERMINE AND ELSA CROSS

G   D7   G   etc.

My boat is sail - ing, sail - ing, — sail - ing, My boat is

1.
D7   G   2.   G

sail - ing o - ver the wa - ter. o - ver the sea. —

Refrain
D7   G

Will you go with me? Will you go with me? Will you go

D7   G   D7

with me o - ver the wa - ter? Yes, I'll go with you, Yes, I'll go

G   D7   G

with you, Yes, I'll go with you o - ver the sea. —

Also play and sing *Hokey Pokey* (p. 14) using G and D7 chords.
Try this tune in the key of F major, using F and C7 chords.

Play this song with one full stroke and two short strokes on the upper strings.
Use a light, gliding stroke for harp effect.

LULLABY

BRAHMS

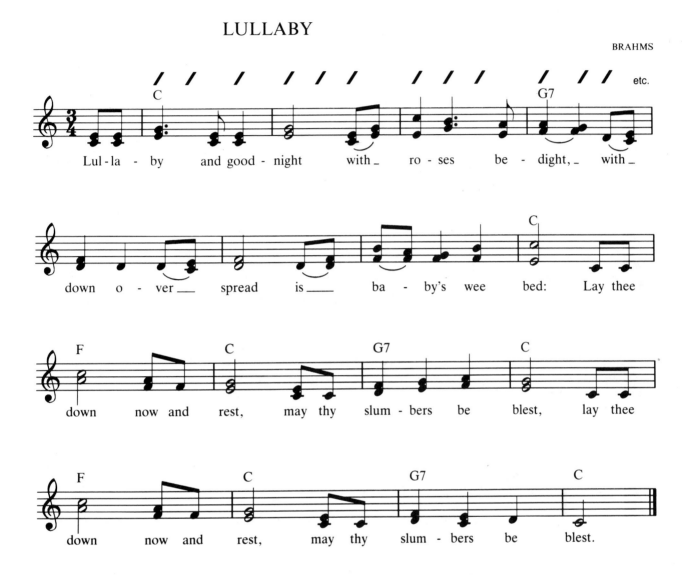

Lul - la - by and good - night with _ ro - ses be - dight, _ with _

down o - ver _ spread is _ ba - by's wee bed: Lay thee

down now and rest, may thy slum - bers be blest, lay thee

down now and rest, may thy slum - bers be blest.

Also play and sing *Harmonizing* (p. 261).

Accompanying with Autoharp

OH SUSANNA

STEPHEN C. FOSTER

Also play and sing *Auld Lang Syne* (p. 263).

Playing in Minor Keys

Songs in minor keys are played with the chord hand moved up to the second row of chord bars. The following spiritual can be played with two firm strokes per measure, changing to four in the next-to-last bar. Play the A7 chord at the end of the verse with a long, slow stroke to create a broken chord.

JOSHUA FIT THE BATTLE OF JERICHO

SPIRITUAL

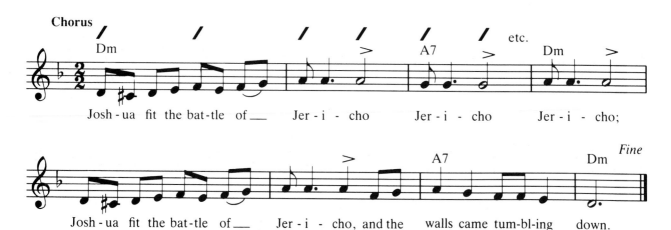

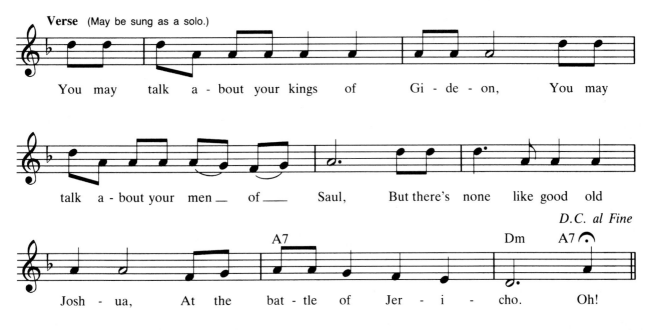

Also play and sing *Shalom Chaverim* (p. 249).

Strum *Minka* with four easy strokes per measure or two strong strokes if sung briskly.

MINKA

LOUISE GARNETT

RUSSIA

When using the alternate harmony in measure 7 below, press the C7 chord bar
with the index finger. Practice it both ways. Which sounds better?

OVER THE RIVER AND THROUGH THE WOOD

THANKSGIVING SONG

LYDIA MARIE CHILDS

Also play and sing *Aura Lee* (p. 75).

BEAUTIFUL BROWN EYES

U.S.

Also play and sing *Buffalo Gals* (p. 188), *Old Paint* (p. 215), *Good News* (p. 215),
Lavender's Blue (p. 187), and *Frankie and Johnny* (p. 216).

Accompanying with Autoharp

Transposing to Different Keys

It is helpful for the classroom teacher to be able to transpose accompaniments for songs to lower and sometimes higher keys to fit the vocal abilities of singers. The following chart[1] will serve as a guide.

Transposition for Autoharp

Key	I	IV	V7
C	Ceg	Fac	Gbdf
F	Fac	B♭df	Cegb♭
G	Gbd	Ceg	Df♯ac
Am	Ace	Dfa	Eg♯bd
Dm	Dfa	Gb♭d	Ac♯eg

To transpose songs for the Autoharp, refer to the chart above in making these changes:

Key of	to	Beginning note will be
D	F	1½ steps higher
D	C	1 whole step lower
E	F	½ step higher
E	C	2 whole steps lower
A	G	1 whole step lower
Em	Dm	1 whole step lower
Em	Gm	1½ steps higher

For example: Key of D (chords D G A7) change to key of C (chords of C F G7), or to key of F (chords F B♭ C7).

The Omnichord

The Omnichord

An exciting electronic accompaniment instrument, the *Omnichord,* has been introduced by Suzuki, Electronics Division of San Diego, California, as a teaching aid for classroom use. Weighing only four pounds and completely portable, it can be played to include twenty-seven major, minor, or seventh chords at the touch of a button. The fingers may also be run over its electronic four-octave "Sonic Strings" touchplate to actually strum (like an Autoharp) a selected chord—even though it has no strings. Bass notes can be added and various patterns of a full electronic rhythm section can be turned on. The *Omnichord* can be used effectively in combination with bells, Orff instruments and other classroom instruments.

1. From *Guitar in the Classroom* by Maurine Timmerman and Celeste Griffith. 2d ed. Wm. C. Brown Company Publishers, 1976. Used by permission. (Good reference for Autoharp as well as guitar.)

Photo Courtesy of Suzuki Corporation P.O. Box 261030, San Diego, California 92126

Suggested Assignments

1. Play Autoharp accompaniments to songs in state and local music series that indicate the letter names for the chords; then sing and play.
2. Create accompaniments for songs in texts that do not indicate the chords to be played.
3. Practice finding and sounding the keynote, starting note, and key chord of various children's songs.
4. Create two- and four-measure introductions to songs in the keys of C, F, G, D, and B♭ major and A and D minor. For some of these introductions use all three chords of the key (see p. 200).
5. Create your own rhythmic patterns for accompaniments in 2/4, 3/4, 4/4, and 6/8 time.
6. Combine bells, wind melody instruments, and Autoharp to form a classroom orchestra.
7. Transpose children's songs up or down a step. Refer to the transposition chart.

10 Accompanying with Guitar

The guitar, a descendant of the ancient lute family, rapidly has become one of the most popular social instruments of this generation. Even though it is more difficult to play than the Autoharp or the ukulele, it now holds a prominent place as an instrument for accompanying singing in the schools. The teacher who can play the guitar has a distinct advantage in motivating children's and teenagers' singing activities. Moreover, since both melody and harmony can be played on the guitar, this versatile instrument is now recognized as a first-rate solo instrument for the concert stage. Recordings by Andres Segovia, Julian Bream, John Williams, Oscar Ghiglia, Christopher Parkening, Narciso Yepes, and many others are a colorful asset in motivation for listening lessons in the classroom.

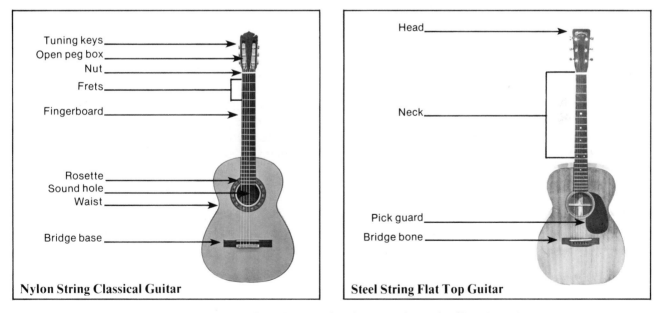

Tuning keys
Open peg box
Nut
Frets
Fingerboard
Rosette
Sound hole
Waist
Bridge base

Nylon String Classical Guitar

Head
Neck
Pick guard
Bridge bone

Steel String Flat Top Guitar

From Jerry Snyder's *Beginning the Guitar*. Charles Hansen Publishing Co., 1974. Used by permission.

Description of the Guitar

There are numerous models and makes of guitars manufactured today for various uses and types of playing. The two most common types of guitars, especially for classroom use, are the nylon string classical guitar and the steel string flat top guitar. Both of these may be either *acoustic* (not amplified) or *electric* (amplified). The basic difference in the two types is the tone quality; the nylon string classical guitar has a dark, mellow quality, and the steel string flat top has a bright, brassy sound. The classical guitar is recommended for beginners because the nylon strings are less taut and are therefore easier on the fingers.

Care of the Instrument

1. Keep the guitar covered at all times when it is not in use.
2. Store in a dry place with an even temperature.
3. Change the strings about every three months or whenever there are signs of wear or corrosion. If one string breaks or shows wear, all of the strings probably need changing.
4. Do not slacken strings after playing. Loose strings go out of tune faster than those kept up to pitch.
5. Do not use steel strings on guitars made for nylon strings or nylon strings on guitars made for steel strings.

Tuning the Guitar

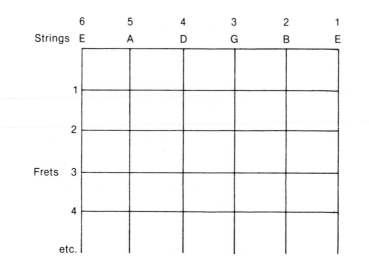

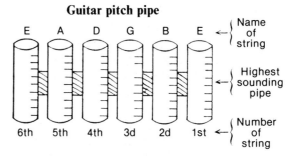

Guitar pitch pipe

Tuning with a Pitch Pipe

A guitar pitch pipe can be purchased at most music stores. Each of the individual pipes is tuned to the correct pitch for each of the six open strings of the guitar. The strings must be tuned one octave below the corresponding notes of the pitch pipe. (See exact notes on the piano diagram.)

1. Start by tuning the high E string, which is the first and thinnest string of the guitar. Blow gently into the corresponding high E of the pitch pipe. Adjust the tuning peg for this string while plucking it until it matches the pitch.
2. Tune each of the remaining strings to the other five pipes in succession.
3. Retune each string, starting with the first, as necessary.

Tuning with the Piano

The same procedure can be applied in tuning the guitar with the piano. The first string, high E, is to the right of middle C on the piano. Proceed downward, to the left on the keyboard, tuning B, G, D, A, and low E. Some guitarists prefer the reverse order, tuning low E, the sixth string, first.

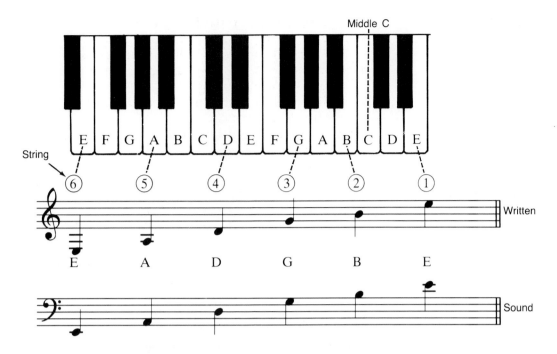

Tuning with the Guitar Itself

The guitar can be tuned to its own strings. Use any fixed-pitch instrument or estimate the pitch of the first string, high E, or the sixth string, low E, and proceed.

As a method of relative tuning, each string is used as an aid for tuning the string that lies adjacent to it.

Beginning with the first string (high E):
Press 5th fret of 2d string to match pitch of 1st string (E).
Press 4th fret of 3d string to match pitch of 2d string (B).
Press 5th fret of 4th string to match pitch of 3d string (G).
Press 5th fret of 5th string to match pitch of 4th string (D).
Press 5th fret of 6th string to match pitch of 5th string (A).

Beginning with the sixth string (low E):
Press 5th fret of 6th string to match pitch of 5th string (A).
Press 5th fret of 5th string to match pitch of 4th string (D).
Press 5th fret of 4th string to match pitch of 3d string (G).
Press 4th fret of 3d string to match pitch of 2d string (B).
Press 5th fret of 2d string to match pitch of 1st string (E).

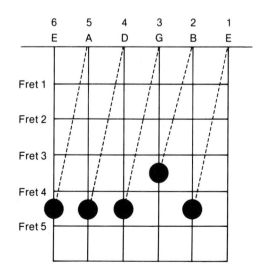

Courtesy of Jerry Rouse, Chairman, Music Department, El Toro High School, Mission Viejo, California.

Playing the Guitar

Holding the Guitar

The guitar should be held in a position that is comfortable for the individual player. The following suggestions may help.

1. Sit erect in an armless chair, crossing the right leg over the left.
2. Place the guitar on the lap with the lower curved side resting on the right thigh and the upper part of the instrument against the chest. Tilt the guitar so that all six strings can be seen clearly.
3. Raise the head slightly toward the left shoulder, as shown in the photograph above.
4. Rest the right arm on the body of the guitar with sufficient pressure to balance the instrument.

Using the Left Hand and Fingers

The strings of the guitar are depressed (fretted) with the fingers of the left hand (1—index, 2—middle, 3—ring, 4—little finger). The tips of the fingers are used, so the fingernails must be short. A few hints for successful fretting follow:

1. Place the thumb of the left hand well in back of the neck of the guitar. Press gently against the back of the neck with the ball of the thumb.
2. Keep the left wrist away from the fingerboard to allow better finger position for fretting the chords.
3. Curve the hand slightly to avoid touching neighboring strings or muting with the hand.
4. Press the fingers firmly and depress the string just back of the fret, without touching the fret itself.

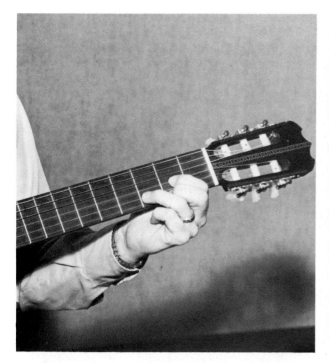

Left-hand Finger Position

Right-hand Position

Strumming the Guitar

The guitar is strummed with the right hand, either *finger-style* or *pick-style*. Finger-style strumming is recommended for beginners. This is done with the thumb and first three fingers. Fingernails must be cut short.

Rest the right forearm on the edge of the guitar directly above the base of the bridge. The hand should hang downward above the strings with the thumb rigid and extended toward the middle of the sound hole. Curve the fingers slightly and bunch them together over the third, second, and first strings and above the rosette, as shown.

Try strumming down across the open strings (low to high) with the back of the index and middle fingernails of the right hand. The motion is from wrist and fingers.

Reading Strum Notation

Finger-style strums are difficult to read in standard musical notation. To simplify this, symbols and tablature are used; for example, in guitar tablature the six lines represent the six open strings of the guitar. The strings to be brushed (brush strum) may be written either as quarter notes or as a slash (/). These receive one count or beat. The vertical wavy line (⌇) means to strum the strings.

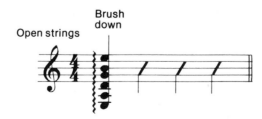

Brush down

Open strings

Reading Chord Frames

The positions for the fingers of the left hand are as follows:

1 = index finger
2 = middle finger
3 = ring finger
4 = little finger
X = do not play
0 = open string

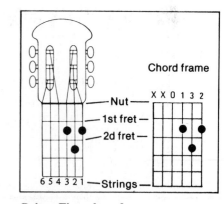

**Guitar Fingerboard
(D Major Chord)**

Playing in the Key of D Major

First learn to play the D chord and the A7 chord, the two most commonly used chords in D major, by practicing the following exercises using the brush strum.

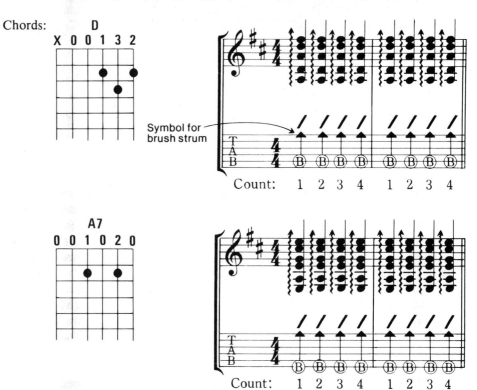

GAILY THE TROUBADOUR

THOMAS H. BAYLY

THOMAS H. BAYLY

Gai – ly the trou –ba –dour touched his gui – tar,

When he was has –ten – ing home from a – far.

OLD PAINT

COWBOY SONG

U.S.

Good – by, Old Paint, I'm a – leav – in' Chey – enne, Good –

by, Old Paint, I'm a – leav – in' Chey – enne; I'm a –

leav – in' Chey – enne, I'm— bound for Mon – tan'; Good –

by, Old Paint, I'm a – leav – in' Chey – enne.

GOOD NEWS

SPIRITUAL

Good news, char-i-ot's com-in', good news, char-i-ot's com-in', good

news, char-i-ot's com-in' and I don't want it to leave-a-me be –hind.

Also play and sing *Buffalo Gals* (p. 188).

The G Major Chord

The basic fingering for the G major chord is shown below. The fingering at the left is difficult for the beginner; simplified alternate G chords are also shown.

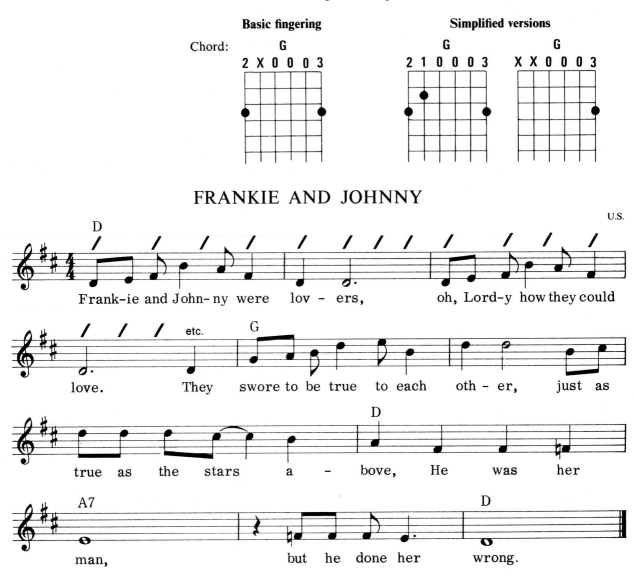

FRANKIE AND JOHNNY

U.S.

Frank-ie and John-ny were lov - ers, oh, Lord-y how they could love. They swore to be true to each oth - er, just as true as the stars a - bove, He was her man, but he done her wrong.

Also play and sing *Beautiful Brown Eyes* (p. 206).

Playing in the Key of G Major

The D7 chord, the next most commonly used chord in G major, is played as follows:

Chord: **D7**

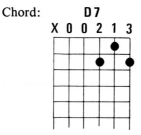

Brush strum the following preparatory exercises several times.

HUSH, LITTLE BABY

U.S.

Hush, lit – tle ba – by, don't say a word,

Ma – ma's gon – na buy you a mock – ing bird. And

if that mock – ing bird won't sing,

Dad – dy's gon – na buy you a dia – mond ring.

TOM DOOLEY

Hang down your head Tom Doo - ley, Hang down your head and cry,

Hang down your head Tom Doo - ley, Poor boy, you're bound to die.

Also play and sing *Recorder Band* (p. 173), and *My Boat* (p. 202).

The C Major Chord   Chords:

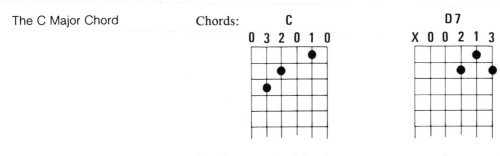

Brush strum the following preparatory exercises several times. Keep the index finger of the left hand down when going from the C to the D7 chord, and vice versa.

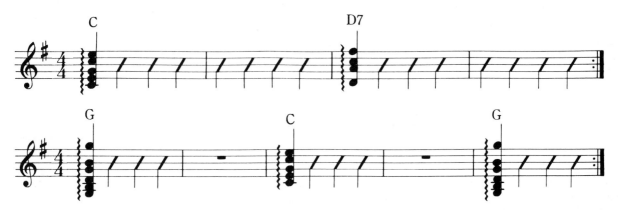

Even though the fourth finger is weak, the following alternate fingering for the G chord is both easier and faster when going to and from the C chord.

Chord:

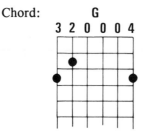

WORRIED MAN BLUES

U.S.

It takes a wor-ried man to sing a wor-ried song, It

takes a wor-ried man to sing a wor-ried song, It

takes a wor-ried man to sing a wor-ried song, I'm wor-ried

(Count 1 — 2 — 3 — 4)

now, _____ but I won't be wor-ried long.

PAPER OF PINS

BRITISH ISLES

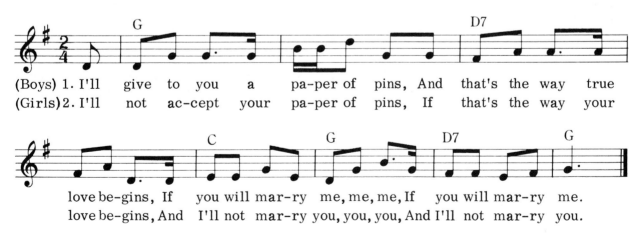

(Boys) 1. I'll give to you a pa-per of pins, And that's the way true
(Girls) 2. I'll not ac-cept your pa-per of pins, If that's the way your

love be-gins, If you will mar-ry me, me, me, If you will mar-ry me.
love be-gins, And I'll not mar-ry you, you, you, And I'll not mar-ry you.

FOGGY, FOGGY DEW

R. W. W.

ENGLAND

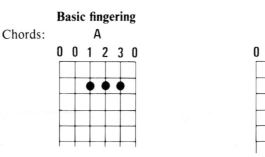

When I was a bache-lor, I lived all a-lone, ___ I

worked at the weav-er's trade; _____ and the on-ly, on-ly thing I

ev-er did wrong was to woo a fair young maid. ___ I

wooed her in the sum-mer time and in the win-ter

too; and the on-ly, on-ly thing I

ev-er did wrong was to shield her from the fog-gy, fog-gy dew.

Also play and sing *Flow Gently Sweet Afton* (p. 25), *Bingo* (p. 14), *Jingle Bells* (p. 145), *The Papaya Tree* (p. 192).

The A Major Chord

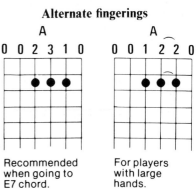

Basic fingering

A
0 0 1 2 3 0

Alternate fingerings

A
0 0 2 3 1 0

A
0 0 1 2 2 0

Recommended when going to E7 chord.

For players with large hands.

The E7 Chord

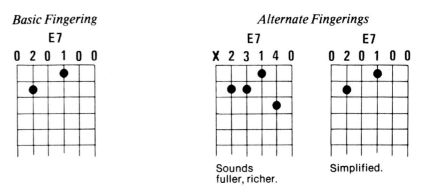

Basic Fingering

E7
0 2 0 1 0 0

Alternate Fingerings

E7
X 2 3 1 4 0

Sounds
fuller, richer.

E7
0 2 0 1 0 0

Simplified.

Brush strum the following preparatory exercises several times.

SLEEP, BABY, SLEEP

FOLK SONG

GERMANY

Sleep, ba - by, sleep, Thy fa - ther guards the sheep. Thy

moth - er shakes the dream - land tree, And down fall pleas - ant

dreams for thee. Sleep, ba - by, sleep. Sleep, ba - by, sleep.

Singers with low-pitched voices should sing *Sleep, Baby, Sleep* down one octave.

WHEN THE SAINTS GO MARCHING IN

NEW ORLEANS PROCESSIONAL

U.S.

Oh, when the saints ———— go march-ing in ———— oh, when the saints go march-ing in, ———— how I want to be in that num-ber, ———— when the saints go march-ing in. ————

OLD SMOKY

U.S.

On top of old Smo - ky, ———————— all cov - ered with snow ———————— I lost my true lov - er ———————— by court - ing too slow.

Accompanying with Guitar

Chords:

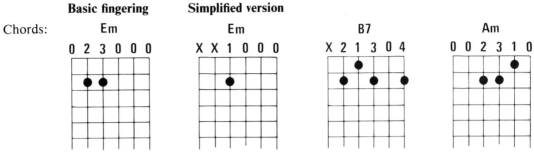

Brush strum the following preparatory exercises several times. In moving from the Em chord to the B7 chord, and vice versa, do not lift the second finger of the left hand. Let it serve as a pivotal guide between these two chords.

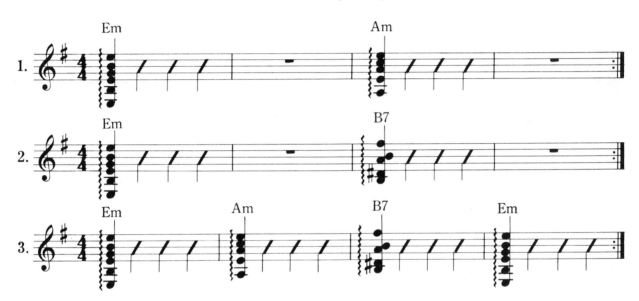

HAIDA

ISRAEL

Hai - da - da - da, hai - da — hai - da, Hai - da hai - da - da,

Hai - da, hai - da - da hai - da, Hai - da hai - da - da.

ZUM GALI GALI

Zum ga - li, ga - li, ga - li, Zum ga - li, ga - li.

He - cha - lutz le 'man a - vo - dah; ___

___ A - vo - dah le 'man he - cha - lutz.

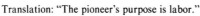

Translation: "The pioneer's purpose is labor."

Playing Accompaniments, Using Bass Notes

To add interest to the accompaniment pattern, guitarists often pick the bass note (root of the chord) with the thumb on accented beats, strumming the remaining notes of the chord with the index and middle fingers on the unaccented beats (low to high). This is called the *thumb brush strum.*

Play the following preparatory exercises. Keep the thumb rigid.

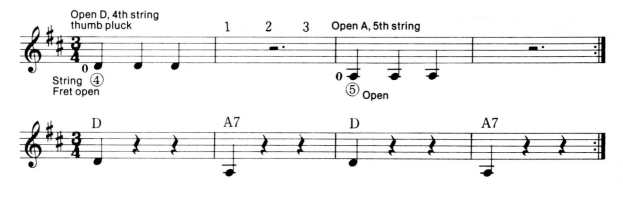

Thumb Brush in 3/4 Time

Practice the following thumb-brush accompaniment. Then apply it as you play and sing *Down in the Valley.*

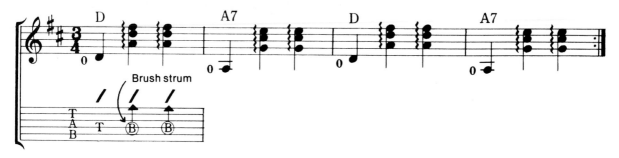

DOWN IN THE VALLEY

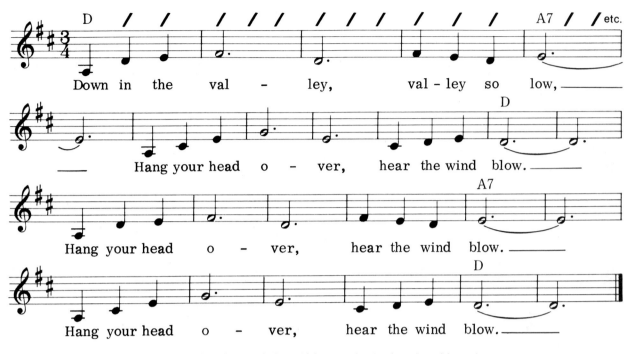

Down in the val - ley, val - ley so low,

Hang your head o - ver, hear the wind blow.

Hang your head o - ver, hear the wind blow.

Hang your head o - ver, hear the wind blow.

Also play and sing *Old Paint* (p. 215), using this style.

Thumb Brush in 4/4 Time

Example 1.

Example 2. (T = Thumb, B = Brush)

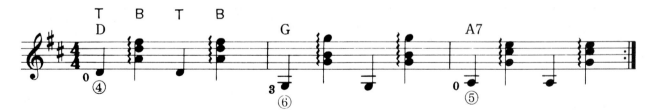

Play and sing *Red River Valley*, using both thumb-strum examples.

RED RIVER VALLEY

Also play and sing *Gaily the Troubadour* (p. 215), *Good News* (p. 215), *Frankie and Johnny* (p. 216), *Lavender's Blue* (p. 187), and *Buffalo Gals* (p. 188), using thumb-strum techniques.

Using the Capo

The *capo* is a clamp that can be placed on the guitar neck to shorten the length of the strings, thereby raising the pitch a half step for each fret ascending the fingerboard. This device makes transposition (changing the key) to higher keys quick and easy when a song is written too low for the singers.

Red River Valley, for example, may be pitched too low for young children and some adult sopranos. Clamping the capo on the first fret makes it possible to use the easy fingerings for the written key of D major while actually playing in the key of Eb, a relatively difficult key to play on the guitar. With the capo on the second fret, the sounding key moves up to E; with the capo on the third fret, the sounding key moves up to F; and so on. Using the capo can be very helpful in classroom music.

Picture from *Guitar in the Classroom*, Second Edition, by Maurine Timmerman and Celeste Griffith. Wm. C. Brown Company Publishers, 1976. Used by permission.

Transpose the following songs to the keys of Eb, E, and F, using the capo: *Down in the Valley* (p. 225) and *Red River Valley* (p. 226). Also transpose *When the Saints Go Marching In* (p. 222) and *Old Smoky* (p. 222) to the keys of Bb, B, and C.

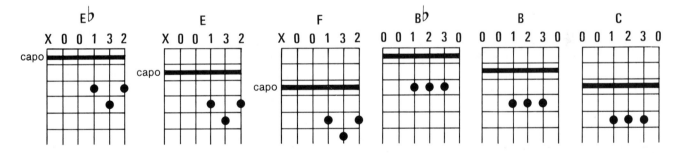

It is beyond the aim and scope of this textbook of introductory music skills to present a complete guitar methods course.

11

Creating Music

Various creative activities have been suggested in relation to the main topics of the preceding chapters. In this chapter systematic approaches to creating music are explored. Creating music, one of the most gratifying personal experiences, requires neither exceptional talent nor extensive training. On the contrary, uninhibited children express themselves spontaneously with rhythms and pitches. The value of creativity is widely recognized by music educators. The following exercises are designed to stimulate the creative imagination and to show mature students how to utilize previously acquired skills in notating original musical ideas—their own and those of their future pupils.

The Word Approach

Since expressing ideas with words is more common than expressing ideas with music, adding words to existing melodies is a logical first step. The melody and suggested words for two verses of an old chantey are given. Retaining the framework of the repeated phrases, add several verses of your own that develop the story. Notes may be divided and combined within the 3/4 metric pattern to accommodate more or fewer syllables.

BLOW THE MAN DOWN

CHANTEY

BRITISH ISLES

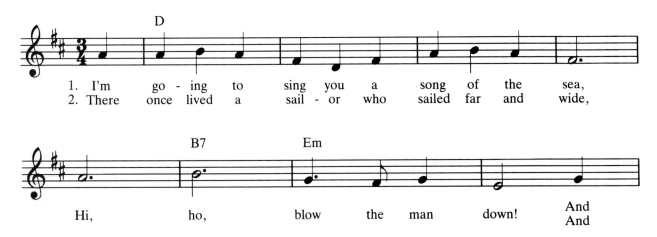

1. I'm go - ing to sing you a song of the sea,
2. There once lived a sail - or who sailed far and wide,

Hi, ho, blow the man down! And / And

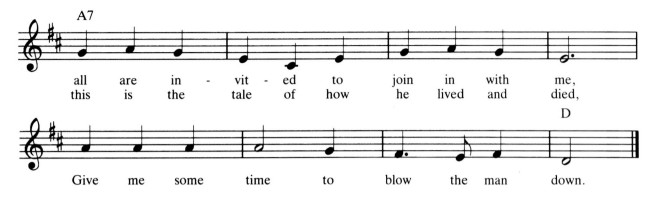

all are in-vit-ed to join in with me,
this is the tale of how he lived and died,

D

Give me some time to blow the man down.

Write original verses for other familiar songs. Then, learn the following melody and create words for it, choosing your own title and subject.

SCHUBERT (adapted)

Write words for additional melodies, perhaps adapting them from instrumental pieces. Try to capture the mood of the music in the words.

The Rhythmic Approach

In adding words to melodies, no doubt you were careful to have accented words and syllables coincide with accents in the music. This is one of the principles observed in making effective musical settings for poems. The poetic meter and the mood of a poem influence the choice of time signature for its musical setting. The relationship between poetic rhythm and musical rhythm is such that a poem usually suggests a musical rhythm, but not necessarily the same rhythm to everybody.

Read the following nursery rhyme aloud as a rhythmic chant, and see whether you can discover its rhythm. Dividing the words into syllables and adding the poetic scansion signs will help. The line before each accented syllable shows where bar lines are likely to occur in the music.

— ∪ ∪ | — ∪ | — ∪ | —
Lit-tle Bo-Peep has lost her sheep,

∪ | — ∪ | — ∪ | — | — |
And can't tell where to find them;

— ∪ ∪ | — ∪ | — ∪ ∪ | — |
Leave them a-lone, and they will come home,

— ∪ ∪ | — ∪ | — | — ||
Wag-ging their tails be-hind them.

Here are three possible rhythmic settings of *Little Bo-Peep*. The one in 3/4 time most closely approximates the natural rhythm of the words. The accents in the other two versions coincide, but the relative durations do not. The slurred half notes in the 2/2 version indicate two notes of different pitch used with a single syllable to preserve the musical flow.

LITTLE BO-PEEP

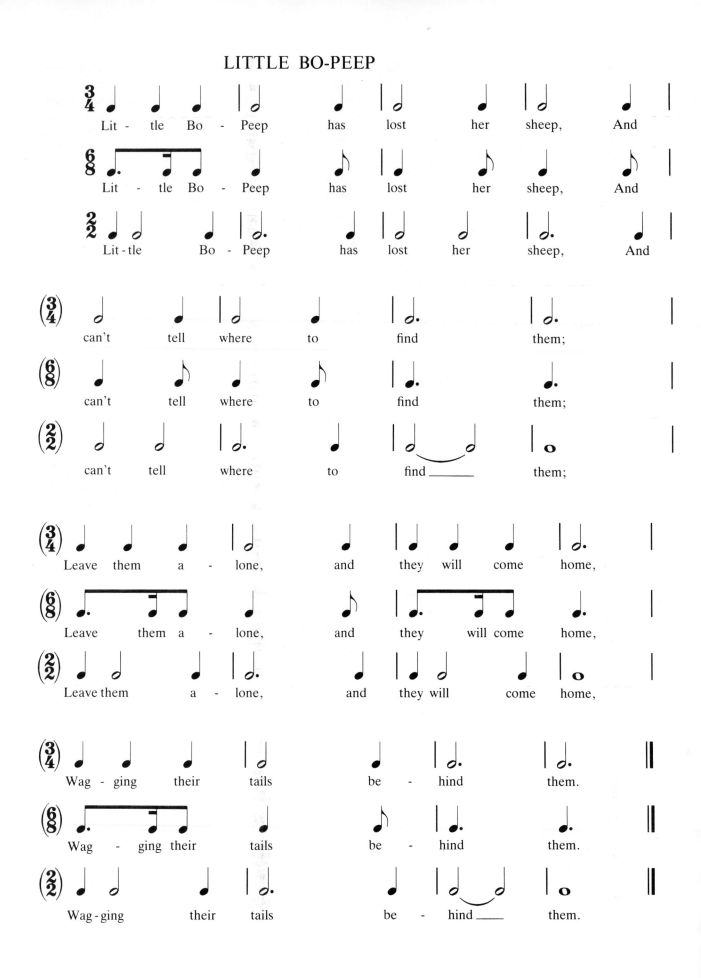

Creating Music

Establish a suitable background beat, and read each of the three versions rhythmically. Which do you prefer? Why?

Using the procedures described in arriving at the rhythms for *Little Bo-Peep*, provide appropriate rhythms for the following nursery rhymes and poems. For each one write the time signature at the beginning and draw in bar lines as required.

LITTLE TOMMY TUCKER

Lit - tle Tom - my Tuck - er sings for his sup - per;

What shall he eat, white bread and but - ter?

How shall he cut it, with - out e'er a knife?

How shall he be mar - ried, with - out e'er a wife?

WEE WILLIE WINKIE

Wee Wil - lie Win - kie, runs through the town,

Up - stairs and down - stairs, in his night - gown;

Rap - ping at the win - dow, cry - ing at the lock,

"Are the child - ren in their beds, for now it's eight o'clock?"

LITTLE THINGS

Lit - tle drops of wa - ter, lit - tle grains of sand,

Make the might - y o - cean and the pleas - ant land.

Thus the lit - tle min - utes, hum - ble though they be,

Make the might - y ag - es of e - ter - ni - ty.

—Julia A. Fletcher

THE SWING

How do you like to go up in a swing, up in the air so blue?

Oh, I do think it the pleas - ant - est thing ev - er a child can do!

Up in the air and ov - er the wall, till I can see so wide,

Riv - ers and trees and cat - tle and all, ov - er the coun - try - side,

Till I look down on the garden green, down on the roof so brown,

Up in the air I go fly - ing a - gain, up in the air and down!

—Robert Louis Stevenson

Now, write an original poem and notate a suitable rhythm for it, complete with time signature, note values, and bar lines.

The words were the determining factor in the rhythmic patterns and phrase divisions of the preceding exercises. Rhythms and phrases can be conceived independently, however, as they are in instrumental music. The following rhythm is an incomplete, abstract musical idea. After establishing the beat, clap the given rhythm and then add an appropriate conclusion.

It is very likely that most of the class will conclude with a rhythm that exactly balances the given pattern, quite possibly something like this:

The two measures of the initial rhythm are balanced by two additional measures. This produces a four-measure phrase that illustrates several aspects of musical organization. Between its two halves there is a proper balance between unifying and contrasting elements. The repeated rhythmic pattern in the first two measures provides a unifying element, and the contrasting rhythms of the third and fourth measures provide variety. The long note on the accented beat of the fourth measure creates a rhythmic cadential effect.

Using the sample phrase as a model, complete the following phrases.

Write the rhythm for a phrase in each of the meters indicated, observing the same principles as in the foregoing exercise.

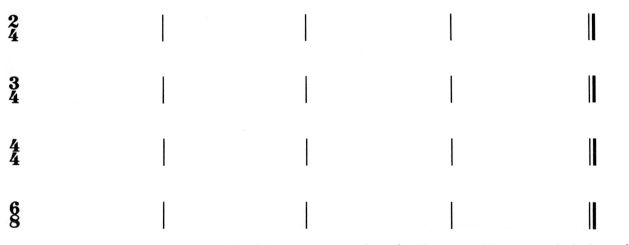

The following rhythms from familiar songs illustrate typical plans of rhythmic organization in two-phrase sentences. Observe the repetitions of a limited number of patterns, the balance between unifying and contrasting elements, and the construction of the cadences as you perform the rhythms in one or more of the ways suggested for the rhythm exercises in chapter 3.

The Girl I Left Behind Me (Irish)

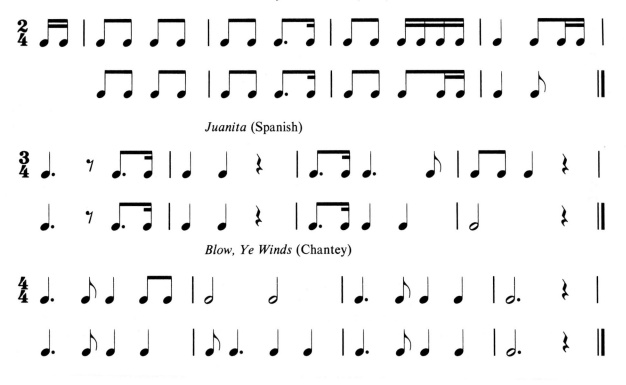

Juanita (Spanish)

Blow, Ye Winds (Chantey)

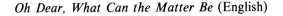

Write original rhythms for two-phrase sentences in the manner of the models.

2/4

3/4

4/4

6/8

Select one of the rhythms written for the previous exercise and write words for it. Be sure the accents in the poetry coincide with the accents in the music and that the ends of the phrases in the poetry coincide with the cadences in the music. The musical sentence may be repeated as necessary to accommodate the stanzas of the poem.

The Harmonic Approach

A harmonic background can serve as the point of departure for musical invention.[1] Limiting the choice of harmony to I, IV, and V(7) and changes to one per measure simplifies the problems, yet provides ample latitude for creativity.

Musical sentences begin and end with a I chord. The two phrases may have the same harmonic pattern. Following this plan, a suitable sequence using only two chords, I and V7, could be as follows:

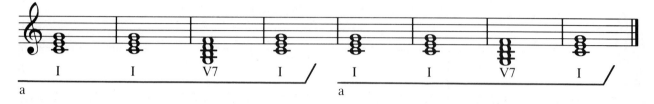

Any chord tone can be used in the melody and may be repeated freely. Rhythmic patterns are unrestricted, but the general principles of rhythmic organization outlined in the preceding section should be observed. Many attractive melodies complying with these guidelines can be conceived for each suitable harmonic background. Here is one possibility.

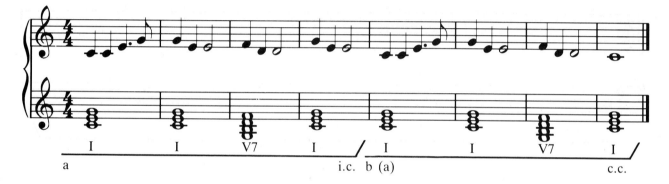

The melody and the chords cannot be played together on the piano when they use the same notes, and the progressions as written are not smooth. This can be remedied by writing the chords in the bass clef and connecting them in the manner suggested in chapters 5 and 6. The seventh of the V7 chord is in the melody, so it is not included in the left-hand part.

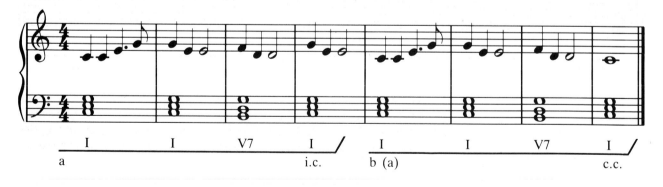

1. This approach was suggested by the late Dr. Charles Neiswender, California State University, Long Beach.

Melody notes that are not chord members are *nonchord tones,* or *nonharmonic tones.* The two most common types of nonchord tones are *neighboring tones* and *passing tones.* Neighboring tones are approached and left by step from the same chord tone. Passing tones occur in a scale line between different chord tones. Nonchord tones in the next example are indicated by a diagonal line through the note head.

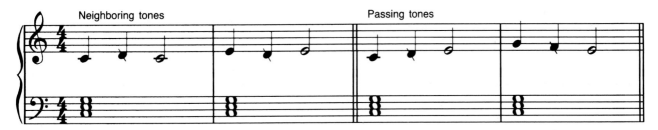

The next example, which has the same harmonic background and general contour as the initial melody in this section, shows how neighboring and passing tones can be used to embellish and animate a basic melody line.

Sentences ordinarily begin with a I chord and end with a I chord with *do* in the melody. The V(7) chord usually precedes the final I chord and often serves as the cadence chord of the first phrase. Interest can be increased by adding the IV chord to the harmonic vocabulary. The IV chord usually occurs within phrases, but rarely as the first or last chord of a phrase. The following progressions are typical. Add original melodies to them, using nonchord tones sparingly. Mark the phrases and cadences.

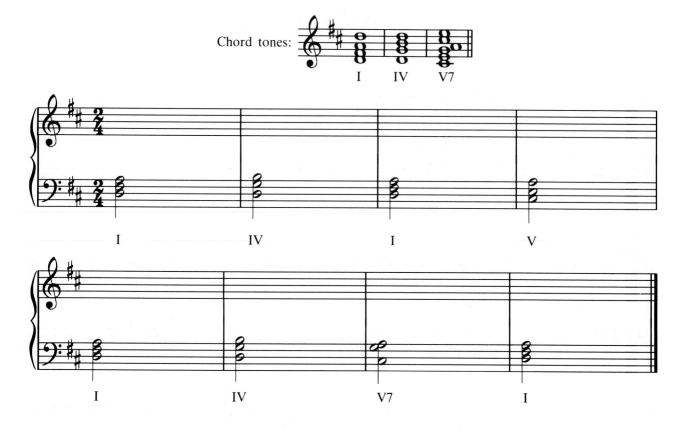

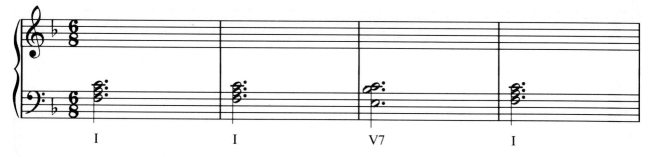

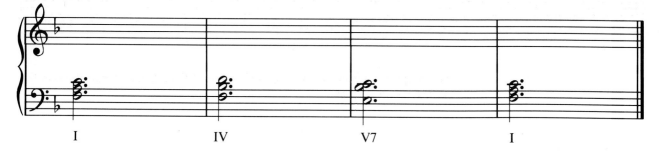

Determine the notes in the primary chords of G major, and add a melody to the given harmonic background. Mark the phrases and cadences.

Select a key and a time signature. Write the chords indicated by the symbols and an original melody. Mark the phrases and cadences.

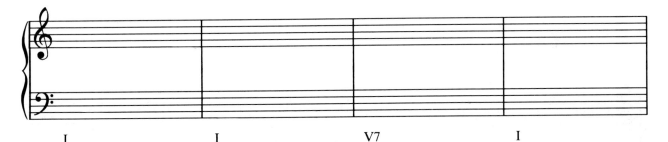

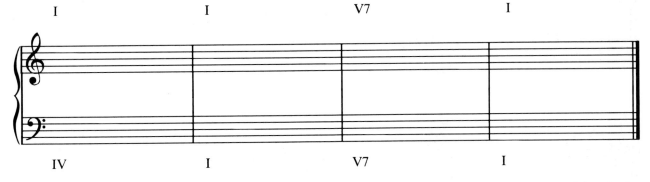

Select appropriate harmonic progressions, and write original compositions in the manner of the models.

More interesting piano accompaniments can be devised when they are independent of the vocal line. The right hand is then free to play multiple chord tones in a rhythmic pattern while the left hand provides the bass, frequently the note with the same letter name as the chord, on the primary accents. The following setting of *Bobby Shafto* illustrates one such accompaniment pattern and some of the less usual nonchord tones.

BOBBY SHAFTO

FOLK SONG

ENGLAND

Completing a Composition

Add original words to any of the melodies you have written, and you will have composed a song. Finding a melody for words and rhythms is only slightly more difficult. *Little Bo-Peep,* for which appropriate rhythms have been found (p. 230), will serve as a model. Memorize the words and rhythm and chant them aloud several times, exaggerating the natural inflections of the voice. This exaggeration will suggest a melody. As soon as you can remember the tune, substitute syllables

Creating Music

for the words. Select a suitable key for a good vocal range, and transcribe the syllables into notes on the staff with the previously determined rhythm. Perhaps your melody will resemble this one:

LITTLE BO-PEEP

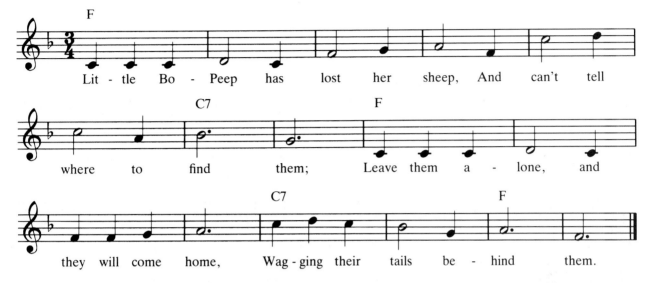

Lit - tle Bo - Peep has lost her sheep, And can't tell where to find them; Leave them a - lone, and they will come home, Wag - ging their tails be - hind them.

To compose an instrumental melody, start by humming the tune or by playing it on the piano, Melody Bells, or recorder. Syllables are useful for finding the notes of hummed melodies. The notes of melodies improvised on an instrument are known by their location or fingering on the instrument. Employing the skills developed in notating rhythms for poems to determine the appropriate time signature and rhythmic values, write melodies for various instruments.

Blues Style

Blues style is more sophisticated than the styles implied by the previously suggested approaches to creating music, but it affords an ideal medium for exercising creativity. The poetic and musical forms are structured but not unduly restrictive, giving direction to the creative impulse without inhibiting it. The essential features of the style can be summarized succinctly.

Blues are based on a more or less standard 12-bar harmonic progression that has served three generations as a point of departure for melodic invention, both improvised and notated. In C major the chords would be C for four measures, with a seventh added in the fourth, and then F, C, G7, and C for two measures each. Sometimes an F7 chord replaces the G7 chord in the tenth measure. This innovation gained acceptance about 1960, probably as a result of rock influence.

The words of blues most often consist of three lines, the second of which is a repetition or slightly altered version of the first. The third line completes the thought and ends with a terminal rhyme. The poetic meter is predominantly iambic pentameter (U—U—U—U—U—), or a rough approximation of that meter.

The distinctive character of blues melodies is partially due to the use of *blue notes,* notes written as lowered third, fifth, and seventh degrees of the scale but of variable pitch in performance. The effect of blue notes is particularly striking when they conflict with chord tones. Blues rhythms are free and improvisational, so that they often look more complicated than they sound. Long notes or rests at the end of melodic phrases provide opportunities for instrumental fill-ins, a specialty of early jazz performers. The approach to the final tonic note is frequently from a third above or below, thus avoiding the *ti-do* cadence formula of art music.

Sunday Evening Blues illustrates the traditional blues features. Study it as a model of blues form and style. Then allow your imagination free rein in creating any or all of the following:

1. A piano accompaniment for the melody—the basic chord tones are written in whole notes in the bass clef as a guide.
2. Fill-ins, improvised or notated, appropriate for preserving the rhythmic motion during the long notes in the melody—fill-ins sometimes echo or elaborate motives from the melody.
3. Additional verses to go with the melody.
4. A version of the melody altered or embellished in the manner of a jazz improvisation.
5. An original melody to go with the blues chords—the chord in the tenth measure can be either F7 or G7.
6. A complete blues, with words and music.

SUNDAY EVENING BLUES

12 Singing in Harmony

Learning to sing in harmony is an important phase of the elementary teacher's basic musical training. Skill in part singing is especially useful for the teaching of fourth-, fifth-, and sixth-grade classroom music.

In this chapter various part-singing experiences are introduced in the sequence frequently found in the upper-elementary school music curriculum. Chants and ostinati with familiar tunes, rounds, canons, and partner songs prepare for two- and three-part singing.

Singing Chants

The easiest part-singing experience is that of adding one or more repeated note patterns (called chants, or ostinati) to familiar melodies. Small groups of singers may be selected, with several others playing bells, Orff instruments, and recorders.

ROW, ROW, ROW YOUR BOAT

ROUND

LONDON BRIDGE

ENGLAND

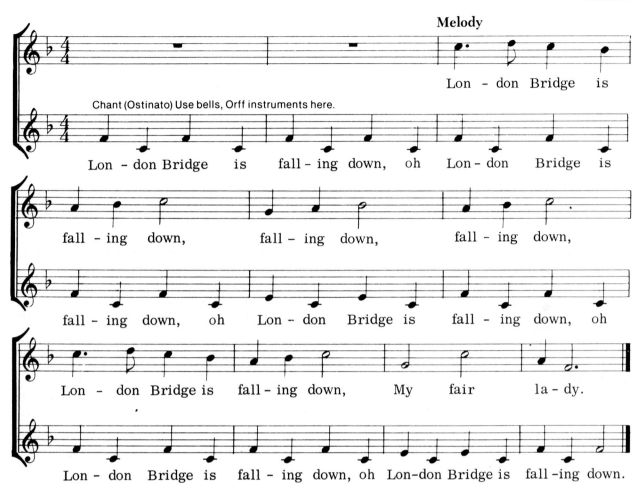

Singing Rounds

Learn the melody well before singing a song as a round. Then divide the class into sections. When group 1 reaches number 2, group 2 begins, and so forth. Repeat as many times as there are sections.

SCOTLAND'S BURNING

TRADITIONAL ROUND

Singing in Harmony

After learning this two-part round, have several strong singers sing the following chant. Also play it on bells. Create other chants.

1. See the fire,   See the fire.
2. Put it out,   Put it out.

The three-part round *Lovely Evening* lends itself well to the blending of voices. Slow down or stop at various points and listen to the harmony. Listen to the other parts.

LOVELY EVENING

ROUND

Oh, how love - ly is the eve - ning, is the

eve - ning, When the bells are sweet - ly ring - ing,

sweet - ly ring - ing, Ding, dong, ding, dong, ding, dong.

Add the ostinato below, first with unison melody and then as a round.

Ding dong bell.   Ding dong bell.

CHRISTMAS IS COMING

ROUND

ENGLAND

1. Christ - mas is com - ing! The goose is get - ting fat!
2. If you've no pen - ny, a ha' - pen - ny will do,

Please to put a pen - ny in an old man's __ hat,
If you have no ha' - pen - ny, then God bless __ you,

Please to put a pen - ny in an old man's hat.
If you have no ha' - pen - ny, then God bless you.

Ostinato

Christ - mas is com - ing! Christ - mas is com - ing!

The following folk round, *Ifca's Castle,* may be sung in from two to eight parts. Boys sing the opening chant as an introduction, repeating it two or four times. The introduction can be sung or played as an ostinato through the entire song.

IFCA'S CASTLE

ROUND   CZECHOSLOVAKIA

A hu-ya-ya, A

A - bove the plain of gold and green, A

young boy's head is plain - ly seen; A

hu - ya, hu - ya, hu - ya - ya, Swift - ly flow - ing riv - er, A

hu - ya, hu - ya, hu - ya - ya, Swift - ly flow - ing riv - er.

Several students sing this ostinato while others play it on bells or Orff instruments:

Hu - ya, hu - ya, hu - ya - ya!

Clap or play this ostinato on rhythm instruments:

Sing the following ever-popular rounds, first without ostinati. Then create your own ostinati.

HEY, HO! NOBODY HOME

ROUND   ENGLAND

Gm   Dm   Gm   Dm   Gm   Dm

Hey,   ho!   No - bod - y   at home,   Meat   nor   drink,   nor

Gm   Dm   Gm   Dm   Gm   Dm

mon - ey have I none,   Yet   will   I   be   mer - ry. _____

Observe the dynamics (**_f_** = loud, **_p_** = soft) as you sing *The Echo*.

THE ECHO

ROUND   GERMANY

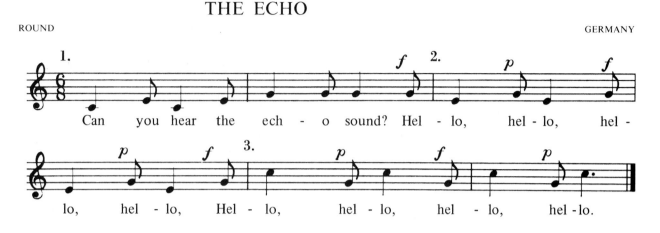

Shalom Chaverim can be sung in as many as eight parts. ("Shalom chaverim lehitraot" is pronounced "shall-ohm chah-vay-reem lay-hee-trah-oht.")

SHALOM CHAVERIM

ROUND   ISRAEL

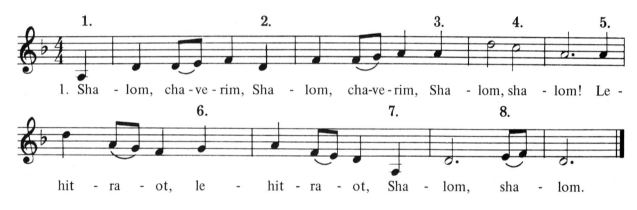

2. Goodbye, good friends, goodbye, good friends, goodbye, goodbye!
   Till we meet again, till we meet again, goodbye, goodbye.

Also sing the rounds *Are You Sleeping* (p. 72), *Good Night* (p. 73), *White Coral Bells* (p. 145), *My Goose* (p. 201), *Clocks and Watches* (p. 201), *Row, Row, Row Your Boat* (p. 244), and *The Bell Doth Toll* (p. 291).

Singing Canons

Canons in school music are sung in two parts, the second group of voices usually beginning after the first group has sung one measure. It is effective to have boys sing one part and girls the other.

Li'l Liza Jane, based on the notes of the pentatonic scale, offers numerous possibilities for Orff improvisation. Some are provided on the following page.

Important: As in singing rounds, be sure to learn the melody well before singing these canons.

LI'L LIZA JANE

U.S.

ORFF OSTINATI FOR *LI'L LIZA JANE*

1.

2.

3.

4.

5.

O, E - li - za, Li'l Li - za Jane.

Singing in Harmony

REUBEN AND RACHEL

TRADITIONAL CANON

1. Reu - ben, Reu - ben, I've been think - ing, What a grand world
   gra - cious Ra - chel, What a queer world

1. Reu - ben, Reu - ben, I've been think - ing,
2. O! my good - ness, gra - cious Ra - chel,

this would be If the men were all trans - port - ed
this would be If the men were all trans - port - ed

What a grand world this would be If the men were
What a queer world this would be If the men were

Far be - yond the North - ern Sea. 2. O! my good - ness
Far be - yond the North - ern Sea.

all trans - port - ed Far be - yond the North - ern Sea.
all trans - port - ed Far be - yond the North - ern Sea.

Important: Twinkle, Twinkle, Little Star (p. 126) is especially effective when sung and played as a canon.

Singing in Harmony

When singing these songs, sing them first with a leader, teacher, or other strong singer, then divide the class into two groups *with strong singers in each group.* The antiphonal effect helps develop independence in singing (or playing) one's own part.

FOLLOW ON

CANON

WHO DID?

U.S.

2.   Whale did, (whale did,) whale did, (whale did,)

Both: Whale did swallow Jo-Jo-Jo-Jo.
            Whale did, (whale did,) whale did, (whale did,)

Both: Whale did swallow Jo-Jo-Jo-Jo.
            Whale did, (whale did,) whale did, (whale did,)

Both: Whale did swallow Jo-Jo-Jo-Jo.
            Whale did swallow Jonah. (whale did swallow Jonah.)

Both: Whale did swallow Jonah down.

3.   Daniel (Daniel) Daniel (Daniel)

Both: Daniel in the Li Li Li Li
            Daniel (Daniel) Daniel (Daniel)

Both: Daniel in the Li Li Li Li
            Daniel (Daniel) Daniel (Daniel)

Both: Daniel in the Li Li Li Li
            Daniel in the Lion's (Daniel in the Lion's)

Both: Daniel in the Lion's Den.

Also sing *The Echo* (p. 249).

Create Orff-like tonal patterns on the following pentatonic tune, using the notes F, G, A, C, and D. Coconut shells or wood blocks of two different sizes can be used to create the effect of horse's hooves: e.g., play and sing.

Clop, clop, clop, clop

OLD TEXAS

COWBOY SONG

U.S.

1. I'm goin' to leave _____ old ___ Tex-as

I'm goin' to leave _____

now   They've got   no   use _____

___ old ___ Tex-as   now   They've got   no

___ for the long-horn   cow. _____

use _____   for the long-horn   cow.

2. They've plowed and fenced my cattle range,
   And the people there are all so strange.
3. I'll take my horse, I'll take my rope,
   And hit the trail upon a lope.
4. Say adios to the Alamo
   And hit the trail toward Mexico.

The following folk song should be sung like a canon, just as you sang *Old Texas*. To create the antiphonal effect, at each pause in the melody echo the words and tune that have just been sung. Note the blues effect created by the lowered seventh step (Bb).

EVERY NIGHT WHEN THE SUN GOES DOWN

APPALACHIAN SONG

U.S.

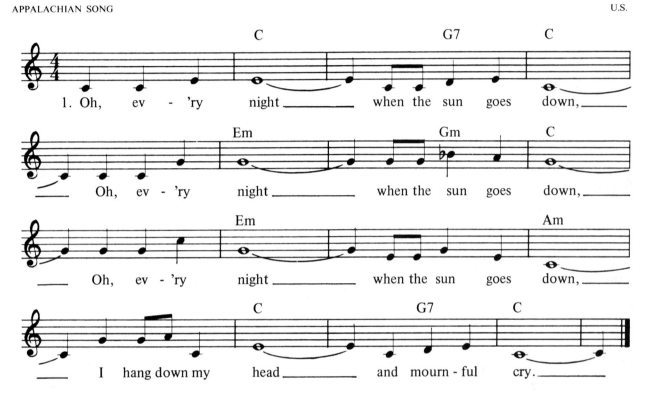

2. True love, don't weep, true love don't mourn, *(3 times)*
   I'm going away from this old town.
3. Oh, how I wish that train would come, *(3 times)*
   To take me back to where I'm from.
4. And when that train does finally come, *(3 times)*
   I'm going back to my old home.
5. Oh, how I wish my babe was born,
   And sitting on his daddy's knee,
   And I, poor girl, was dead and gone,
   With green grass growing over me.
6. My love is gone, where can he be? *(3 times)*
   He no longer gives his love to me.

Singing Partner Songs

Partner songs, two songs that can be sung together, help to establish the ability to hold one's own part while something else is being sung. They are particularly useful in fun songfests. Have the class learn each song separately before combining them. See next page.

THREE BLIND MICE/ARE YOU SLEEPING

TRADITIONAL ROUNDS

Next, sing and play these ostinati with these rounds.

Singing in Harmony

Sing the American spiritual *He's Got the Whole World in His Hands*, tapping the foot on strong beats and clapping the hands on weak beats ("pattin' juba"). Create additional verses. This song can be sung effectively with *Rocka My Soul*, on the next page.

HE'S GOT THE WHOLE WORLD IN HIS HANDS

SPIRITUAL

See chapter 1 (p. 8) for three-way partner songs.

The spiritual *Rocka My Soul* should be performed in the style and mood suggested for *He's Got the Whole World in His Hands*. Create simple harmony parts in bouncing rhythm, repeating only "Rock, rock, rock-a my soul."

ROCKA MY SOUL

SPIRITUAL

Oh, a - rock-a my soul, in the bo-som of A - bra-ham; A-
rock - a my soul, in the bo-som of A - bra-ham; A-
rock-a my soul, in the bo-som of A-bra-ham; Oh, rock-a my
soul. So high, you can't get o - ver it;
So low, you can't get un - der it; So wide, you
can't get 'round __ it; You must go in at the door.

Additional Partner Songs

The following songs also have matching chord patterns and two or more in each group may be combined.

1. *This Old Man, Ten Little Indians, Skip to My Lou, Sandy Land, Pawpaw Patch.*
2. *Santa Lucia, Juanita, Bicycle Built for Two.*
3. *Frère Jacques, London Bridge, The Old Grey Mare.*

Frederick Beckmann's *Partner Songs* (Boston: Ginn and Company, 1958) and *More Partner Songs* (Boston: Ginn and Company, 1962) are excellent sources for partner songs.

THE DEAF WOMAN'S COURTSHIP

U.S.
ARR. R. W. W.

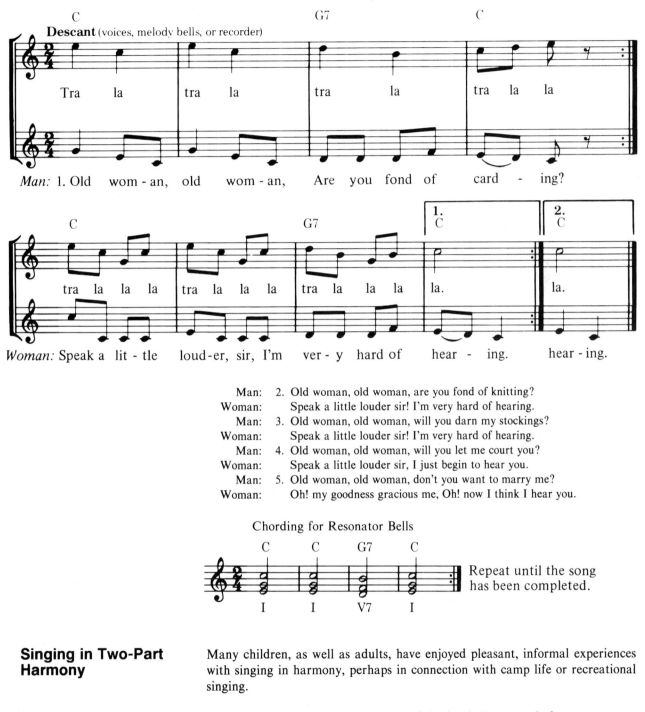

Descant (voices, melody bells, or recorder)

Tra la   tra la   tra   la   tra la la

Man: 1. Old wom-an, old wom-an, Are you fond of card - ing?

tra la la la   tra la la la   tra la la la la   la.   la.

Woman: Speak a lit-tle loud-er, sir, I'm ver-y hard of hear - ing.   hear-ing.

Man:	2. Old woman, old woman, are you fond of knitting?
Woman:	Speak a little louder sir! I'm very hard of hearing.
Man:	3. Old woman, old woman, will you darn my stockings?
Woman:	Speak a little louder sir! I'm very hard of hearing.
Man:	4. Old woman, old woman, will you let me court you?
Woman:	Speak a little louder sir, I just begin to hear you.
Man:	5. Old woman, old woman, don't you want to marry me?
Woman:	Oh! my goodness gracious me, Oh! now I think I hear you.

Chording for Resonator Bells

C   C   G7   C

I   I   V7   I

Repeat until the song
has been completed.

Singing in Two-Part Harmony

Many children, as well as adults, have enjoyed pleasant, informal experiences with singing in harmony, perhaps in connection with camp life or recreational singing.

Adding Barbershop Descants (Tenor)

One of the most popular social uses of singing in harmony is for two or more singers to blend their voices, usually by ear, in close harmony by adding a barbershop descant, or tenor part, to a familiar tune.

TELL ME WHY

COLLEGE SONG

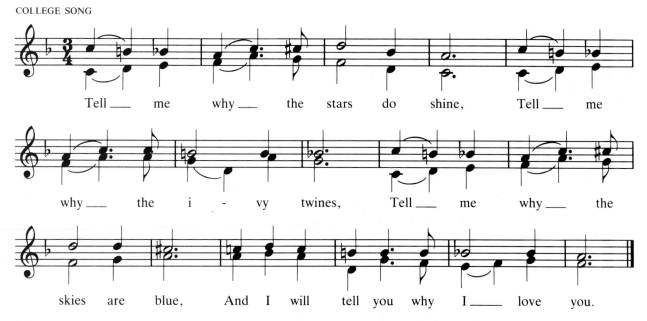

Tell __ me why __ the stars do shine, Tell __ me

why __ the i - vy twines, Tell __ me why __ the

skies are blue, And I will tell you why I __ love you.

Create your own barbershop harmony for such familiar tunes as *Home on the Range* and *Good Night Ladies*. Also sing the descant with *Aloha Oe* (p. 298).

Chording in Thirds and Sixths

Singing exercises in parallel thirds and sixths helps prepare the student for successful two-part singing. Practice the following exercises slowly, using the neutral syllable "loo," *so-fa* syllables, and numbers. Listen carefully for blend and balance. Always exchange parts in both exercises and songs.

In teaching part songs, having the entire class learn the melody first is usually helpful. Next, some or all of the class can be taught to sing the harmony part, after which the teacher will sing or play the melody on the piano or bells with them. Then, groups are formed to sing the parts. The teacher can assist by singing or playing an instrument for whichever part needs support. If the harmony part is difficult, some of the class members can hum the melody while others are learning the harmony. While it is sometimes necessary to rehearse the harmony part alone, the learning of parts separately should be kept to a minimum. The first notes should be held until everyone has them.

HARMONIZING

R. W. W.

AUSTRIA

Melody

C ... **G7** ... **C**

We like to har - mo - nize, when we're to - geth - er, Oh

G7 ... **C**

we sing so joy - ful - ly where e'er we go.

F ... **C** ... **G7** ... **C**

We raise our voic - es high, sing - ing so loud and clear.

G7 ... **C**

Let's sing in har - mo - ny, for all to hear. **Recorder and Bells**

STEAL AWAY

SPIRITUAL

F ... **Dm** ... **F** ... **C** **F**

Steal a - way, steal a - way, steal a - way to Je - sus!

Dm **F** ... **C7** **F** *Fine*

Steal a - way, steal a - way home. I ain't got long to stay here.

1. My Lord ___ calls me, He calls me by the thun - der, The
2. Green trees are bend - ing, poor sin - ners stand ___ trem - bling, The
3. My Lord ___ calls me, He calls me by the light - ning, The

D.C. al Fine

Dm **F** ... **C7** **F**

trum - pet sounds with - in ___ my soul, I ain't got long to stay here.

Singing in Harmony

OH HANUKKAH

HASIDIC FOLK SONG

ADAPTED R. W. W.

Oh Ha - nuk - kah, Oh Ha - nuk - kah good cheer it is bring - ing. Oh

Ha - nuk - kah we cel - e - brate with sing - ing and danc - ing.

Mer - ri - ly for eight days the drë - dl we spin.

Crisp - y lit - tle lat - kes, tast - y and thin. tast - y and thin. And

night - ly so bright - ly, the can - dles we light for Ha - nuk - kah.

Shin - ing with glo - ry, re - call - ing the sto - ry, the

won - ders of God long a - go. won - ders of God long a - go.

For additional songs with thirds, sing *Jacob's Ladder* (p. 146), *Upidee* (p. 185), *The Papaya Tree* (p. 192), *Las Pollitas* (p. 293), *Alouette* (p. 295), and *Lullaby* (p. 203).

Bass Chanting

Many folk songs and familiar tunes can be harmonized with I, IV, and V7 chords. An extra harmony part can be added to melodies simply by singing the root of the appropriate chord. Groups of students can sing *do, fa,* or *so,* or 1, 4, or 5, or a neutral syllable. Also, the words of the song can be used in the melody rhythm. Boys enjoy singing this added part because the notes are relatively low.

Singing in Harmony

Auld Lang Syne provides an easy introduction to three-part singing. The teacher or selected students can accompany by chording on the Autoharp and piano. Add Orff effects to this pentatonic tune.

AULD LANG SYNE

ROBERT BURNS   SCOTLAND

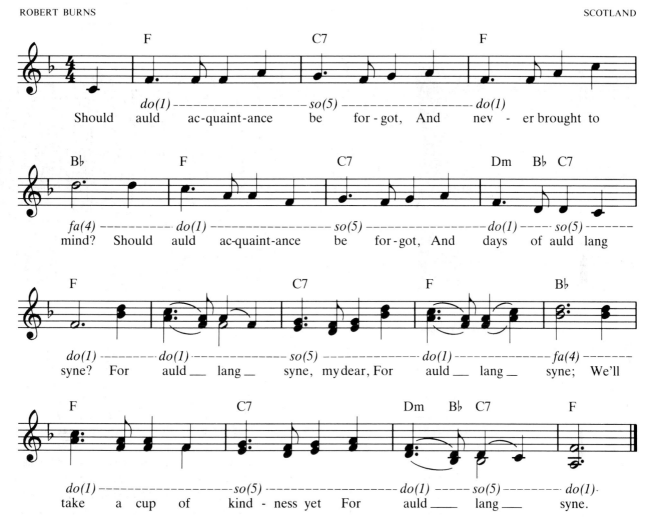

Singing in Three-Part Harmony

One of the highlights of the elementary school music program is the singing of songs in three-part harmony. If a good foundation of readiness activities and two-part singing has been established, three-part music can be used effectively in the classroom. The procedure for learning three-part music is similar to that used in two-part music. However, there is usually greater need to rehearse individual parts. To establish harmonic relationships, it is advisable to have students hum their part while other parts are being taught. The use of the piano and bells on difficult passages may be helpful. The interchange of singers on the various parts is recommended unless a program is in preparation.

Chording in Triads

Singing triad chord progressions helps the student to develop security in three-part singing. For practicing these exercises, follow the procedures used for chording in thirds and sixths.

hum, Loo
or
La

BOATING

R. W. W.

GERMANY

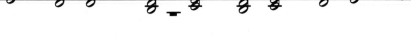

Sil - ver boats sail at night, Drift - ing

Sil - ver boats sail at night, o - ver the

by, drift - ing by. In the sky

wa - ter are drift - ing; In the sky

stars are bright, Soft - ly clouds are lift - ing.

stars are bright, Soft-ly the clouds are now lift - ing.

Singing in Harmony

In singing *Koom Bah Yah* a good antiphonal effect can be created. Have a soloist sing the first part, "Someone's crying Lord," with the chorus answering in three-part harmony on "Koom Bah Yah!"

KOOM BAH YAH
(DRAW NEARER, LORD)

AFRICA
ADAPTED R. W. W.

Also sing *Marching Song* (p. 195) and *Upward Trail* (p. 302) in three-part harmony.

Suggested Assignments

1. Sing additional rounds and other song materials that provide readiness for part singing. These may be selected from the standard school music series and community songbooks and from the rounds and part songs found elsewhere in this book.
2. Create your own chants and descants (tenor parts) for several familiar songs.
3. Sing partner songs like these: *Three Blind Mice* with *Row, Row, Row Your Boat; There's a Long, Long Trail* with *Keep the Home Fires Burning; Old Folks at Home* with *Humoresque; Ten Little Indians* with *Skip to My Lou;* and *Goodnight Ladies* with *When the Saints Go Marching In.*
4. Create your own bass chanting *(do, fa, so)* for folk songs and familiar tunes.
5. Form a classroom orchestra of simple instruments to play along with part singing.
6. Use standard band and orchestral instruments played by members of the class or outside talent with the singing of part music. Orchestral parts for various school music series and community songbooks are readily available.

13   Listening Concepts

Music listening is a universal, lifetime activity and a significant part of every school music program. Listening to music does not involve skills in the same sense that reading and writing music and playing instruments do, but perceptive listening requires a background of knowledge and listening experiences. The concepts explored in this chapter are useful in giving music listening a point of focus and a sense of direction in both cognitive and affective domains. They can be applied by students seeking to enhance their own responses to music and by teachers guiding the listening activities of others. The objectives are to cultivate attentive listening habits, to encourage receptivity to a wide range of musical styles, to provide essential information about some aspects of music, and to make music listening more meaningful and rewarding.

Concepts of Musical Sound

Sound originates when an object or surface vibrates in the frequency range between approximately 20 and 20,000 *Hertz* (cycles per second). If the sound waves resulting from the vibrations have a regular pattern, they are perceived as tones, otherwise as noise. Each tone has a distinctive wave pattern that produces a corresponding *tone quality,* or *tone color.* We are able to recognize the sound of a clarinet or a violin because of the unique tone qualities of these musical instruments. Other factors that affect the sound of tones are attack and decay, that is, the way tones begin and end. Striving to recognize the various instruments and voice types as they are heard individually and in combinations contributes to the development of perceptual skills and concentrates the listeners' attention on the music being performed.

Voices

Mature voices are classified according to sex and range, as follows:

Female	**Male**
High: Soprano	*High:* Tenor
Low: Alto (Contralto)	*Low:* Bass

The approximate ranges of the voices in four-part vocal music are shown. The ranges of immature and untrained voices are more restricted, and the ranges of professional singers exceed these limits in both directions. The unchanged voices of boys normally fall within the soprano range, so young male singers are called *boy sopranos.*

The terms *soprano, alto, tenor,* and *bass* are applied not only to voices and singers but to the parts they sing in ensembles and to the corresponding parts in instrumental music. Female singers with a range lower than sopranos but not as low as altos are called *mezzo-sopranos.* Male singers with a range lower than tenors but not as low as basses are called *baritones.* These terms are usually reserved for performing artists and opera roles.

Compare and contrast the range and quality of the four basic voice types as they are heard individually in solos and collectively in choruses. The suggested selections from Handel's *Messiah,* for which many recordings are available, are appropriate for this purpose.

G. F. Handel: *Messiah* **(1741)**

Air: I know that my Redeemer liveth (soprano)
Air: He shall feed His flock (alto)
Air: Every valley shall be exalted (tenor)
Air: The trumpet shall sound (bass)
Chorus: Hallelujah (sopranos, altos, tenors, basses)
Chorus: For unto us a Child is born (sopranos, altos, tenors, basses)

Instruments

Sound is produced on conventional instruments in five different ways—by *bowing, plucking, blowing, striking,* and by means of *keyboard mechanisms.* These methods of producing sound are associated with specific instruments and types of instruments, as listed below.

Bowing/String Instruments
violin
viola
cello (violoncello)
bass (string bass, contrabass, double bass)

Plucking/String Instruments
harp
guitar
banjo
ukulele
all other string instruments as a special effect

Blowing/Wind Instruments

Woodwind	*Brass*
Aperture	Valve
piccolo	trumpet
flute	cornet
Single Reed	horn (French horn)
clarinets	baritone (euphonium)
saxophones	tuba
Double Reed	sousaphone
oboe	Slide
English horn	trombone
bassoon	bass trombone
contrabassoon	

Striking/Percussion Instruments

Definite Pitch	*Indefinite Pitch*	
timpani	snare (side) drum	castanets
glockenspiel	tenor (street or field) drum	tom-tom
xylophone	bass drum	whip (slap-stick)
marimba	cymbals	maracas
vibraphone (vibes)	triangle	bongos
tubular bells (chimes)	tambourine	temple blocks etc.
	gong (tam-tam)	

Keyboard Instruments

piano (acoustic, electronic)	celesta
organ (acoustic, electronic)	synthesizers
harpsichord	various electronic instruments

On the basis of their range and functions, basic orchestral instruments of the string, woodwind, and brass families can be equated with the four main voice types, as follows:

	Soprano	**Alto**	**Tenor**	**Bass**
String	violin	viola	cello	bass
Woodwind	flute	oboe	clarinet	bassoon
Brass	trumpet	horn	trombone	tuba

The following illustration shows the ranges of voices and instruments in relation to the piano keyboard and to each other. Frequencies have been rounded to whole numbers. Ranges are approximate for voices and some instruments, and extremes are not always practical.

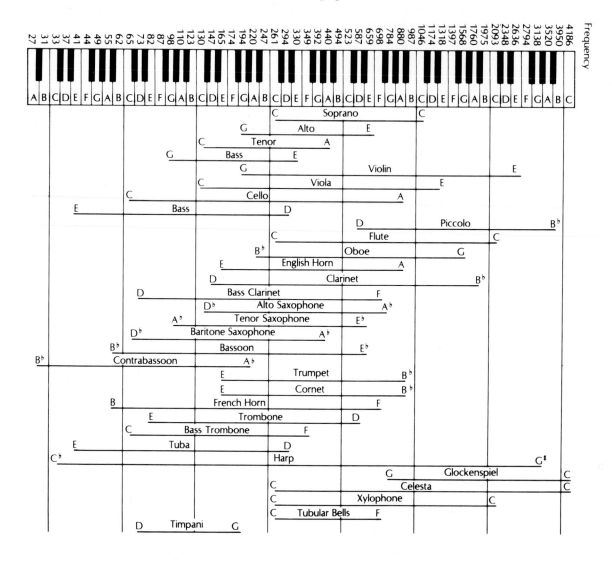

String Instruments

The violin is the smallest in size, the highest in pitch, and the most brilliant in quality of the string instruments. Violins most often play the melody, but they are equally effective in a variety of supporting roles. Violas are slightly larger than violins but not as much as would be suggested by their difference in pitch, which is a fifth lower, and their quality, which is less brilliant.

Photographs courtesy of Scherl & Roth, Inc., Cleveland, Ohio.

Violin   **Viola**

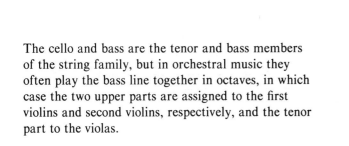

The cello and bass are the tenor and bass members of the string family, but in orchestral music they often play the bass line together in octaves, in which case the two upper parts are assigned to the first violins and second violins, respectively, and the tenor part to the violas.

Photographs courtesy of Scherl & Roth, Inc., Cleveland, Ohio.

Cello   **Double Bass**

The harp is the only orchestral instrument played exclusively by plucking. It has just seven strings per octave, corresponding to the seven letter names of notes. Whether the notes are sharp, flat, or natural depends upon the position of the seven pedals, three of which can be seen in the illustration, around the base of the instrument.

Photograph courtesy of Lyon & Healy, Chicago, Illinois.

Harp

Woodwind Instruments

On the flute and its smaller counterpart, the piccolo, the tone is produced by a stream of air from the player's lips striking the edge of the hole in the mouthpiece. The principle can be demonstrated by blowing over the open top of a small bottle.

On the clarinets, a finely shaped piece of cane called a *reed,* attached to the underside of the mouthpiece, is the primary source of the vibrations that produce the tone.

Photographs courtesy of F. E. Olds & Sons, Lincolnwood, Illinois.

Photographs courtesy of Fox Products Corporation, South Whitley, Indiana. Joe Schnurr, photographer.

Flute   **Piccolo**   **Clarinet**   **Bass Clarinet**

Saxophones, which have mouthpieces and reeds similar to those on clarinets, come in several sizes. The three most common are the alto, tenor, and baritone saxophones, which are shown.

Photographs courtesy of G. Leblanc Corporation, Kenosha, Wisconsin.

Alto Saxophone   **Tenor Saxophone**   **Baritone Saxophone**

Two pieces of cane fastened together with an air passage between them form a *double reed,* the primary source of the tone-producing vibrations on oboes and English horns. The distinctive tone quality produced by the double reed on these instruments is often associated with plaintive and pastoral melodies.

Photographs courtesy of G. Leblanc Corp., Kenosha, Wisconsin.

Oboe   **English Horn**

Bassoons and contrabassoons are also double-reed instruments. The bassoon plays in the same pitch range as the cello, and they frequently share melodic lines in orchestral music. The contrabassoon range is an octave lower than the bassoon range—lower than that of any other orchestral instrument.

Fox Products Corporation, South Whitley, Indiana. Joe Schnurr, photographer.

Bassoon   **Contrabassoon**

Brass Instruments

The trumpet and the cornet are similar in appearance and sound. Trumpets are ordinarily used in orchestras and jazz groups. Cornets, which have a somewhat mellower tone, are featured in bands.

Photograph courtesy of Conn Corporation, Elkhart, Indiana.

Trumpet

Photograph courtesy of G. Leblanc Corporation, Kenosha, Wisconsin.

Cornet

The French horn, often called simply the horn, is a versatile instrument with a surprisingly wide range. It has enough power to dominate an orchestra and enough control to blend with delicate string passages.

French Horn

The tuba provides the foundation for the brass section—and indeed, for the whole orchestra—when it plays the bass line in loud passages, which is its normal function. Sousaphones, named for John Philip Sousa, the March King, are designed to be carried over the shoulder. They replace the tubas in marching bands.

Tuba   **Sousaphone**

The trombone and bass trombone are the only instruments that have a slide mechanism. The position of the slide controls the pitch, as the valves do on the other brass instruments, by varying the amount of tubing the air passes through between the player's lips and the bell at the other end of the instrument.

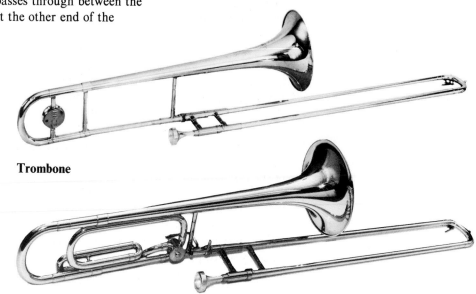

Trombone

Photographs courtesy of Conn Corp., Elkhart, Indiana.

Bass Trombone

Percussion Instruments

A representative assortment of percussion instruments is shown here. The compact collection of drums and cymbals on the riser in the center is typical of the instruments, known collectively as *traps,* played by the drummer in jazz and popular music. The four similarly shaped instruments on the left are the timpani. The instruments from left to right at the top of the picture are the vibraphone (vibes), tubular bells, xylophone, gong, and marimba. Also shown are drums of various types and sizes, cymbals, and several smaller percussion instruments.

Photograph courtesy of Ludwig Drum Company, Chicago, Illinois.

Percussion Instruments

To familiarize yourself with the sounds of the orchestral instruments, listen to a recording of Benjamin Britten's *Young Person's Guide to the Orchestra* in a version with narration that names and describes the instruments before they are heard. This work, with narration, is included in the specially prepared record and cassette albums that accompany *LISTENERS GUIDE to Musical Understanding* on record or cassette side 8 number 2—or, as it will be abbreviated in subsequent references, LG 8/2.[1]

When you are familiar with the sounds of the instruments, listen to a recording of *Young Person's Guide to the Orchestra* without narration, such as the one conducted by the composer on London recording Lon. 6671. The work, subtitled *Variations and Fugue on a Theme of Purcell,* consists of six versions of the theme, thirteen variations based on the theme, and a fugue—as listed in the left column of the following outline. The first and last statements of the theme are for full orchestra; each of the other four statements of the theme is for one family of instruments. As you listen to a recording, circle on the outline the name of the family of instruments heard in the themes that are not for full orchestra. In each variation (except the one for harp), two or more similar instruments are featured. Circle the name(s) of the instrument(s) most prominent in each of the variations. The fugue begins with a sprightly tune played successively by the various instruments, which are introduced in the same order as in the variations. Check your responses for the variations as the instruments enter in the fugue.

Benjamin Britten: *Young Person's Guide to the Orchestra* op. 34 (1946)

Theme A	(full orchestra)				
Theme B	string	woodwind	brass	percussion	
Theme C	string	woodwind	brass	percussion	
Theme D	string	woodwind	brass	percussion	
Theme E	string	woodwind	brass	percussion	
Theme F	(full orchestra)				
Variation A	violins	oboes	flutes	piccolo	trumpets
Variation B	clarinets	violas	horns	oboes	bassoons
Variation C	flutes	clarinets	cellos	bassoons	violins
Variation D	bassoons	oboes	violas	clarinets	trombones
Variation E	violas	cellos	violins	basses	clarinets
Variation F	cellos	violas	bassoons	violins	flutes
Variation G	bassoons	clarinets	violas	violins	cellos
Variation H	basses	violins	cellos	bassoons	clarinets
Variation I	trombones	horns	harp	xylophone	flutes
Variation J	trumpets	tuba	oboes	trombones	horns
Variation K	horns	trombones	trumpets	tuba	clarinets
Variation L	trumpets	trombones	tuba	bassoons	horns
Variation M	flutes	trombones	bassoons	percussion	oboes
Fugue					

Electronic Instruments

The newest musical instruments are electronic music synthesizers. Handmade prototypes of electronic instruments were exhibited in 1964, but the term *synthesizer* was not in general use until a few years later. The early synthesizers consisted of a complex maze of electronic sound generating and control components, but simplified and standardized makes and models soon developed. More recently, computers have been converted into synthesizers by means of suitable music programs, and computer-based digital synthesizers have been designed specifically for the production of musical sounds.

1. The *Listeners Guide* (LG) records and cassettes are available from Wm. C. Brown Publishers, 2460 Kerper Boulevard, P.O. Box 539, Dubuque, IA 52001.

The new digital synthesizers are capable of producing a full array of distinctive electronic sounds and of imitating with uncanny realism the sounds of any conventional instrument or combination of instruments. Much of the background music heard in current television programs and motion pictures is produced by computer musical instruments, though the electronic origin of the sound is not always apparent. Synthesizers are also used extensively in pop and rock music. Some of the less familiar electronic sounds are illustrated in Barton McLean's *Etunytude,* a composition conceived for and realized on a Fairlight Computer Musical Instrument (recorded on LG 8/3 and Folkways FSS 37465).

Courtesy of Fairlight Instruments, Los Angeles, CA

Fairlight Computer Musical Instrument

Mediums

The tone colors of voices and instruments are heard individually and in many varied combinations that informed listeners learn to recognize. The combinations that, by virtue of special qualifications, have become standardized constitute the common performance mediums of music. Their designations, which should be learned, are not always consistent with the literal meaning of the terms applied to them.

Solo literally means "alone," but in music the term is applied not only to works for a single instrument but to a piece, passage, or song for one predominant instrument or voice with accompaniment. The one instrument commonly played by itself is the piano, and a performance on a piano alone is a *piano solo.* A song for one voice with piano accompaniment is a *vocal solo.* An *art song,* or *lied* (plural, *lieder*), is a special type of vocal solo highly developed by nineteenth-century German composers. An instrumental solo is identified by the name of the featured instrument, such as a *violin solo.*

The term *sonata* originally meant a piece that was played, as opposed to a *cantata,* which meant a piece that was sung. *Sonata* is now applied to extended works, usually in three or four distinct parts, or *movements,* for one or two instruments, one of which is ordinarily the piano. A *piano sonata* is for piano alone. When a sonata is for two instruments, piano is implied and the other instrument is named; for example, a *violin sonata* is for violin and piano.

Chamber music is a general classification for music played by a small group with a different part for each player and with no doubling or duplication. Preeminent among the many chamber music combinations is the *string quartet,* consisting of two violins, a viola, and a cello. When a piano is added to the string quartet instrumentation, the group and the music it performs are identified as a *piano quintet.* Woodwind, brass, and percussion instruments are not as prominent in classical chamber music as string and keyboard instruments are, but contemporary composers have been attracted by the wide range of tonal colors available in the *wind quintet,* also known as a *woodwind quintet* even though it includes a brass instrument. The instrumentation of a wind quintet is flute, oboe, clarinet, horn (the brass instrument), and bassoon. The horn is also a member of *brass quintets,* usually in conjunction with two trumpets and two trombones. All of the jazz and popular music played by small combos fits the definition of chamber music. The instrumentation of such combos is as varied as the music they play. Examples of all types of chamber music, both standard and modern, abound in the recorded literature.

The larger musical organizations differ from chamber groups in that many performers are assigned to a limited number of parts. Music for choirs and choruses is most often written in four parts, one each for sopranos, altos, tenors, and basses. The sections may be divided into first and second parts, for a total of eight. Choirs may be as small as twenty or thirty singers, but festival choruses sometimes have hundreds of singers, with fifty or more for each part. The size of the group has a pronounced effect upon the tone quality. For comparison, listen to a recording of a *madrigal,* such as Thomas Morley's *My bonny lass she smileth* (LG 1/11) and a recording of a work for a large chorus, such as a choral selection from Handel's *Messiah.* Madrigals are a type of vocal chamber music originally intended for performance with one singer on each part, but they are frequently performed now by small choirs and choruses.

A *string orchestra* is a sort of instrumental counterpart of a chorus. A string orchestra includes many players, usually the full string section of a symphony orchestra, but only four different kinds of instruments and only four or five parts. The violins are divided more or less equally into first violins and second violins, accounting for two of the parts. The first violins ordinarily play the melody; the second violins are relegated to a lower, subservient part (hence the expression "playing second fiddle"). The violas play the third part. The cellos and basses may play the bass line in octaves, or they may have independent parts in a five-part texture. The instruments in a string orchestra are the same as those in a string quartet, plus basses. The difference in the sound of the two mediums is due more to the effect produced by one instrument on a part in a string quartet as opposed to the multiple instruments on each part in a string orchestra than to the addition of the basses. To compare the sound of a string orchestra with that of a string quartet, listen to a recording of a movement of a string quartet by Haydn, Mozart, or Beethoven and to the waltz from the *Serenade in C* for string orchestra by Tchaikovsky.

A string orchestra forms a nucleus to which wind and percussion instruments are added in varying numbers to make a *symphony orchestra.* The classic orchestra used by Haydn and Mozart consisted of the basic string section plus two each of the following: flutes, oboes, sometimes clarinets, bassoons, horns, trumpets, and timpani (one player). A full orchestra like the one used by Beethoven for his *Leonore Overture No. 3* has all of the instruments of the classic orchestra plus two horns (for a total of four) and three trombones. A modern large orchestra includes all of these, the specialized instruments, and several percussion players. Samuel Barber's *Symphony No. 1 in One Movement,* for example, is scored for two flutes, piccolo, two oboes, English horn, two clarinets, bass clarinet, two bassoons, contrabassoon, four horns, three trumpets, three trombones, tuba, timpani, percussion, harp, and the usual strings. The seating plan of the Philadelphia Orchestra shows how the 106 instruments of one large orchestra are arranged on the stage. An asterisk (*) by an instrument indicates the principal or first chair of each section.

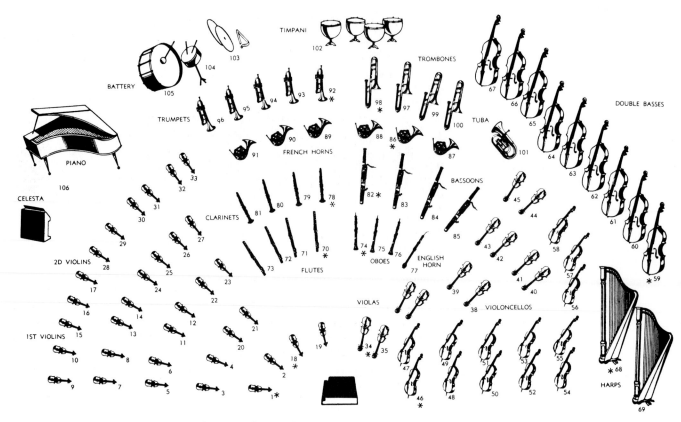

Courtesy of the Philadelphia Orchestra Association

Philadelphia Orchestra seating plan

Bands are instrumental ensembles comparable in size to symphony orchestras but with only three sections: woodwind, brass, and percussion. Bands are classified according to function as *marching bands* and *concert bands,* though they have many instruments and often many players in common. Marching bands are featured attractions in parades and football halftime shows. Concert bands are increasingly important as a concert medium. Band instrumentation is not uniform, but in general, bands have all of the wind instruments found in large orchestras plus cornets, saxophones, and baritones or euphoniums, which are like small tubas with the same range as trombones. There are many clarinets in various sizes and all of the specialized instruments such as piccolo, English horn, and contrabassoon. Concert bands usually have one or two string basses.

Symphonic wind ensembles are elite bands that have the same three sections and the same instruments as concert bands, but in symphonic wind ensembles the number, distribution, and uses of the instruments are significantly different. There are fewer players and much less doubling (more than one player on the same part), and the instrumentation is adjusted to the precise requirements of each work performed. The Eastman Symphonic Wind Ensemble is widely known through its recordings under the direction of its founder, Frederick Fennell, and its present conductor, Donald Hunsberger. It can be heard playing Sousa's *Hands Across the Sea,* a staple in the repertoire of both marching and concert bands (LG 6/5).

Photograph courtesy of Eastman School of Music. Rochester, New York.

**Eastman Wind Ensemble, Donald Hunsberger
Conductor**

For *pop and rock* music the number of players is small, as for chamber music, but in live performances the sound is amplified to a level exceeding that of a massive unamplified ensemble going full blast. A typical rock group consists of two or three electric guitars, an elaborate set of traps, usually an electronic keyboard instrument or a synthesizer, and one or more singers. Pop and rock groups can be heard at almost any hour of the day or night on radio stations that play recordings of current hits.

Concepts of Form

Music can be defined as "organized sound." Melodies are pitches and durations shaped into pleasing contours. Accompaniments are made up of chords, which in turn are made up of rational combinations of tones, occurring in a planned order. Melodies and accompaniments are organized in phrases delineated by cadences. Phrases are combined in various patterns to form sentences. A sentence may be an independent one-part form or part of a larger design, such as a binary or ternary form. These aspects of musical form are explored in chapter 5.

Conceptually, musical form results from repetition. Repetitions can be immediate and note for note, or they can be varied, in another part (voice), at a different pitch level, after contrasting material, or any combination of these. The patterns and types of repetition used in a song or an instrumental composition determine its form.

Strophic Song Form

Immediate, note-for-note repetition is the simplest and most obvious type. This type of musical repetition is illustrated in every folk and familiar song that has more than one stanza set to the same music. In this category are such songs as *America the Beautiful* (p. 305), *Prayer of Thanksgiving* (p. 77), *Sweet Betsy from Pike* (p. 74), and *Bow Belinda* (p. 93). Immediate, literal repetition of the complete musical idea also occurs in art songs (lieder), such as Schubert's immortal *Who Is Sylvia* (LG 5/2), in which three stanzas of Shakespeare's words from *Two Gentlemen of Verona* are set to the same music. When each stanza, or strophe, of a poem is set to the same music, the resulting form is a *strophic song form*.

Themes and parts of musical forms are often represented by letters assigned in alphabetical order. The letter *A* indicates the first theme, or part, in its initial statement at the beginning and in all subsequent appearances. In a strophic song form, the melody usually consists of one complete musical idea that is repeated with each stanza of the words. A strophic setting of a three-stanza poem, like *Who Is Sylvia,* produces the following design:

Music	Words
A	First stanza
A	Second stanza
A	Third stanza

Variation Form

Varied repetition is intrinsically more interesting than literal repetition. Nearly all music contains elements of varied repetition, but the principle is most systematically exploited in the variation forms. In variation forms one or more of the elements—melody, harmony, bass line, and/or structure—is constant while the other elements are varied. In the classic *theme and variation form,* the theme melody is the source of the constant elements, though the melody itself may be elaborately embellished. The structure and cadences of the theme are retained, so each variation comes to a complete close like the theme. Each variation typically has a distinctive character, the individual variations are clearly delineated, and the overall form is sectional.

Schubert composed an art song, *The Trout,* from which he later derived the theme for the variation movement in his *Quintet* for violin, viola, cello, string bass, and piano. Listen first to the song (on Angel record S-36341) and then to the fourth movement of the *Quintet* (on Angel record DS-37846), which provides a clear introduction to theme and variation form. In the outline of the variation form, the prime signs indicate varied repetitions.

Franz Schubert: ***The Trout (Die Forelle), op. 32* (1818)**
**   *Quintet in A, op. 114, "The Trout"* (1819)**
                    4. Andante

Theme and Variations

A	Theme	The first two sentences of the song melody with the first sentence repeated, the rhythm altered, and a different accompaniment.
A′	Variation I	Slightly embellished version of the melody in the piano with an animated accompaniment in the strings.
A″	Variation II	Melody in the viola. Elaborate figuration in the violin. Fragmentary imitation in the piano.
A‴	Variation III	Melody in the cello and bass. Elaborate figuration in the piano.
A⁗	Variation IV	Change to minor mode. Melody fragmented and submerged in figuration.
A′′′′′	Variation V	Transformed theme in remote keys played by cello. Transition leads to A′′′′′′
A′′′′′′		Like variation VI but not numbered as a variation in the score. Melody returns to version of the theme, but tempo is faster and accompaniment is like that of the song. Both sentences repeated and varied. Brief extension concludes movement.

For a twentieth-century example of variation form, listen to Dohnanyi's *Variations on a Nursery Song* (London recording STS-15406).

The concept of varied repetition is the stock-in-trade of jazz musicians. Their spectacular improvisations are, in effect, variations on a melody and the chord progressions that accompany it. In jazz improvisation the structure and basic harmony of the original melody are preserved, as in classic theme and variation form, but the treatment of melodic elements is limited only by the player's imagination and technique. The point of departure for jazz improvisation is most often a popular song, customarily consisting of thirty-two bars (measures) and an A A B A sentence pattern, or a twelve-bar blues (see p. 242). Since the tunes and chord progressions that serve as the theme in jazz improvisation are presumably familiar, a jazz performance may begin with what is essentially a variation rather than the straightforward statement of the theme found in classic variations. The improvisation may be no more than an ornamented version of the original melody in which all of the essential features are preserved and immediately recognizable, or a totally free melodic line may be improvised over the predetermined harmonic background. Since jazz improvisations are spontaneous and not notated, no two are alike. Each player cultivates a personal style. It is illuminating to listen to two or more jazz interpretations of the same piece. Ideal for this purpose are the recordings of *Body and Soul* by the Benny Goodman Trio and by Coleman Hawkins, both of which appear on record side 4 of the *Smithsonian Collection of Classic Jazz*.[2]

Imitative Forms

A plan of musical organization can be based on the concept of repetition in another voice after a short time interval. This type of repetition is called *imitation,* and continuous imitation between two or more parts produces a *canon.* Familiar rounds like *Are You Sleeping* (p. 72) and *Lovely Evening* (p. 246) are a special type of canon in which the end of the melody leads around to the beginning, permitting any number of repetitions.

Repetition in another voice after a short time interval can be at a different pitch level. This is the type of repetition and imitation found in *fugues.* A fugue normally begins with a single melodic line that states the main thematic idea, called the *subject,* which is stated in turn by each voice as it enters. As soon as the statement of the subject by the first voice is completed, the second voice enters and states the subject, or a slightly modified form of it, at the dominant pitch level (a fourth lower or a fifth higher). A brief linking passage leads to the entrance of the third voice, most often in an octave relationship to the first voice. The fourth voice, if there is one, then enters like the second voice but an octave lower or higher. Following the statement of the subject in the third voice in a three-voice fugue or the fourth voice in a four-voice fugue, the subject appears in various keys and may be in any voice. Between some of the subject entrances there are modulatory *episodes* based on motives derived from or associated with the subject or, less frequently, on new material. Toward the end of the fugue, the subject returns in the original key, sometimes with overlapping statements in the different voices.

No two fugues are the same, but the following fugue is a simple model of the form. Its subject is given, and the diagram shows the appearances of the subject in each voice. The lines represent the subject. The number of the measure in which it enters and the letter name of the first note, which is the keynote, are given above the line. The letter name of the key is followed by a small *m* when

2. Distributed by W. W. Norton & Company, Inc., 500 Fifth Avenue, New York, New York 10110.

the mode is minor. Follow the diagram as you listen to a recording of this fugue, which—like all fugues—illustrates musical organization predicated upon repetition in another voice and at a different pitch. The statement of the subject that begins in measure 25 in voice 3 moves in measure 26 to voice 1, where it is completed.

J. S. Bach: *Organ Fugue in G Minor, "Little"* **(c. 1700)**[3]

Voice 1: 1—Gm   26 (Gm)

Voice 2:   6—Dm

Voice 3:   12—Gm   25—Gm

Voice 4:   17—Dm

1:   50—Cm

2: 33—B♭

3:

4:              41—B♭   63—Gm

Part Forms

When the statement of a musical idea is followed by contrasting material rather than some kind of repetition, aesthetic instinct seems to require a return to the opening idea to bring the musical experience to a satisfactory conclusion. The most prevalent plans of musical organization are governed by this principle, which produces a statement-departure-return design. The statement-departure-return concept functions in a wide range of dimensions. It is most concisely illustrated in simple ternary forms (see pp. 98–100) of which *The Ash Grove,* with its AA B A design, is typical. The immediate repetition of the initial A is included in the statement. The function of the B part is to provide an element of contrast between the statements of A and its return, which may be literal, altered, abridged, or extended as long as its identity is unmistakable. Many popular songs have an AA B A design. The *Russian Dance (Trepak)* from Tchaikovsky's *Nutcracker Suite* is an example of ternary form, as outlined, in the symphonic literature.

3. A recording is included in *Bach Organ Favorites,* Columbia MS-6261.

P. I. Tchaikovsky: *Nutcracker Suite, op. 71a* **(1892)**

4. Russian Dance (LG 6/4)[4]

Ternary Form

A   Four phrases with an a-b-a-c(b) design.
A   Repeated with somewhat fuller scoring.
B   Melody moves to bass; four phrases with the same design as A.
A   First three phrases essentially as before; fourth phrase extended, delaying the final cadence.

In many instrumental ternary forms, especially those found in minuets and scherzos, the ternary design is expanded still further by the repetition of the BA as a unit. The complete pattern then becomes AA BA BA. This pattern is heard in the first part of the minuet (*menuetto*) and again in the trio of Mozart's *Haffner Symphony.* The statement-departure-return principle can function on multiple levels. In a typical minuet the first part, or minuet proper, is ordinarily a simple ternary form with repeats. The second part is a contrasting trio which, as a rule, is also a simple ternary form with repeats. A sign at the end of the trio, *D.C.* (from the beginning), indicates a return of the minuet without repeats. Simple forms combined in a larger ternary design, like minuet-trio-minuet, result in a *compound ternary form,* the form of the minuet outlined below and of most minuets and scherzos.

W. A. Mozart: *Symphony No. 35 in D, "Haffner"* **(1782)**

3. Menuetto (LG 3/3)

Compound Ternary Form

Minuet: Ternary, D Major
A   Two phrases—the first loud, vigorous, ascending; the second quiet, lyric, descending.
A   Repeated.
B   Two phrases paralleling the stylistic relationships of A.
A   As before.
BA   Repeated together.

Trio: Ternary, A major
A   Two phrases that begin alike.
A   Repeated.
B   Two phrases, the second extended.
A   As before.
BA   Repeated together.

Minuet: D.C. without repeats
A   As before.
B   As before.
A   As before.

Sonata Form

On a very sophisticated level, *sonata form* has a ternary design in which the three large parts are the *exposition,* the *development,* and the *recapitulation.* The themes, usually three, are stated in the exposition, which may be repeated in its entirety. The themes are developed and transformed in the development section.

4. See fn. 1, p. 277.

They return in the recapitulation essentially as they were in the exposition, except that the second and third themes, which initially appear in a related key, return transposed to the tonic key of the work or movement. The basic form is often preceded by an *introduction* and followed by a concluding section called a *coda*. The following selection is an example of sonata form with an introduction and a coda.

L. van Beethoven: *Piano Sonata no. 8, "Pathetique"* **(1799)**

1. Grave—Allegro di molto e con brio (LG 4/2)

Sonata Form	
Introduction	Slow tempo, sombre mood.
Exposition	Fast tempo and vigorous rhythms, three contrasting themes.
Development	Brief return to slow tempo and thematic material of introduction, then fast tempo and development of first theme.
Recapitulation	Essentially a return of the exposition with the second and third themes transposed.
Coda	Begins with the material and slow tempo of the introduction, ends with a final reference to the first theme in a fast tempo.

Rondo Forms

The statement-departure-return concept can be expanded by additional departures and returns. Forms that have two or more departures and returns are *rondo forms,* and their recurring theme is called the *rondo theme.* In a five-part rondo form, there are two contrasting themes, and the contrasting themes alternate with the rondo theme to produce an A B A C A design. The individual themes may be one-part, two-part, or ternary forms, with or without repeats. Between the themes, transitions are customary, and rondos usually end with a coda. The third movement of Brahms's *Second Symphony* is an example of five-part rondo form. The three themes are linked by a common motive.

Johannes Brahms: *Symphony no. 2 in D* **(1877)**

3. Allegretto grazioso (LG 6/2)

Rondo Form, Five-Part	
Theme I/rondo theme	Moderate tempo, 3/4 time, ternary form.
Theme II	Fast tempo, 2/4 time, ternary form.
Theme I/rondo theme	Moderate tempo, 3/4 time, reduced to one part.
Theme III	Fast tempo, 3/8 time, structure closely parallels that of theme II.
Theme I/rondo theme	Moderate tempo, 3/4 time, ternary form.
Coda	Continues tempo and meter of preceding theme.

More complex rondo forms theoretically have a design represented by the letters A B A C A B′ A, though the final return of A is frequently merged with the coda. The B′ is a return of the first contrasting (second) theme transposed to the key of the rondo theme. The last movement of Beethoven's *Piano Sonata no. 2 in A* is an example of this type of rondo form. An unmistakable soaring figure, with which the movement begins, signals each return of the rondo theme.

L. van Beethoven: *Piano Sonata no. 2 in A* (1795)
4. Rondo: Grazioso (LG 4/1)

Rondo Form, Seven-Part

Theme I/rondo theme	Ternary, tonic key.
Theme II	One part, dominant key.
Theme I/rondo theme	Ternary, tonic key, slightly embellished.
Theme III	Ternary with repeats (AA BA′ BA′), parallel minor key and its relative major key, loud and vigorous.
Theme I/rondo theme	Ternary, tonic key, additional embellishments.
Theme II	One part, transposed to the tonic key but otherwise essentially as before.
Theme I/rondo theme and coda merged	Tonic key, developmental in character, ornate versions of the rondo theme at beginning and end separated by contrasting material derived from theme III.

After this exploration of formal concepts, it should be apparent that repetition is the foundation of musical organization and that repetition is employed systematically in a variety of musical plans. The most common plans have been described and illustrated. Listening to the suggested examples provides background in the perception of musical organization, which is essential for full understanding and appreciation. Consciously striving to remember themes and to recognize them when they reappear develops the habit of attentive listening, which elevates the musical experience to the highest cognitive and emotional levels.

Concepts of Style

The styles of music reflect and are the product of many interacting forces. Every musical expression is influenced by the culture, language, resources, state of development, and habitat of the people who create it and by the purpose for which it is intended. Furthermore, music develops continuously within each ethnic group and region, and over the centuries styles change dramatically. The masterpieces and major achievements of each era tend to survive and to exist side by side with current creations. The amount of viable music literature and the range of styles within our direct Western European heritage is enormous. Improved travel, communication, and recording facilities have made non-Western music increasingly accessible and awareness of its values increasingly important. A few random examples are suggested on the following pages to provide some concept of the infinitely varied musical styles available to twentieth-century listeners and about which they should be informed.

Music and Religion

Music has figured prominently in religious observances since the dawn of civilization. A hymn inscribed on a clay tablet about 1400 B.C. and recently discovered in Syria is the oldest known piece of religious music, but the ritual uses of music in several earlier cultures have been documented. Through the centuries, each religion has developed its own musical traditions. Some styles have been preserved virtually intact for extended periods, while others have changed with the times and reflected concurrent secular influences. The following examples give some idea of the broad spectrum of musical styles associated with religion.

Mesomedes: *Hymn to the Sun* (A.D. **130**)

This hymn, ascribed to Mesomedes of Crete, is grouped with the examples of Greek music in histories and anthologies, but its authenticity and dating have been questioned. The words contain references to Olympus, abode of the Greek gods, and Phoebus, the sun god Apollo, but Crete was a Roman province in the time of Mesomedes, and he was attached to the court of the Roman emperor Hadrian (A.D. 76–138). The style is *monophonic* and *syllabic,* that is, a single melodic line and, with few exceptions, one note for each syllable. (LG 1/2)

Anonymous: *Kaddish (Song of Praise)*

The *Kaddish* is still sung in synagogues at the Passover, but it represents an old tradition—the Aramaic words date from the eighth or ninth century. The unaccompanied melody often has several notes on a single syllable, a style of text setting known as *melismatic.* (*2,000 Years of Music,* Folkways FT 3700)

Anonymous: *Navajo Night Chant*

The *Night Chant* is part of a nine-day ceremony in which boys and girls are initiated into tribal life. The belief is that the ceremony was given to the first Navajos by the gods and that it has been preserved by an unbroken succession of medicine men. Gourd rattles provide a rhythmic accompaniment to the singing, which alternates between a normal vocal quality and a high falsetto. (*Music of the Sioux and the Navajo,* Folkways FE 4401)

G. P. da Palestrina: *Pope Marcellus Mass—Kyrie* (**1555**)

This model of Catholic liturgical music and of Renaissance choral style is sung *a cappella* (without instruments "in the chapel manner"). The different voice parts usually enter imitatively, and multiple melodic lines are combined in an elaborate *polyphonic texture.* (LG 1/10)

J. S. Bach: *A Mighty Fortress Is Our God—Chorale* (**1730**)

The style of this Protestant church music from the baroque period is vastly different from that of the preceding example. Instruments are added to the voices, and the rhythm is more clearly metric. The principal melody is in the top part, and the lower parts move more or less synchronously with it. Musical texture is classified as *homophonic* when one melody predominates and the other parts have supporting or accompanying functions. This chorale concludes Bach's *Cantata No. 80* of the same name, known in German as *Eine feste Burg ist unser Gott.* (Deutsche Grammophon DG ARC-2533459)

Stephen Schwartz: *Godspell—Day by Day* (**1973**)

The latest style in religious music is rock. The rock opera *Godspell* created a sensation when it first appeared on the stage and again in the motion picture version. The hit tune *Day by Day* is featured in the original cast recording. (Arista ALB6-8304)

Music and Dance

Religious ceremonies, especially those of primitive peoples, often involve dancing, and the music of *Godspell* can be danced to as well as any rock music. The dance influence on such music is incidental to its primary function, but there exists a large body of music in which dance influences are preeminent. This includes not only music directly associated with dancing, but also stylized dance music intended for performance in concert halls and other places of entertainment that feature passive listening. The styles of dance-inspired music are as varied as those of religion-inspired music, a premise demonstrated by the following examples.

Anonymous: *Greetings from Podor*

Podor is a town on the Senegal River, which marks the border between Senegal and Mauritania in West Africa. The inhabitants are principally Wolofs and Mandingos. Their dress and dietary customs reflect their Moslem religion, but their intricate drumming is distinctly West African in style. In a favorite form of entertainment, drummers and spectators gather in a circle. An individual from among the spectators moves to the center of the group, where he or she dances impromptu, alone or with a partner, until exhausted or displaced by another dancer. Meanwhile, complex rhythms like those on the suggested recording continue. Drum sounds predominate in *Greetings from Podor,* but individual voices, group singing, and handclapping can also be heard. (LG 10/1)

Anonymous: *Overture—Kapi Radja*

Music and the dance are inseparable from daily life in Bali. No temple ceremony or village festival, and there are many of them, is complete without music and dancing. The orchestras of Bali, which consist principally of gongs, metallophones, drums, and cymbals, are known as *gamelans*. The 25-piece gamelan heard on the suggested recording is from the village of Pliatan, where it plays ceremonial temple music and accompanies both traditional and modern forms of the dance. *Kapi Radja* is an overture to a dance program. (LG 10/4)

G. F. Handel: *Water Music—Bourrée* (**1717**)

The bourrée, a dance of French origin in fast duple meter, is frequently included as one of the stylized dance movements in suites of the baroque period (1600–1750). This piece preserves the style and spirit of the French dance, but it was written by a German composer for a royal entertainment held on barges floating on the Thames River in England. (RCA LSC-3226)

W. A. Mozart: *Serenade "Eine kleine Nachtmusik"—Minuet* (**1787**)

The minuet, a stately dance in a moderate triple meter, was adopted as the official dance in the court of Louis XIV of France during the mid-seventeenth century. Its popularity quickly spread throughout Europe, revolutionizing the styles of dancing and dance music. The symphonies and string quartets of Mozart and his contemporaries usually have a stylized minuet as the third movement, as does this serenade.

Johann Strauss: *The Blue Danube Waltz* (**1867**)

The styles of dancing and dance music were again revolutionized in the nineteenth century by the waltz, in which partners danced for the first time in the then-scandalous embracing position. Though its detractors characterized waltzing as a "vulgar habit," it achieved immediate, universal, and enduring popularity. (Strauss: *Famous Waltzes,* Angel DS 37892)

Duke Ellington: *Old King Dooji* (**1938**)

There are many styles of jazz and most of them have been danced to, but the one that had the whole nation dancing in the decade before and during World War II was *swing*. Duke Ellington was a master composer and performer whose brilliant career spanned the history of jazz from its beginnings into the seventies. *Old King Dooji* is typical dance music from the era of swing. (LG 9/4)

Aaron Copland: *Appalachian Spring* (1944)

Appalachian Spring is a ballet, an art form in which music and dance elements are highly integrated. Opportunities to see good ballet performances are limited, but they have great popular appeal. *Appalachian Spring* is particularly appealing, because the action depicts a tender story of Pennsylvania pioneer newlyweds, and the music has a style recognized as distinctly American. (RCA LSC-2401)

Periods and Styles

Western music is divided into style periods, as follows:

Ancient	Before 850	Monophonic (one-part) music.
Medieval	850–1450	Beginnings of polyphony (multipart music); staff invented.
Renaissance	1450–1600	Perfection of vocal polyphony.
Baroque	1600–1750	Ascendancy of instrumental music and homophonic (harmonic) texture.
Classic	1750–1825	Reflects classic ideals of simplicity, symmetry, refinement, objectivity.
Romantic	1825–1900	Emphasis on emotion and personal expression; emergence of nationalism and program music.
Modern	Since 1900	Diverse styles, complex rhythms and sonorities, new methods of organization, and more recently, music by synthesizers and computers.

The dates for these periods are somewhat arbitrary, and between periods there is much overlapping of style traits. The selections already cited in this chapter illustrate the main periods and styles of Western music and provide a sampling of music from other cultures. For more comprehensive listening experiences, see the complete *Listeners Guide* recordings, which include a chronological survey of Western art music and jazz and additional examples of music from other cultures. A background of listening experiences directed toward the perception of stylistic features enables students to relate the music they hear to its function and time and place of origin, significant factors in the appreciation of music.

14 Applying Your Music Skills with Songs and Instruments

The purpose of this chapter is to provide a repertoire of song literature that is readily adaptable to school music programs and useful for additional practice in developing skills that have been introduced throughout this book. The following songs have been selected to increase the student's skill in unison and part singing, provide experience singing in foreign languages, and present supplementary material for playing classroom instruments.

Rounds

THE BELL DOTH TOLL

ENGLISH ROUND

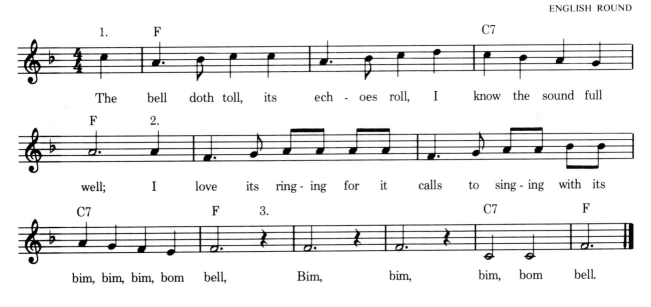

The bell doth toll, its ech - oes roll, I know the sound full

well; I love its ring - ing for it calls to sing - ing with its

bim, bim, bim, bom bell, Bim, bim, bim, bom bell.

Chords for Resonator or Tone Educator Bells:

F (I) C7 (V7)

Repeat this ostinato three times, using bells and Orff instruments.

MUSIC ALONE SHALL LIVE

GERMANY

All things shall per - ish un - der the sky;

Mu - sic a - lone shall live, Mu - sic a - lone shall live,

Mu - sic a - lone shall live, nev - er to die.

Folk Songs Around the World

HEY, BETTY MARTIN

U.S.

1. Hey, Bet - ty Mar - tin, tip - toe, tip - toe, Hey, Bet - ty

Mar - tin, tip - toe fine. Hey, Bet - ty Mar - tin,

tip - toe, tip - toe, Hey, Bet - ty Mar - tin, tip - toe fine.

2. Can't find a boy, a boy to please her,
Can't find a boy to please her mind;
She hopes to find a boy to please her,
She hopes to find a certain kind.

3. I found a boy, a boy to please me,
I found a boy to please my mind.
I found a boy, a boy to please me,
I found a boy, a certain kind.

Applying Your Music Skills with Songs and Instruments

LAS POLLITAS

Pin - ti - tas de co - lo - ra - do, Son las pol - li - tas que

ten - go, Pin - ti - tas de co - lo - ra - do, Son

las pol - li - tas que ten - go, Pero est - a - ca - pe - ton

ci - ta No la ven - do___ no la ven - do, Pero

est - a - ca - pe - ton ci - ta No la ven - do___ no la ven - do.

Chorus

No la se lle - van la pol - la Que no se la lle - va - ran, Que

si a la polla se lle - can Ca - ram - ba yo voy al - lá.

Rhythm instruments played as follows:

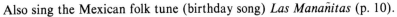

Rhythm sticks

Castanets

Tambourine

hit   shake   shake

Also sing the Mexican folk tune (birthday song) *Las Manañitas* (p. 10).

To make *Alouette* an action fun song, have the class point to the parts of the body corresponding to those mentioned in the song.

ALOUETTE

CANADA

4. Le dos (*the back*)
5. Les pattes (*the claws*)
6. Le cou (*the neck*)
7. Les jambes (*the legs*)
8. Les pieds (*the feet*)

LES ANGES DANS NOS CAMPAGNES

CAROL

FRANCE/ENGLAND

2. Bergers, pour qui cette fête!
   Quel est l'objet de tous ces chants?
   Quel vainqueur, quelle conquête
   Mérite ces cris triomphants?
   Refrain

2. Shepherds, why this celebration?
   Why this burst of heav'nly song?
   What could cause such jubilation?
   What inspired the heav'nly throng?
   Refrain

Play on the piano and sing the A pentatonic scale to help capture the oriental mood of *Cherry Blossoms*.

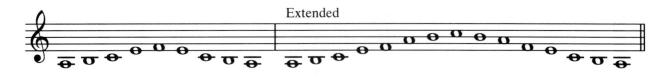

Extended

Pluck rather than strum the individual strings of the guitar, Autoharp, or ukulele for accompaniment to imitate the *Japanese Koto*. Also use finger cymbals and triangle.

Create your own ostinati using the notes of this scale. Use Orff instruments.

CHERRY BLOSSOMS
SAKURA

ADAPTED R.W.W.   JAPAN

Sa - ku - ra, Sa - ku - ra, Cher - ry blos - soms wave in the trees, Love - ly blos - soms dance in the breeze. Pink and white the blos - soms will fall. Pe - tals send - ing scent to __ all. Sa - ku - ra, Sa - ku - ra, Smell - ing sweet Sa - ku - ra.

Sa-ku-ra Sa-ku-ra
Ya-yo-i no so-ra-wa
Mi-wa-ta-su ka-gi-ri
Ka-su-mi ka ku-mo-ka
Ni-o-i zo i-zu-ru
I-za-ya I-za-ya
Mi ni yu-ka-un

Puccini used this melody in his opera *Madame Butterfly*. It was popularized in the film score of *Sayonara*.

Applying Your Music Skills with Songs and Instruments

First sing *Hava Nagila* on the syllable "la." Then, attempt the words. Free translation: "Come, let us sing and be happy; Wake up, brothers, with a happy heart."

HAVA NAGILA

ISRAEL

Also sing the popular Jewish round *Shalom Chaverim* (p. 249).

ALOHA OE
FAREWELL TO THEE

QUEEN LILIUOKALANI   QUEEN LILIUOKALANI

Dear the thoughts I take a-way with me, Sweet mem-'ries of our hap-py past, It is sad that we must say "Fare-well," In our dreams we shall meet a-gain at last.

Chorus

Fare-well to thee, Fare-well to thee, the breeze will sing a-gain my sad re-frain. ___ One fond em-brace be-fore we say "a-dieu," un-til we meet ___ a-gain.

O ka halia aloha kai hiki mai Ke hone ae nei i kuu manawa,
O oe no ka'u ipo aloha A loko e hana nei.
Aloha oe, aloha oe, E ke ona ona noho i ka lipo;
One fond embrace a hoi ae au, Until we meet again.

HARMONY PART FOR ALOHA OE

Sing "oo" or hum or sing the words.
Play on bells or recorder.

Chorus

For a German language folk song sing *Du, du, liegst mir im Herzen* (p. 128).

Action and Game Songs

The following action and game songs are especially appropriate for children in the lower grades.

THE MUFFIN MAN

ENGLAND

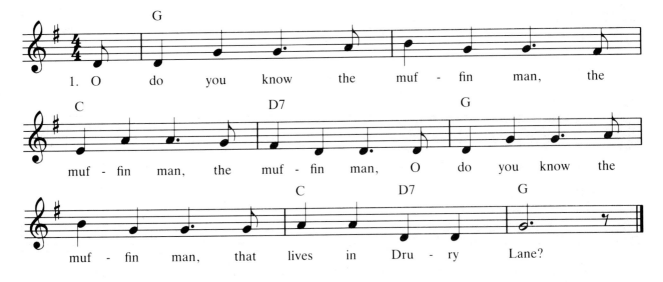

2. O yes I know the muffin man, etc.
3. O have you seen the muffin man, etc.
4. Where did you see the muffin man, etc.

This old English game song has rhythm suitable for skipping and marching. It often is used as a question and answer song, and offers excellent opportunity for the singers to make up verses about a variety of activities. See next page.

For Halloween, sing these words to the tune of *The Muffin Man.*

THE PUMPKIN MAN

Oh do you know the Pump-kin man, the Pump-kin man, the Pump-kin man,
Oh do you know the Pump-kin man who comes on Hal - low - een?

Also sing in G minor for a more "spooky" Halloween mood.

The primary grade action song *Pussy Willow* can be useful to teach scale steps by having the teacher and children show the direction of the melody with hand and body levels.

PUSSY WILLOW

TRADITIONAL

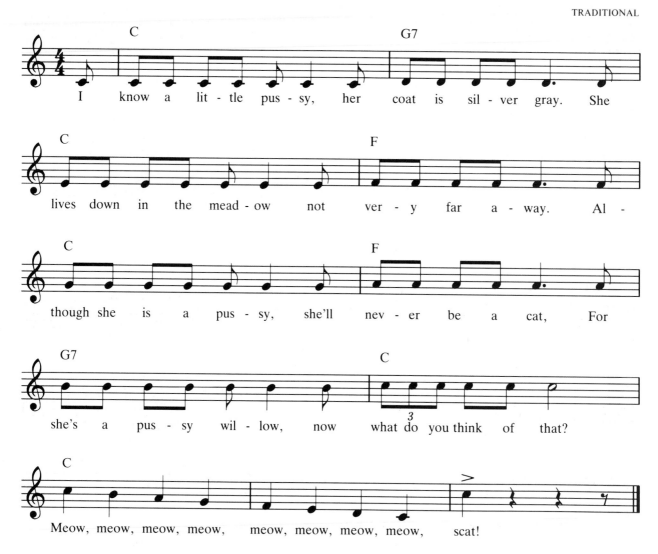

I know a lit - tle pus - sy, her coat is sil - ver gray. She

lives down in the mead - ow not ver - y far a - way. Al -

though she is a pus - sy, she'll nev - er be a cat, For

she's a pus - sy wil - low, now what do you think of that?

Meow, meow, meow, meow, meow, meow, meow, meow, scat!

THE BUS SONG

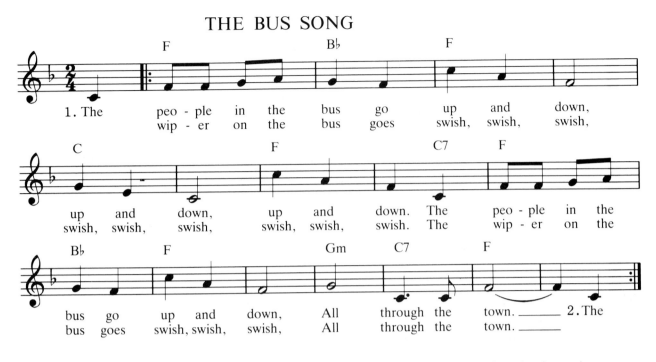

1. The peo-ple in the bus go up and down,
   up and down, up and down. The peo-ple in the
   bus go up and down, All through the town. _____ 2. The

   wip-er on the bus goes swish, swish, swish,
   swish, swish, swish, swish, swish, swish. The wip-er on the
   bus goes swish, swish, swish, All through the town. _____

3. The money in the bus goes, clink, clink, clink,
   Clink, clink, clink; clink, clink, clink!
   The money in the bus goes, clink, clink, clink!
   All through the town.

4. The wheels on the bus go 'round and around,
   'Round and around; 'round and around.
   The wheels on the bus go 'round and around,
   All through the town.

For additional verses have children suggest other things that happen on the bus.

THIS OLD MAN

SINGING GAME

ENGLISH

1. This old man, he played one, He played nick - nack
   on my thumb, With a nick - nack pad - dy whack
   give the dog a bone! This old man came roll - ing home.

(Roll hands)

2. This old man, he played two,
   He played nick-nack on my shoe; (tap shoe) etc.
3. This old man, he played three,
   He played nick-nack on my knee; (tap knee)
4. This old man, he played four,
   He played nick-nack on my door; (tap forehead)
5. This old man, he played five,
   He played nick-nack on my hive; (shoo bees away)
6. This old man, he played six,
   He played nick-nack on my sticks; (tap two fingers)

7. This old man, he played sev'n,
   He played nick-nack up in heav'n; (flying motion)
8. This old man, he played eight,
   He played nick-nack on my pate; (tap top of head)
9. This old man, he played nine,
   He played nick-nack on my spine; (tap spine)
10. This old man, he played ten,
    He played nick-nack once again;
    Nick-nack, paddy whack, give a dog a bone,
    Now we'll all go rolling home.

Song for Classroom Orchestra

Play and sing this rousing folk tune in three-part harmony, the first section in march time and the second with rhythmic swing. Also create your own instrumentation. Guitar and Autoharp strum the rhythms of the cymbals or drums. Include thumb-strum techniques with root bass on accents for guitar accompaniment.

UPWARD TRAIL

R. W. W.

GERMANY

Applying Your Music Skills with Songs and Instruments

The following typical jazz-rock rhythmic patterns can be used to accompany *Upward Trail* in swing time.

The rhythms indicated above may be used also with guitar and Autoharp. Now, create introductions and codas, using the same rhythm patterns.

Patriotic Songs

America, America the Beautiful and *The Star-Spangled Banner,* which are sung regularly in classrooms and school assembly programs throughout the United States, should be a part of the basic song repertoire of all teachers. Four-part harmonizations of these songs are included for students and teachers who play the piano. The more experienced singers in college classes may be taught to sing the parts.

When only the melody is played or sung, the simplified chording can be used for Autoharp, piano, or Resonator Bells.

AMERICA

S. F. SMITH

HENRY CAREY

1. My coun-try 'tis of thee, Sweet land of lib - er - ty, Of thee I sing; Land where my fa - thers died! Land of the Pil - grim's pride! From ev - ry— moun-tain-side, Let— free-dom ring!

2. My native country, thee,
   Land of the noble free,
   Thy name I love.
   I love thy rocks and rills,
   Thy woods and templed hills;
   My heart with rapture thrills,
   Like that above.

3. Our fathers' God, to thee,
   Author of liberty,
   To Thee we sing.
   Long may our land be bright
   With freedom's holy light;
   Protect us by Thy might,
   Great God, our King.

AMERICA THE BEAUTIFUL

KATHERINE LEE BATES

SAMUEL A. WARD

1. O beau-ti-ful for spa-cious skies For am-ber waves of grain,_____ For pur-ple moun-tain maj-es-ties A-bove the fruit-ed plain._____ A-mer-i-ca! A-mer-i-ca! God shed His grace on thee,_____ And crown thy good with broth-er-hood From sea to shin-ing sea!

2. O beautiful for pilgrim's feet,
Whose stern impassioned stress;
A thoroughfare for freedom beat
Across the wilderness;
America! America!
God mend thine ev'ry flaw;
Confirm thy soul in self-control,
Thy liberty in law.

3. O beautiful for patriot's dream,
That sees beyond the years;
Thine alabaster cities gleam
Undimm'd by human tears;
America! America!
God shed his grace on thee,
And crown thy good with
brotherhood,
From sea to shining sea.

THE STAR-SPANGLED BANNER

FRANCIS SCOTT KEY

JOHN STAFFORD SMITH

1. O say! can you see, by the dawn's ear-ly light, What so

proud-ly we hailed at the twi-light's last gleam-ing? Whose broad

stripes and bright stars, thro' the per-il-ous fight, O'er the

ram-parts we watch'd, were so gal-lant-ly stream-ing! And the

rock-ets' red glare, the bombs burst-ing in air, Gave

Applying Your Music Skills with Songs and Instruments

proof thro' the night ___ that our flag was still there.

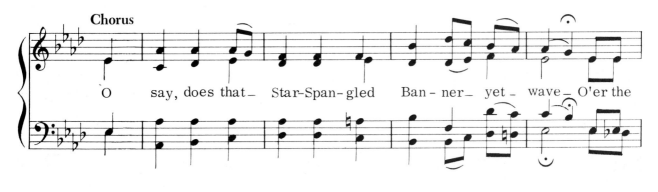

Chorus

O say, does that ___ Star-Span-gled Ban-ner ___ yet ___ wave ___ O'er the

land ___ of the free and the home of the brave?

2. On the shore, dimly seen thro' the mists of the deep,
   Where the foe's haughty host in dread silence reposes,
   What is that which the breeze, o'er the towering steep,
   As it fitfully blows, half conceals, half discloses?
   Now it catches the gleam of the morning's first beam;
   In full glory reflected now shines on the stream;
   'Tis the Star-Spangled Banner, oh, long may it wave
   O'er the land of the free and the home of the brave!

3. O, thus be it ever when free men shall stand
   Between their loved homes and the war's desolation!
   Blest with vict'ry and peace, may the heav'n rescued land
   Praise the Pow'r that hath made and preserved us a nation!
   Then conquer we must, when our cause it is just,
   And this be our motto: "In God is our trust!"
   And the Star-Spangled Banner in triumph shall wave
   O'er the land of the free and the home of the brave!

Appendix 1
Performance Directions

Certain signs and terms, largely Italian, are used to convey directions to performers.

Tempo Indications

The *tempo* is the pace of music. It is often specified by one of the following Italian terms, which are arranged in order from the slowest to the fastest.

Extremely slow	Largo (broad, large)
	Lento (slow)
	Adagio (leisurely)
	Andante (going along, flowing)
Moderate	Moderato (moderate)
	Allegretto (cheerful, lively)
	Allegro (brisk, rapid, lively)
	Vivace (quick, lively)
Extremely fast	Presto (very fast)

A *metronome* is a mechanical device used to establish and maintain tempos in music. A metronome mark is another way of indicating tempo. A metronome mark consists of a note symbol representing the beat and a number showing the number of beats per minute. Thus:

♩ = 72 means a tempo of 72 quarter-note beats per minute.

𝅗𝅥 = 84 means a tempo of 84 half-note beats per minute.

Gradual slowing of the tempo is indicated by *ritardando* (abbreviated *rit.* or *ritard.*). Gradual acceleration is indicated by the Italian word *accelerando* (abbreviated *accel.*). A return to the preceding tempo after *ritardando* or *accelerando* is indicated by *a tempo.*

Dynamic Marks

Italian words, or more often their abbreviations, are used to indicate degrees of loudness and softness.

Word	Abbreviation	Meaning
pianissimo	*pp*	very soft
piano	*p*	soft
mezzo piano	*mp*	moderately soft
mezzo forte	*mf*	moderately loud
forte	*f*	loud
fortissimo	*ff*	very loud
crescendo	*cresc.*	gradually louder
decrescendo	*decresc.*	gradually softer
diminuendo	*dim., dimin.*	gradually softer

Spreading lines are often used in place of *crescendo* (*cresc.*) and contracting lines in place of *decrescendo* (*decresc.*), as shown below.

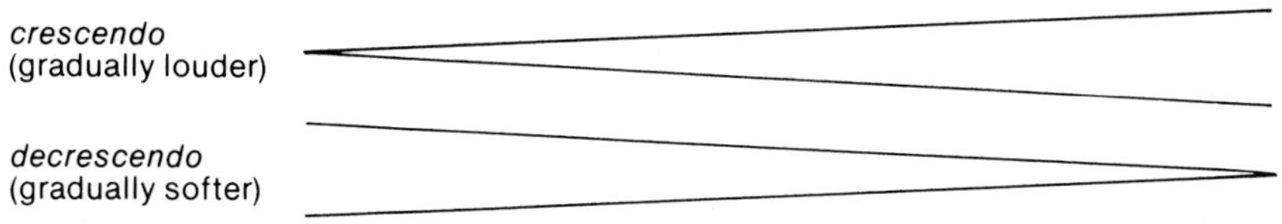

crescendo
(gradually louder)

decrescendo
(gradually softer)

Several pocket dictionaries that give translations and definitions of musical terms are available in book stores and music stores.

Appendix 2
Guitar and Ukulele Fingering Charts

This appendix presents the principal chords for the keys used in this book. Some keys are not practical for beginners on the guitar and ukulele.

C Major

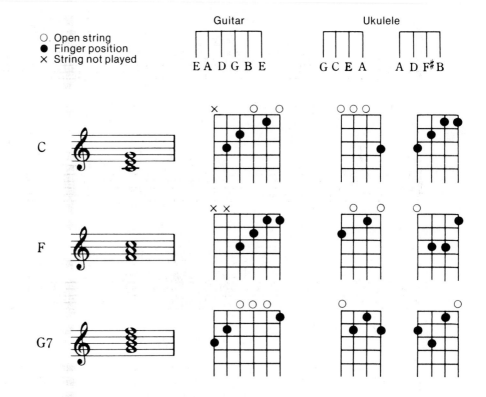

From *Heritage Songster,* by Leon & Lynn Dallin. Copyright © 1966, 1980 by Wm. C. Brown Company Publishers.

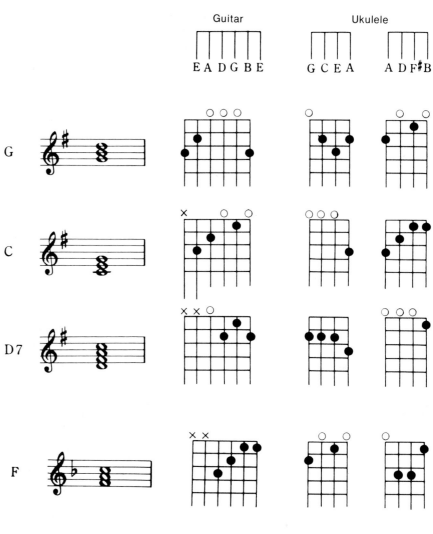

D Major

B♭ Major

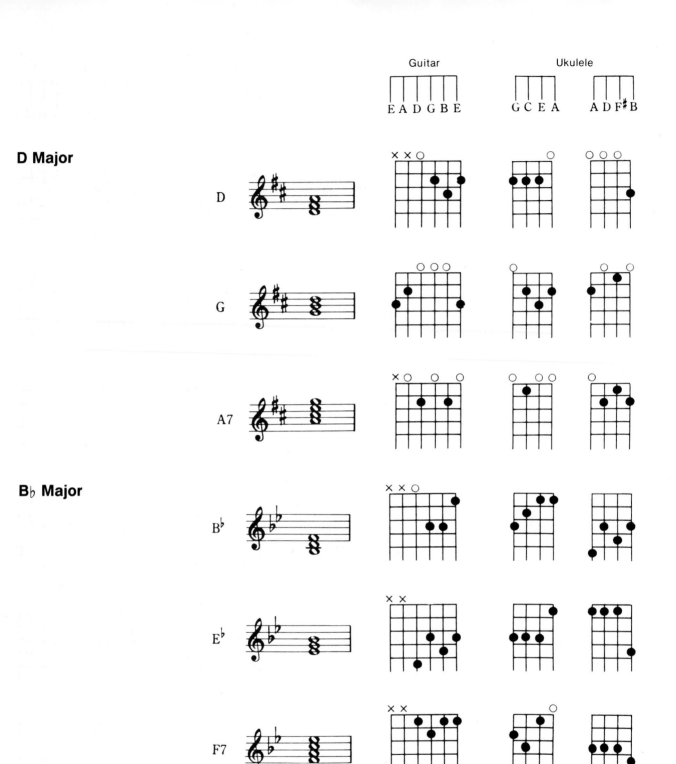

Appendix 2 Guitar and Ukulele Fingering Charts

A Major

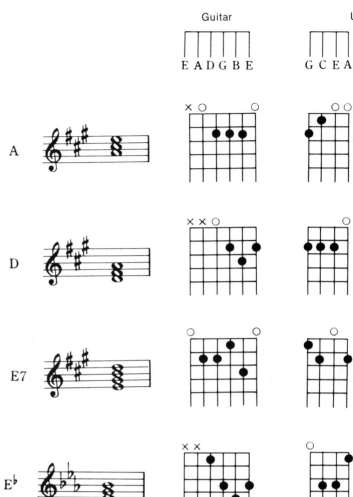

E♭ Major

Guitar

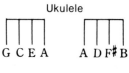
Ukulele

E A D G B E   G C E A   A D F# B

A♭ Major

A♭

D♭

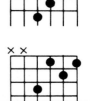
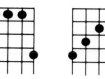

E♭7

A Minor

Am

Dm

E7

E A D G B E

G C E A   A D F# B

E Minor

Em

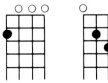

Am

 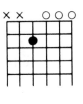

B7

 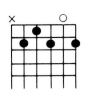

D Minor

Dm

Gm

A7

G Minor

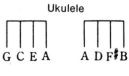

E A D G B E   G C E A   A D F♯ B

Gm
 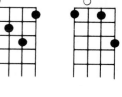

Cm

D7

Appendix 3
Piano Chord Chart

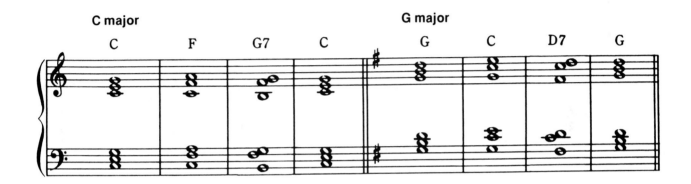

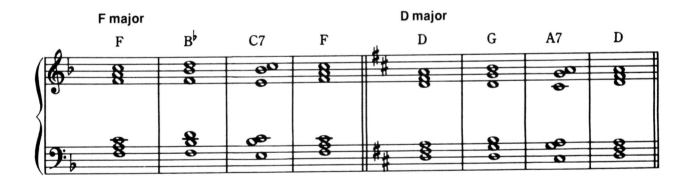

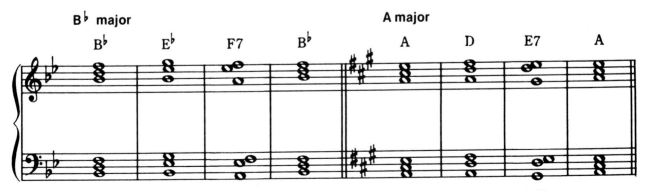

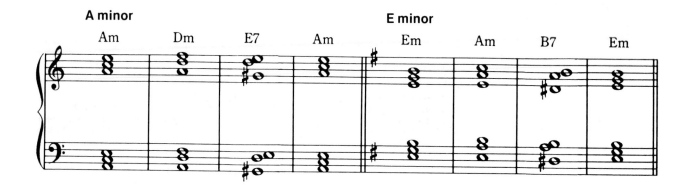

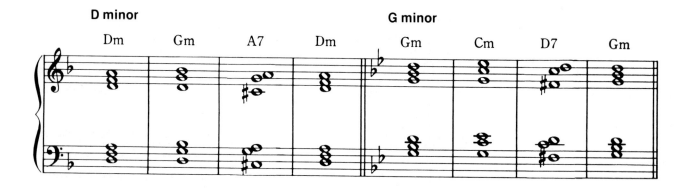

Appendix 3 Piano Chord Chart

Glossary and Index of Terms

A cappella in the manner of the chapel, i.e., without accompaniment, 288
Accelerando increase the tempo gradually, 308
Accents, 31
    Primary, 38 Secondary, 38
Accidental a sharp, flat, or natural not in the key signature
Adagio a slow, leisurely tempo, 308
Al fine to the end, 36
Alla breve, 42
Allegretto a lively tempo, 308
Allegro a brisk, rapid tempo, 308
Alto voice, 267
Anacrusis upbeat, 47
Andante a moderately slow, flowing tempo, 308
A tempo return to the preceding tempo, 308
Autoharp, 196

Ballet a theatrical performance by a dance troupe accompanied by music, 290
Band, 280
Bar a measure, 31
Baritone voice, 268
Bar line a vertical line between measures in musical notation, 31
Baroque, 164, 290
Bass, string, 271
Bass chanting, 262
Bass clarinet, 272
Bass clef, 76
Bassoon, 274
Bass trombone, 276
Bass voice, 267
Beat the pulse in music, 30
    Divisions, Subdivisions, 52
Bells, 140 Handbells, 148 Resonator, 141 Song (melody), 140 Step, 140 Swiss Melodé, 141 Tone Educator, 141
Binary (two-part) form, 96
Blue notes a feature of blues melodies, 242
Blues an early jazz style and form, 242
Bourrée a dance of French origin in fast duple time, 289
Brass instruments, 269

Cadence a closing effect associated with the ends of phrases, 93
Canon a single melody performed in two or more parts starting at different times, 249, 283
Cantabile in a singing style
Cantata, 278
Capo a guitar attachment, 227
Castanets, 133
Cello, 271
Chamber music, 278

Chant rhythmic speech or a repeated tone or figure, 149
Chorale a Protestant hymn tune, 288
Chord builder, in the endleaf pocket
Chord chart (piano), 317
Chords, 90
    Dominant Seventh, 92 Primary, 91
Chorus a large group of singers; also the part of a song sung after (or before) each verse
ChromAharp, 196
Chromatic scale, 68
Clarinets, 272
Clef signs, 63 Bass, 76 Treble, 63
Clogs (jingle sticks), 132
Coda a concluding phrase or section
Common time, 39
Conductor's beat, 32 2/4, 32 3/4, 36 4/4, 38 6/8, 44
Consonants, 23
Contrabass string bass, 271
Contrabassoon, 274
Contralto voice, 267
Cornet, 274
Counterpoint two or more melodies combined, 88
Crescendo (cresc.) gradually louder, 309
Cut time, 42
Cymbals, 134

Da capo (D.C.) repeat from the beginning, 36
Decrescendo (decresc.) gradually softer, 309
Descant a harmony part added above the melody, 259
Development the middle section of a sonata form, 285
Diminuendo (dimin., dim.) gradually softer, 309
Diphthong a double vowel sound, 23
Dominant the fifth degree of the scale and the chord built on it, 91
Dot, 40
Double bar bar lines indicating the end of a piece, section, or exercise, 31
Double bass string bass, 271
Downbeat, 32
Drums, 133
Dynamic marks, 309

Electronic instruments, 277
English horn, 273
Enharmonic notes, 67
Episode a passage between themes or statements of a subject, 283
Exposition the section of a sonata form in which the themes are first stated, 285

Falsetto a method of vocal tone production used to produce pitches above the normal range

Range the compass of a voice or instrument, 268 Voices, 269 Voices and instruments, 270

Recapitulation the third section of a sonata form in which the themes return in the tonic key, 285

Recorder, 162 Fingering chart, 167

Reed, 272 Double, 273

Relative keys a major and a minor key with the same key signature, 79

Repeat signs, 35

Repertoire a collection of music ready or available for performance

Rests the symbols for silence, 46

Rhythm the temporal aspect of music, 30 Duple, 32 Triple, 32

Rhythm sticks, 132

Ritardando (ritard., rit.) slowing the tempo gradually, 308

Rock, 281, 288

Rondo forms, 286

Rote, learning by imitation, 1

Rounds, 71, 245, 283

Sand blocks, 132

Saxophones, 273

Scale, 64

Scale builder, in the endleaf pocket

Scales, 65 Chromatic, 68 Major, 70 Minor, 78 Pentatonic, 68

Scherzo a piece or movement characterized by vivacious rhythm, 285

Semitone a half step, 65

Sentence a complete musical idea, 93

Sharp the symbol that raises the pitch a semitone, 67

Slur a curved line indicating that notes are to be performed smoothly as a group, 177

Solfège a method of sight singing in which notes are associated with syllables, 34

Solo a piece or prominent part for one instrument or voice, 278

Sonata, 278

Sonata form, 285

Song Flute, 164 Fingering chart, 168

Soprano voice, 267

Sousaphone, 275

Staccato detached, separated, 21

Staff, 62

String bass, 271

String instruments, 271

Subdominant the fourth degree of the scale and the chord built on it, 91

Subject the theme of a fugue, 283

Submediant the sixth degree of the scale and the chord built on it, 91

Subphrase a structural unit smaller than a phrase, 96

Subtonic the seventh degree of the scale and the chord built on it, 91

Suite previously a group of stylized dance movements in the same key, now the term is applied to a variety of multi-movement compositions

Supertonic the second degree of the scale and the chord built on it, 91

Swing a jazz style of the '30s and '40s, 289

Syllabic a style of text setting in which each syllable is associated with a single note, 288

Syllables euphonious sounds used in solfège, 34 Pitch, 64 Rhythm, 34, 52

Symphony orchestra, 279

Syncopation, 58

Synthesizers, 277

Tambourine, 133

Tempo the pace of the beat, 45 Terms, 308

Tenor voice, 267

Ternary form, 98, 284

Tie, 40

Time signatures, 32 2/4, 32 3/4, 36 4/4, 38 2/2, 42 3/8, 43 6/8, 44

Timpani, 155, 276

Tone a musical sound, 30

Tone blocks, 132

Tone color (quality), 267

Tonette, 164 Finger chart, 168

Tonic the first degree of the scale and the chord built on it, 91

Transition a passage between two thematic elements in a form

Transpose to write or perform in a higher or lower key, 20, 207

Traps, 276

Treble clef, 63

Triads three-tone chords, 90 Primary, 91

Triangle, 133

Trio the contrasting second part in minuets and related forms, 285

Triplets, 57

Trombones, 276

Trumpet, 274

Tuba, 275

Two-part form, 96

Ukulele fingering chart, 310

Upbeat, 32, 47

Variation form, 282

Viola, 271

Violin, 271

Violoncello the complete name for the cello, 271

Vivace a quick, lively tempo, 308

Voices, 267 Classifications, 267 Ranges, 268 Registers, 17

Vowels, 22

Waltz, 289

Whole step (tone), 65

Wind instruments, 269

Woodwind instruments, 269

Xylophones, 153, 276

Classified Song Index

Patriotic and Military Songs

America, 304
America the Beautiful, 305
Anchors Aweigh, 42
George Washington, 6
Star-Spangled Banner, 306
This Land Is Your Land, 4
When Johnny Comes Marching Home, 82
Yankee Doodle Dandy, 5

Popular Songs

Aloha Oe, 298
Do-Re-Mi, 2
Farewell to Thee, 298
It's a Small World, 3

Recreational Songs
Action, Game, Stunt, and Camp

Barnyard Song, 69
Bingo, 14
Bow Belinda, 93
Bus Song, 301
Chopsticks, 171
Come on and Join into the Game, 13
Down by the Station, 13
George Washington, 6
Good Morning to All, 16
Hokey Pokey, 14
If You're Happy, 15
London Bridge, 245
Merrily We Roll Along, 118, 174
Muffin Man, 299
Polly Put the Kettle On, 158
Pumpkin Man, 300
Pussy Willow, 300
Tell Me Why, 260
This Old Man, 301
Three Cornered Hat, 183
Upidee, 185

Rounds and Canons

Are You Sleeping, 72, 256
Bell Doth Toll, 291
Christmas Is Coming, 246
Clocks and Watches, 201
Echo, 249
Every Night When the Sun Goes Down, 255
Follow On, 252
Good Night, 73
Hey, Ho! Nobody Home, 248
Ifca's Castle, 247
Li'l Liza Jane, 250
Lovely Evening, 246
Music Alone Shall Live, 292
My Goose, 201
Old Texas, 254
Reuben and Rachel, 251
Row, Row, Row Your Boat, 244
Scotland's Burning, 245
Shalom Chaverim, 249
Three Blind Mice, 256
White Coral Bells, 145

Songs of Other Lands

A-hunting We Will Go, England, 130
All through the Night, Wales, 26
Aloha Oe, Hawaii, 298
Alouette, French Canada, 294
Are You Sleeping, France, 72, 256
Ash Grove, Wales, 98
Au Clair de la Lune, France, 24
Auf Wiedersehen, Germany, 121
Auld Lang Syne, Scotland, 263
Barbara Allen, Scotland, 94
Bee, Germany, 172
Bell Doth Toll, England, 291
Big Ben Clock, England, 144

Blow the Man Down, England, 228
Boating, Germany, 264
Bobby Shafto, England, 240
Calypso Joe, Caribbean, 138
Charlie Is My Darling, England, 80
Cherry Blossoms, Japan, 296
Christmas Is Coming, England, 246
Cuckoo, Germany, 120
Dame Get Up, England, 80
Dance, Hungary, 124
Down in Mexico, 136
Du, du, liegst mir im Herzen, Germany, 128
Echo, Germany, 249
Fais Do Do, France, 169
Farewell to Thee, Hawaii, 298
Fiddle-dee-dee, England, 174
Foggy, Foggy Dew, England, 220
Folk Tune, Russia, 122
French Tune, 169
German Folk Tune, 116
German Tune, 189
God Rest You Merry, Gentlemen, England, 95
Good Night, England, 73
Haida, Israel, 223
Harmonizing, Austria, 261
Hava Nagila, Israel, 297
Hey, Ho!, Nobody Home, England, 248
Ifca's Castle, Czechoslovakia, 247
In the Shining Moonlight, France, 24
Johnny Has Gone for a Soldier, Ireland, 78
Koom Bah Yah, Africa, 265
La Raspe, Mexico, 137
Las Mañanitas, Mexico, 10
Las Pollitas, Spain, 293
Lavender's Blue, England, 125, 187
Les Anges dans nos Campagnes, France/England, 295
Lightly Row, Germany, 112, 172
London Bridge, England, 245
Marching Song, Silesia, 195
Merry Bells, Wales, 143
Mexican Folk Song, 181
Minka, Russia, 205
Muffin Man, England, 299
Music Alone Shall Live, Germany, 292
My Boat, Hawaii, 202
Norwegian Dance, 130
Oh Hanukkah, Hasidic folk song, 262
Papaya Tree, Philippines, 192
Paper of Pins, England, 219
Prayer of Thanksgiving, Netherlands, 77
Recorder Band, Germany, 173
Sakura, Japan, 296
Scarborough Fair, England, 12
Shalom Chaverim, Israel, 249
Singing on the Playground, Germany, 115
Sleep, Baby, Sleep, Germany, 221
Sleep My Baby, Sweden, 123
Steeple Bells, France, 144
This Old Man, England, 301
Three Cornered Hat, Germany, 183
To Paree, France, 171
Turtle Dove, England, 27
Twinkle, Twinkle, Little Star, France, 126
Under the Spreading Chestnut Tree, England, 62, 63, 64
Upward Trail, Germany, 302
We Wish You a Merry Christmas, England, 177
White Coral Bells, England, 145
Zum Gali Gali, Israel, 224

Spirituals and Hymns

Chorale from Jesu, Joy of Man's Desiring, 173
Draw Nearer, Lord, 265
Good News, 170, 215
He's Got the Whole World in His Hands, 257
Jacob's Ladder, 146
Joshua Fit the Battle of Jericho, 204

Alphabetical Song Index

Keys are major unless otherwise indicated.